THE RUSSIANS ARE COMING

1939 – 1944

Based on the

DIARY

Written by

BRITA VON TROIL

Translation by Stella von Troil

The Survival of a Paper Mill Town in Finland under the Threat of a Russian Invasion during World War II in Finland

To my father
for bringing Brita's writing to life

To my mother
for creating a loving home

I would also like to thank

Laura
Jessie
Steve
Bosse and Leena
Matti and Aili
Poka

Table of Contents

THE FAMILIES

KNUT (Pulle)
BRITA (Musti), born VON HAARTMAN
- Märtha (Mi)
- Britta (Pi)
- Sten (Trolle)

BROTHER'S FAMILIES

HOLGER
CONSTANCE
- Isabella
- Jeanne-Marie
- Werner

STEN (Lasse)
LISA
- Lars
- Knut (Tommy)

UNO (Dulle)
MAJ-LIS

NILS (Nisse)
MARGIT
- Barbro
- Ebba
- Olof

SISTER'S FAMILIES

MÄRTHA
HARRY ELVING

MARGA (Maggie)
HUGO ÖSTERMAN
- Margaretha

EBBA
TOR ASCHAN

BRITAS SISTER'S FAMILIES

GRETA
VERNER GUSTAFSSON
- Margaretha (Tippan)
- Paul

KARIN (Caja
RAINER MANDELIN
- Bubi
- Gunnar (Murre)
- Tytti

FRIEND'S FAMILIES

WILLY VON KOSKULL
BRITA (Muku)
- Ulla
- Willy
- Peter

CARL-GUSTAF
TIGERSTEDT
LISBETH
- Axel
- Peter

FREDRIK
AF FORSELLES
TYTTI
- Eva
- Marita (Mita)

EINAR RHEN
EINE
- Ebba
- Kurt-Erik

VIKTOR SERCK
STINA
-Gunnar

THE AUTHOR AND HER FAMILY

Written by Stella von Troil

Brita von Troil, was born in 1902 in Kotka, Finland. Her father, Berndt von Haartman, was an engineer, her mother, Anna, was a housewife; they had three daughters, Brita was the youngest. The family moved numerous times during her childhood. She spent several years in Russia, including St. Petersburg, but her father's business failed and they were forced to move back to Helsinki, Finland. They continued to struggle and were forced to sell some of their possessions, however, they were able to afford a maid, which was customary at the time for a family of an engineer.

Brita completed middle school and went on to study music, focusing on the piano. She made some extra money by playing during silent films. But she was not able to reveal this to her father, as receiving payment was not acceptable for a girl of her status. Her father was a nobleman, and although the nobility did not have any privileges left, she still needed to keep up a certain appearance. Music became Brita's passion in life, she even wrote some piano compositions herself. Her sister, Greta, studied in Paris and became a famous opera singer at the Finnish Opera.

Brita was married at the age of eighteen to Knut von Troil, a nobleman with the rank of baron and a successful lawyer. He was twenty-eight years old at the time. He recognized Brita's love for music and it wasn't long before he gave her a grand piano. They had three children Märtha (Mi), Britta (Pi), and my father, Sten (Trolle). Their home was filled with music, especially classical music, and they all learned to dance at a young age.

Mi

Pi

Trolle

Brita and Knut were part of the Swedish-speaking minority, which was not suppressed, but rather enjoyed relative prosperity and wealth compared to the Finnish-speaking majority at the time. Her command of the Swedish language was remarkable despite her limited schooling. Maybe that is why she was so good at scrabble, a game I remember playing with my grandmother many times in Mustaniemi, the family summer cottage.

Her husband Knut (Pulle), became the Vice President of Kymmene Paper Industries, his grandfather was one of the founding members of the company. The factory was located in the town Kuusankoski, in the Southeast of Finland. The family moved to the small town dominated by the paper mill and the River Kymmene, an important north to south waterway with its connections to the vast lake district.

Brita often refers to Kuusankoski and its factories as just “Kymmene”, the place. But “Kymmene” is also short for the company itself, which was an important part of Finnish industry. The main natural resource in Finland is timber and the river provided the means for transporting the timber. Nearby Kouvola was an important transit point for the railroad going toward the war front in the East. Subsequently, the area became a target for the Russians during the war.

Kymmene Headquarters in Kuusankoski

It was the intention of Brita to write a diary during World War II to help future generations understand the hardships they had to endure; the Russian bombardments, the famine, the lack of basic things like food and clothing, and the evacuations. But she also describes the development of volunteerism, which not only helped to sustain the men on the frontline but also helped to maintain order on the home front. This included the Lotta movement, an all-female volunteer organization, which she also was a part of. She is pictured proudly wearing her uniform on the cover of the book.

Brita describes the mood during the war in astonishing detail, the fear of a Russian invasion is palpable, and the uncertainty of their future sometimes led to desperate actions in order to survive. The idea of surrender or falling into Russian hands was unthinkable, fleeing to Sweden or death was preferable.

Brita gave part of her diary, as a present, to her husband for his 50th birthday in 1942.

After finishing the diary, at the end of the war in 1944, it remained forgotten for more than 50 years. My father, Sten (Trolle) von Troil, began reading it after he retired from the paper industry at the beginning of the 21st century. Brita's handwriting was not easy to decipher, but to my father's surprise, the story fascinated him, and he decided to summarize the hundreds of pages of notebooks into one book in its original language, Swedish. He chose to give it the name "Bolsjevikerna Kommer" (The Bolsheviks Are Coming). My father later translated the book into Finnish with the name "Ryssät Tulevat" (The Russians Are Coming), also used here in the English version.

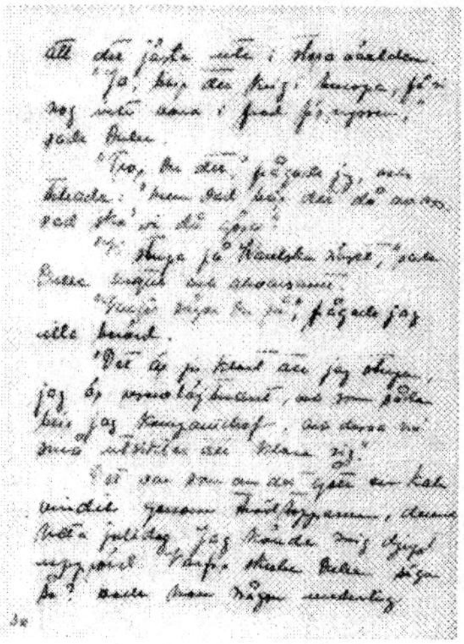

Brita's handwriting

The original, as well as the Finnish version, unfortunately do not include the year 1943. These notebooks were missing. My father, therefore, wrote about his own memories of 1943 and also included the main developments in the war for continuity. The notebooks were found several years after the original book was written. In order to bring the story to a larger audience I decided to translate the book into English and also include a summary of the 1943 notebooks. As a dual citizen of Finland and the United States myself, I especially hope to reach the later generations of Finnish immigrants who may still be interested in Finnish history but have lost the language skills of their family origins.

I am also interested in bringing the story to light now that we again are seeing unrest develop in Europe with the recent events in the Ukraine. After a fairly long period of demilitarization, we are now seeing an increase in troops and military preparedness, including the nations around the Baltic Sea. Like the Ukraine, Finland, Estonia, Lithuania, and Latvia find themselves in the buffer zone between East and West. Who is going to help if Russia decides to expand into the west again? The buffer nations are not able to defend their independence alone. Therefore, some of them have entered into an alliance with the West, NATO, to increase their security.

Finland is relying on its neutrality; hoping war will never come again. But is this naive and wishful thinking? The Finnish people are split on the decision whether to join NATO or not, and the people of the Ukraine have to decide whether they want to belong to the East or the West, risking all-out war to secure true independence, versus accepting continued Russian interference and humiliation. History will tell who is right.

PROLOGUE

Finland declared independence from Russia December 6, 1917, but Finnish desire for independence is a lot older. In a text by Per Brahe in 1757, a time period when Finland was ruled by Sweden, he points out that the country's eastern border should run from the Gulf of Finland up to Lake Ladoga, along the River Svir to Lake Onega, and north to the White Sea. He also suggested that students should learn Finnish instead of French and Italian.

In 1809 Finland was conquered by the Russian empire and became a semi-autonomous territory. But thoughts of nationalism only increased and were often expressed in arts and culture. In 1835, Lönnrot published Kalevala, a national epic piece of literature in the language of its people (and not those in power). The cultural circles in Europe started to pay close attention to the developments in Finland. Kalevala also inspired painters like Gallen-Kallela and Järnefelt. Sibelius led the composers with his Kalevala inspired first major composition Kullervo. The poet Runeberg praised the Finnish warrior and was soon followed by other writers. The architect Saarinen created a Finnish Pavilion, not a Russian one, at the World Exhibition in Paris 1900.

In the early 20th century Finland was a part of the Russian empire and was ruled by Nicolai II, the last Russian tsar. The Russian rule was not popular. Thoughts of independence were brewing. Bobrikov, the hated Russian Governor of Finland, was assassinated and Sibelius composed his most famous symphony, Finlandia, which further fueled the independence movement. It evoked such powerful nationalistic feelings in the listener that the Russian authorities prohibited it.

Even though Finland had some autonomy within the Russian empire, the intention of the Russian government in the 1800‘s and early 1900‘s was to slowly integrate and “Russianize” the Finns into Russian customs and to weaken the Finnish language and culture. Censorship was increased and the sovereign dissolved the parliament whenever he wasn’t pleased with their decisions. This was not acceptable to the majority of the Finnish people. However, with the rise of Lenin in Russia, the Bolsheviks did have some supporters even in Finland.

Hatred of Russia kept growing and independence was seen as a necessity. During a time of weakness in the Russian ranks at the end of World War I, Finland seized the moment and declared independence on December 6, 1917. At the time of the declaration just about the entire nation stood behind the decision. Lenin, preoccupied with the Russian revolution, accepted the declaration, thinking he could later force Finland to rejoin the new Soviet Union with the help of the Finnish Bolshevik supporters.

The dispute over how the country should be run eventually boiled over and a civil war broke out between the Bolshevik supporting “Reds” and the anti-communist “Whites”. In 1918 the Whites, led by General Mannerheim, were victorious. The next step was to get the world to recognize Finnish independence. As a nation with its own culture and language, Finland was quickly recognized as a sovereign state.

Lenin had miscalculated the Finnish resolve, or “Sisu” as it is often called, an unwavering fighting spirit that runs through the veins of the Finnish people. Resistance remained firm and with clever politics Finland was able to keep its independence. Despite the long border with Russia in the East, the countries lived in relative peace until the unrest started again in Europe in the 1930's leading to World War II in 1939. The book is divided into years from 1939-1944, each year starting with a prologue to make it easier for the reader to follow the main developments of the war in Europe and elsewhere. All the photographs come from family albums.

Stella von Troil
Pensacola, Florida, USA, 2017

1939

In August the Soviet Union and Nazi Germany signed the Molotov-Rippentrop Pact, nominally a non-aggression treaty, however, there was a secret agreement dividing the Eastern European nations into spheres of interest. Finland fell into the Soviet sphere of interest.

Germany attacks Poland on September 1st and the Second World War breaks out.

While the German tanks roll into Warsaw unrest is also growing in Finland.

Stalin forces the Baltic nations, Estonia, Latvia, and Lithuania into a pact with the Soviet Union to avoid a full-blown invasion. The small nations on the Eastern Shore of the Baltic Sea reluctantly give up military bases and allow the Russians to station their troops there in defense of Hitler's ambitions to expand into the east.

EASY DAYS OF FALL

It was a beautiful September morning and our beloved summer home in the country, Mustaniemi, was basking in the sun. The whole family was about to travel to Kymmene. Father Pulle was on his way to his office as usual, and the kids were headed to their respective schools, and I did not want to remain in the country by myself, which was downright unthinkable.

Pulle standing by the Studebaker

We sat in our Studebaker and drove the 15 miles to the Kouvola train station, where our oldest girl, Mi, would take the train to Helsinki and from there to Grankulla, to "Klostret", her boarding school, to continue her second year in high school.

After countless kisses and hugs, the rest of us drove on toward the paper mill. Pi and Trolle remained at home, initially, as their Little School was not to start until one a clock. I went to the hospital to visit Dr. Köhler for a minor ailment.

On the way back I met Evy Ramsay, who was married to the technical manager at the mill. She had heard strange rumors about war. A few days earlier we had had a dinner party for a few friends from the mill. It was a great evening with good wining and dining. Apart from the Ramsays, office chief Wiklund, his wife, as well as Allan and Greta Björk were present. Mi was there as well, but she was bored to death and left right after dinner. Around midnight, young Enrst-Adolf Biese and Wolter Ramsay came to pick up mother and father Ramsay. Mi refused to get up and meet with them. She claimed she had a stomachache. But it was probably all the talk about politics that had strained the nerves of her stomach.

As I now stood outside the paper mill and talked to Evy, we continued our conversation from the previous evening. At the hospital, DR. Köhler had just heard that war had broken out in the big world, but he tried to calm me down by telling me that this war had already ended. It had only lasted a few hours.

I did not know what to believe.

I almost ran on the way home. There was to be an extra radio news broadcast and I wanted to hear it. I popped into the home of my neighbor Brita von Koskull, one of my best friends. Together we listened to the radio and heard the war was still raging. Even though we whole-heartedly took part in other nations' trials and tribulations, we, above all, cared for each other. As long as we were able to think about the war as something far away, we were able to remain reasonably calm. But I was struck by terror at the thought of an attack on our country by the Russians. How would we then be able to defend ourselves?

Brita von Koskull
In her Lotta Uniform

The first change in our daily lives was the withdrawal of gasoline sales for private vehicles. Because of this it was necessary for us to move from Mustaniemi back into town. In mid-September, we, along with the kitchen help, Taina, went to prepare the villa for the winter. We turned off the water pipes and emptied the water from the heating units. And then we packed various things to take with us to Kymmene, curtains, blankets etc. I had a feeling this was all done in haste, we had always thought Mustaniemi would actually become the evacuation home for us, Brita von Koskull, and her children, if it came to a war with the Russians.

Mustaniemi

Pulle was an optimist and did not think it would come to war, so we packed most of the things. But I did take one little precaution; I put curtains, blankets and tablecloths in a separate suitcase, which I would not unpack in Kymmene. I thought our stay in the country would become too dreary if we did not have these things. If we were forced to evacuate I would at least try to make our lives as tolerable as possible.

The same September evening, as we sat by the fireplace in Mustaniemi, we heard that the Germans had marched into Warsaw. Maybe the war will be over soon, I thought.

I remembered earlier that summer, Dulle, Pulle's brother, and his wife, Maj-Lis, had visited us in Mustaniemi. We had some beautiful summer days, wonderful weather, and we enjoyed ourselves in every way.

Easy days of summer in Mustaniemi

But one day we started to talk about the unrest out in the big world.

"If war breaks out in Europe the Russians are not going to leave us alone", said Dulle.

"Do you believe that?" I asked, and said: "But what is going to happen to us then, what are we going to do?"

"I am going to die at the Isthmus of Karelia," Dulle said, calm and serious.

"Why do you say that?" I asked, ill at ease.

"Of course, I will be killed, after all, I am a lieutenant in the reserves, and as such I will become a company chief. Their chances of survival are slim".

It was as if a cold wind had blown through the treetops on that hot July day. I was deeply upset. Why did Dulle say such a thing? Did he have some sort of strange premonition of what was going to happen? I looked up into the treetops and wondered if enemy planes were going to fly over Mustaniemi? No, that was impossible, not over such a small peaceful remote place like this. I shook off the somber mood and tried to think about something else.

I could not dwell on my thoughts for long. We had to pack and get ready, the next morning we were going to drive home to Kymmene.

That was the last trip we made with the car while we still had peace in the land. The next time we used it, it was to evacuate to Mustaniemi. We did received gasoline in order to evacuate. But later in September private citizens were not allowed gas anymore for such purposes. It was worse for taxi and bus drivers who only received a quantum of gas, which obviously was going to affect their ability to earn a living. But most of them had cars with wood carburetors, which to some degree secured their outcome.

Both our imports and exports suffered because of the war, and already in September this led to a shortage of sugar and coffee. Later, the same thing happened to most other groceries as well as clothing.

The shortage of coffee was a hardship for many, especially the coffee klatch ladies. No one was going to get hurt by the shortage of coffee, this was not the case with sugar. Many started to lose weight, myself included. But this was probably not because of the reduced ration of sugar, but rather my unrest and nervousness. And, yet, I had less reason for restlessness then most.

In September, the hoarding craze started. The Koskulls blamed such gorging on others, people less well off. Willy, especially, was upset by this. His strong sense of justice immediately reacted to any unfairness. Brita and I tried to live according to our principles and did not hoard anything that could hurt someone else. We only bought some tiny rolls of thread and some soap, but only in such minute quantities that calling it hoarding would have been a joke.

Willy von Koskull

We heard that people in Helsinki were acting crazy. Everything was hoarded: food, fabric, washing powder, simply everything. It turned into a shopping frenzy, a panic.

September turned into October. Politics were discussed everywhere. The European map was

studied in detail. People were hoping there would soon be peace.

On the sixth of October Pulle was sitting in the brown easy chair reading the newspaper. I was sitting in the sofa doing my needlework and really wanted to talk, but decided not to. My thoughts were interrupted by the telephone and a gentleman asking for Pulle.

Pulle answered and I heard him say: “Yes, I will come immediately - but that really isn’t anything to pay attention to”, he said.

Pay attention to? What was he talking about, I wondered.

Pulle told me only that he was supposed to take part in a meeting to discuss army calling-up orders, this was for both men and horses. I continued my interrupted needlework and hoped Pulle would be back home soon. But time went on, it got late and there was no sign of him.

I turned on the radio news broadcast too late and missed the beginning. Suddenly there was an interruption. It sounded as if there was turmoil on the radio and it lasted a long time. It sounded as if chairs had been dragged on the floor, one could hear quiet cursing, single words and agitated voices. I got so scared I ran to the phone to call the Koskulls. No one answered. On the radio, a female voice announced that the electric light had failed, which lead to the interruption in the broadcast. Exhausted and a little ashamed over my fear, I dropped into a chair and felt like a hysterical fool.

When Pulle finally returned home, I told him what I had heard. He took it all in with extraordinary tranquility, just like the meeting he had just been to.

The following day, the 7th of October, the mood was not quite free of nervousness. One still did not know anything with certainty, but we were hoping the calling-up orders were just a precaution, which was nothing to pay much attention to. The same day, Trolle turned 8 years old. He was allowed to invite his classmates for a party in the morning. It was a success in every way. All the children came and they were all in good spirits.

In the afternoon Pulle and I invited the Koskulls over, it was Saturday, after all, so Pulle and Willy finished work early. We sat in the small living room talking in our usual cozy way.

It was also Pi's name day, she was allowed to have her girlfriends over in the evening. But Pi's party became more complicated as there was to be a blackout practice run that same evening. The girls' mothers were worried to send them out on such a night. We were all not used to the October darkness, so we phoned back and forth. In the end, they were allowed to come because I promised they would be taken home by car.

Sunday and Monday became restless days. The mood became more and more nervous. On Tuesday, our needlework club was supposed to meet for its regularly scheduled meeting, but we realized that the political situation was about to come to a point and, perhaps, it was time to evacuate the children to Mustaniemi.

At breakfast, I told Pulle it was silly that the women under such circumstances were called in for needlework. I also thought it could be detrimental with all the talk and rumors that would ensue. In addition, the women surely had something much more important to do at home, especially those who had little children. Maybe some would even start getting ready for the evacuation. Pulle agreed with me and asked me why I didn't cancel the meeting,

since I was the chairwoman. I called the vice chairwoman, Tua Nyberg, and we decided to cancel the meeting.

Consequently, I stayed at home and started to sort the children's clothes.

Wednesday morning the superintendent from "Klostret" called and asked if she could send Mi home from school, which we of course agreed to and she was already at home the same day. When Pulle came home for lunch at noon we started to pack in order to leave the next morning.

The same evening the Lotta volunteers had their usual needlework get-together. Even the passive members were asked to come. As an active member, I had never seen so many people gather in Kymmene, except at festivities or some other event. Brita and I talked about how we were going to organize our trip to Mustaniemi.

I told Kirsti Halme, the chairwoman of the Lotta organization, that we were going to evacuate and that I would be glad to take some of the needlework with me. She promised to take care of it and told me I could stay in the country unless all of the Lotta members were called into duty. Since I had not made the Lotta Promise, I decided that it was my duty to get the children out of harm's way. Trolle, as I mentioned, was only 8 and I could not trust anyone to take care of him. I was the one who carried the main responsibility for him and for Pi. It was different with Mi, she could take care of herself if it came to it. On top of that I was neither a physician or a nurse or any other important person. My job as a Lotta was mainly going to be needlework. Because of my weakness and frail heart, it was impossible for me to do anything more strenuous. Sewing was something I could do in the country just as well as in Kymmene. Therefore, I decided to evacuate together with the children to Mustaniemi.

The chief of Police Mr. Saastamoinen visited the Lotta volunteers that evening and made a pompous speech about the importance of evacuating. A somewhat comical episode happened when he told everyone to put address tags on their luggage. He took me as an example:

"Write it like this: Baroness von Troil, Ranta Street 126, Kymmene Factory, Kuusankoski."

The Family Residence in Kymmene

Evacuations were still not enforced as war had not broken out yet, but according to Saastamoinen it was important to evacuate as many children as possible in order to make it easier for those who stayed behind to continue their work. After the speech, Greta Björk announced that she would stay. She was a childless woman able to work and had no intention of moving. When Brita and I went outside the blackout was in effect. As we slowly made our way home we bumped into Mr. Horelli, chief of staff of the legal department, as well as assistant engineer Baron Cedercreutz. Horelli was among those called up and was about to leave the same night.

Pulle was ordered to take charge of the community population shelters. On top of that he had his own job, and when Horelli left, he also had to take over the judicial department. Later, the company president Karl-Erik Ekholm left the area, and Pulle got his fourth job. So, he certainly had his hands full, especially since the shelter job became very taxing due to the eternal nightly watches.

The most important thing for those leaving was to take food and warm clothes, as well as schoolbooks for the children. Willy von Koskull supported me in saying that it also was important to think about being comfortable.

In the morning on October 12th, a truck came to our door to deliver milk, it made regular deliveries from two of the mill's properties east of the mill, and it was going to make an extra stop in Mustaniemi. The children traveled in the truck, Brita and I took a taxi. We had with us Taina, our kitchen help, and Koskull's maid Siiri. Eino Saari, who had been our construction manager for the villa, was informed of our arrival. He had been called-up but had not left yet.

It was a strange mood that came over me and Brita von Koskull. The trees had lost half of their leaves, all the flowers had faded, and the yellow leaves were rustling under your feet with every step of the way. The light was fading and soon it was pitch dark. We had left our homes, we had left our husbands. When were we going to be able to return?

PULLE IS MOCKING THE AUTHORITIES

It was the time for “additional refresher training” of the reserves. Our first assignment was arranging the curtains for the blackouts. We had taken paper and wood trim with us from Kymmene, and now Brita, assisted by Mi, in her usual energetic way, started cutting and crafting.

It turned out very nice. Mustaniemi is a pretty little villa, and when we hung both Brita’s and my wall rug on the wall, and rearranged the old farmer’s style furniture, it became very warm and cozy.

I was grateful I did not have to sit in an overcrowded train waiting at a station for hours, or squeeze into an overcrowded bus with the children. Oh, how wonderful it was to be home! Yes, indeed, I was at home, even though it was in the country. And we did not have to sleep on hay mattresses on the floor in some drafty elementary school. We had it good while many others were experiencing trying times. Countless families were evacuated under difficult circumstances. And the military trains kept rolling toward the east.

We held classes for the children every day and we took turns as teachers. Mi, no longer a child, was now one of us adults. But, Pi, who was twelve, Ulla, ten, Willy and Trolle, eight, and Peter who was five, had lectures every day between ten and twelve o’clock in a few school subjects. Several times Ulla took “school” too

seriously and cried bitter tears over history and especially when reading poetry. She had a lot of trouble with “Fänrik Ståhl’s Sägner” (The Songs of Ensign Stal), a collection of patriotic military songs.

Pi, on the other hand, enjoyed reading and did her homework well. Most of the time Mi taught Willy and Trolle. She always had a good hand with little kids, but she had a hard time getting respect from these wild boys.

The boys ended up brawling numerous times. One time Trolle threw a fit and tossed a small log at his friend's head. Even Peter came up with a bunch of pranks. But in general, the kids were good friends and were helpful with raking leaves and fetching wood. But the girls were much more diligent then the boys.

Willy loved drawing, as well as Ulla, and she was very skilled for her age. Their drawings were everywhere. Trolle's cars and Peter's playing cards could be found on chairs all over the house. "Musti, you are a pedant", I grumbled at myself, and tried to look at the mess from a more humorous side.

When Ulla had her tenth birthday we celebrated with a wreath-shaped cardamom roll, cake, and other various goodies. We had great fun. We listened to the radio every day, even though, at times, it screamed until our ears nearly bled, and at other times it just whispered so you really couldn't hear anything. But at least we had a radio and were able to follow the events out in the big world.

There, in our little cottage, we listened to the broadcast of the Meeting of the Nordic Kings from Stockholm on the 18th of October, where even our president Kyösti Kallio was present. He was appreciated in broad circles, and we were happy he represented our country at this meeting (to demonstrate Nordic unity and neutrality). We were very moved by the festive atmosphere of this royal gathering that reached us through the radio.

We also heard very good music in these days, like Sibelius, Beethoven, Wagner, and other great composers, as well as patriotic music, marches, and folk music. Sibelius, Palmgren, and other Finnish composers were, of course, played the most.

Every day we called our husbands. It did not take long until they thought we should pay them a visit in Kymmene. It was a relief to me that I wasn't completely cut off from the mill, as I had thought. In consideration of the children we did not travel together, Brita went first and when she returned I left.

It felt strange to be back at the mill again, even though I had only been gone for ten days. In some ways, everything had changed. There were mainly soldiers there, and most, who thought they had any reason at all, actually wore their uniforms or at least wore their Defense Corps' yellow arm bandage. I felt uncomfortably civilian.

Pulle and Willy did not want to live by themselves, so Willy moved into Trolle's room. The Koskulls' kitchen help, Rauha, together with our maid, with the same name, took care of them and looked after Koskull's empty house.

I stayed in Kymmene for a few days. After lunch, we had coffee in the little sitting room, and in the evening, we were talking in the dining room and went for walks on roads in complete darkness. I had to cling onto Pulle's hand as I could hardly see anything in front of me. We listened carefully to the radio broadcasts and commented broadly back and forth. Pulle told us that his brothers Lasse, Dulle, and Nisse, were already headed east.

I went back to Mustaniemi. Mrs. Halme had not forgotten her promise. She sent us assignments: shirts to sew and gloves to knit, as well as simple gas masks that could be fabricated at home (using charcoal). We received food with the milk truck from the factory, or we took the bus to Tillola, were we picked up the groceries with a handcart. The loads were very heavy, and Pi was the anchor in this tug of war. Only milk and potatoes were available at the nearby farm.

We went for a lot of walks. It felt good both physically and psychologically. We were wondering if we weren't soon allowed to go back to the mill with our kids. But nothing had changed yet. We just had to wait. We went to visit the neighboring farm, the Mynttinens, and talked to the young and old hostess, as well as the agronomist himself. We visited our friends, the Tolppalas, and bought apples from them. Everywhere we went we were met with the same patriotic spirit.

Another two weeks passed. During that time, the Lotta volunteers had opened a cafeteria at the Community Clubhouse. I felt bad for Mi, who, at seventeen, was too old to be evacuated like a child, but too young to be responsible for her younger siblings. I talked to Pulle and we decided to ask if she would be allowed to work at the cafeteria. Up until now she did not belong to the Lotta volunteers, but maybe it could be arranged after all? I called one of our neighbors, Eine Rhen, who was the vice chairwoman of the local Lotta organization. She was in charge of the cafeteria and promised Mi would be accepted. We packed a few things for the girl and off she went. She was allowed to work every day except on Sundays when she was off. This was my request that she could rest one day of the week.

My heart was full of pride. Mi was happy and friendly with everyone, something Eine frequently mentioned. She met many different people, mainly Lottas and officers and soldiers. Kymmene had become overrun by the military. Mi was eagerly courted by two young officers and we frequently joked about it with her, but she just laughed wholeheartedly. I was a little worried about the fact that she did not eat breakfast. She was quite chubby when she started her job, but she soon lost five kilos

(10 pounds). It was hard work initially until she got used to standing all day. Her feet and legs were aching, but she never complained.

On Saturday afternoons, she often came out to the country on a bicycle to spend the weekend. At the beginning of November, Pulle and Willy were able to arrange a few days off to come visit with us. The funny thing was that they were not able to agree on what time to leave, so all three arrived and left at different times. But we had a wonderful time together, Saturday night we heated the sauna and took part in conversation, naturally, about the political situation.

One thing Mi later pointed out was that she did not like to get up early on Sunday mornings to get the fire started in the hearth, which allowed the maid to rest that day. This had been Brita's suggestion, which I did not think much about at the time. Later, I felt bad about it. But then again, I did not think getting up at eight o'clock in the morning, for a seventeen-year-old, was such a barbaric time since she had to get up before seven on all the other days. Adding to her annoyance, there were times when she had trouble getting the fire started in the hearth. One Sunday she did not want to come to the country at all, she couldn't get enough rest cycling such a long way, 22 kilometers (13 miles) from Kymmene to Mustaniemi, so she chose to stay in Kymmene and catch up on some sleep. I was worried about her, she was worn out.

Pulle had come to see us with Curt Cedercreutz to go hunting, and Willy had arrived as usual to spend Sunday in peace and quiet with Brita. Around noon engineer Zimmermann called from the mill and asked for Pulle. I told him that he was out hunting and would not be back for several hours. The gentleman wanted us to go out and look for Pulle and do everything we could to find him. When I asked Mr. Zimmerman if something unusual had happened, he said no, but that something could.

All we could do was to go out into the woods with a dinner gong and yell at the top of our lungs. It was very unpleasant since we did not know why Zimmermann wanted to get a hold of my husband. For two hours, we ran about in the woods shouting. Occasionally we heard his loyal dog, Reku, bark which meant Pulle couldn't have been very far away. But, in the end, it was no use, so we returned home. Zimmermann called again and said that he was going to send a car for Pulle, because he absolutely had to return to the mill. When he finally came home, Pulle was surprised to find a military vehicle waiting, and even more amazed when he heard Zimmermann's message. "But Wallenius is in Kymmene," Pulle said. "He is the assistant chief of the shelters and is covering for me today."

After a quick brunch Pulle got up to leave with Cedercreutz, Mi, and Allan Björk, who had come to fetch him. I accompanied them outside. A strange, eerie feeling came over me as I watched the car drive away.

Later I was told that a few Russian planes had flown over nearby Lake Lappträsk which was the reason Pulle had to return to Kymmene immediately.

Little Ulla, who had always been a sensitive child, was very shaken by what happened. She became noticeably more nervous after it.

The days became shorter and colder. Lake Urajärvi lay blank; a thin ice crust had formed along the shore and the weak rays of the sun were not able to melt the frost on the ground any longer.

With winter approaching we were longing to return home to Kymmene. The 15th of November I traveled to Kymmene. Though the weather was bleak, there was finally a bright light on the political horizon. And, what joy, on the 16th Pulle said we could move back into town. I joyfully called Brita and told her I would return to Mustaniemi the next day and we could pack together. But Brita said she could do that without me. She, Siiri and Taina did not want to wait and were going to start right away.

The next day everyone returned to Kymmene by bus, except Pi and Ulla, who came on their bikes. Peter, who turned six that day, had to wait and celebrate the next day. He was honored with mirth and glee, and everybody was happy to be home again and above all that our country had weathered the storm without ending up at war.

Life returned to normal. Even the schools started again. Mi returned to Klostret, and Pi and Trolle walked to their school, at the break of dawn, each November morning. Brita and I organized our homes. It was surely needed, as long as we had been gone.

We lived just as we had in times of profound peace, if one does not count the concern about the food situation, which had made

a turn for the worse. Hoarding was something we wanted to avoid. The World War was discussed constantly. The unrest grew again.

One day some of the Kymmene wives came for coffee. We had not met in a long time. They were Clara Ekholm, Glory Zilliacus, Maggie Sucksdorff, and of course, Brita. Eva Horelli was still in Sweden where she had evacuated with her two children. Glory was convinced that all of us would still have to leave and that she herself probably would spend Christmas close to Heinola in one of the company's properties. She had already been there during the time of the additional refresher training period. I could understand her concern very well. Her husband Olle, chief accountant at the office, was still on active duty. On top of that their daughter was only a few months old. The boys were older, ten and six years old. Brita and I tried to calm her down. We were hopeless optimists.

WAR!

On November 30th Brita and I were supposed to travel to Kouvola to do some shopping. The bus was to leave at 10:30 and I was getting ready when the sirens went off. My first thought was that it was a fire, but I quickly realized it was an air-raid alarm. We needed to take cover in our cellar.

Brita came rushing in, she was agitated and did not want to hear anything about a cellar. She was determined to fetch the children from school. I had to use all my persuasive skills to talk her out of it. No one was aloud in the streets during an alarm. Besides, the children were at school where their teachers would surely take care of them. I also pointed out if she did not trust the teachers, Stina Serck was close by. She lived right across the street from the Little School.

Brita calmed down and we stood outside our ice cellar to take cover if it was needed. As we stood there our neighbor Eine Rhen arrived. I asked her where her children would go if war was going to break out. During the additional refresher training Eine had taken them to stay with her family in Gamle-Karleby. She returned to Kymmene, as she was not allowed to leave the area, being the vice chairwoman of the Lotta volunteers. The kids were at home again and she did not know where they were going to go next.

The telephone rang, I hurried inside but whoever called had hung up. It was forbidden to make calls during an alarm. I phoned the call center, but they couldn't tell me who had called. I asked them to connect me to Stina, as I was certain she had defied the order and made the call. But she had not. However, she was able to assure me that the children were all right. Later we heard that the teachers had gotten pretty hysterical when the alarm went off and if Stina had not stopped her, one of the teachers would have walked through the town and taken the kids home one by one. There had also been some mothers who arrived to take their children home, even though it was forbidden to be out on the roads during an alarm.

Soon the telephone rang again. It was Klostret's principal, Mrs. Björksten, who informed me that Mi's friend's mother had come to Grankulla to pick up her daughter. Somehow, she had gotten a hold of a car. The question was if Mi should go back home with them. I was glad it could be arranged. Mrs. Björksten told me there had also been an alarm in Grankulla as well as Helsinki at the same time. Later we learned that the capital city had been bombed.

It was time to evacuate to Mustaniemi again. After the all-clear signal, we went inside and began packing. We offered to take care of Eine's children as well, and thereby our evacuation family was increased by two kids. Twelve-year-old Ebba and Kurt-Eric who was seven.

Our nation had been attacked by the Russians. But we were going to defend ourselves until the last drop of blood.

On December 1st, a bus arrived to take us to the country. I was feeling pretty gloomy, unhappy that the war had broken out. Pi had cried bitter tears over having to leave home again; there had been an edgy feeling ever since the day before. Pulle looked serious when he followed us outside. As we were about to say our goodbyes he had to rush to the phone. He soon came out again and told us to hurry.

Brita, her kids and maid, the Rhen children, as well as our kids and myself all rushed onto the bus as fast as we could. We were supposed to pick up Mrs. Halme's three-year-old daughter Pirkko and her caretaker Mrs. Kelistö, as well as Tytti af Forselles and her two small girls, Eva, five, and Marita who was three. The ladies were going to move into a little cottage not far from Mustaniemi. On top of that, engineer Spolander's wife and two teenage sons, Erkki and Tauno, were coming along to stay with the Mynttinens at the neighboring farm.

Just as the bus stopped to pick up more passengers the sirens sounded. Now I understood why Pulle wanted us to hurry. As the chief of the shelters, he was informed whenever there was danger approaching, and he was the one to give the order to sound the alarm. The bus was in a very unfavorable spot, in a wide-open area, so we decided to drive to af Forselles who lived in Lautta Street. The bus parked under cover and we were able to go into a cellar.

Ulla got very distraught and started crying. Brita had all the worry in the world trying to calm her down. The alarm was not long and we didn't see any planes, so we were able to continue our journey. Mrs. Spolander told us her younger boy had a nervous breakdown the night before which was why they had come along. But she hoped they would not have to stay away long, as she wanted to go back into town and continue her job at the cafeteria.

I told her that Mi was also going back. She was only coming along to help us get settled in the country again. Tytti sat quietly with her little daughters. The woman had just said goodbye to her husband, lieutenant Fredrik af Forselles. He had been in uniform, which meant

he'd been called up like most of the other men. She looked sad but lovely with her doll-like daughter, Marita, sitting in her lap. It was an adorable sight, but oh so somber. Strength and grace. She was the epitome of the warrior's wife.

Winter came early. The frozen ground was already covered in a thick layer of snow. When we arrived in Mustaniemi we were lucky to have lots of things to do. It was a relief to be able to think about everyday tasks.

The first week Trolle caught a cold. It was nothing serious, just slightly swollen glands, runny nose and cough, for Trolle, nothing out of the ordinary.

But the first week was terribly exhausting, as soon as we had gotten our home in order, Brita tried to convince me to send the children to Sweden. I fought back with all my heart: "Pulle is chief of the population shelters, and as such, he has to set an example in Kymmene. It would look strange if he sent his children to Sweden as soon as the war broke out. It could downright cause panic."

But Brita insisted that it would be the best solution. It would not include Mi, she would stay at the cafeteria. I was desperate. Was the situation really that hopeless? And where could we send the kids? We would have to turn to The Finland Help, for we did not know anyone to send them to privately. It was different for the Koskulls, they had good friends, the Rosenblad family in Stockholm, who, when the war broke out, had sent a telegraph saying they would be willing to take all three kids to stay with them. It was a very generous offer. And all those in Sweden, Norway, and Denmark who helped us during our hard times deserve our utmost recognition.

Brita was negotiating with Willy on the phone. When I spoke to Pulle, he thought Brita and Willy should send their children, but we should not. We weren't even supposed to talk about such things on the phone. Pulle did not contradict himself. He always stuck to his principles and faithfully fulfilled his duties.

All this tormented me like a nightmare for several days. Brita thought that if we did not send Pi and Trolle, she would not send her kids either. I felt as if I was between two fires. I could not ask Pulle to go against his conviction, and I could not stop Brita from sending her children out of danger. This above all, because we knew it was necessary to take Ulla to a calm place due to her nerves. What would become of our country? Nobody knew. Pulle wanted Brita and I to come to Kymmene to discuss the matter.

When Tytti heard that we were planning to go back to Kymmene she was terrified. According to her it was crazy to go into town on December 6th as there were dreadful rumors going around that the Russians would hit us hard on our Independence Day. It was unsettling news, but I decided to not get hysterical. Come what may, I was going to travel to Kymmene!

The grocer, Heinonen, was leaving his nearby villa by truck and we were allowed to join him that evening on his way back to Kymmene. It was a strange feeling to drive through the dark forest and white snow using only blue lights. I could not fathom how Heinonen was able to drive in such darkness.

Once we were home the question about the children was decided very promptly. Pulle made the decision: The Koskull's children would be sent to Sweden, and ours would stay in the homeland. Willy asked several times if I disliked it. I answered that they naturally should do what they thought was right. It was decided that Brita would do some shopping the next day and then we would go back to Mustaniemi with the milk truck. All of the practical things, such as bus tickets, were being arranged. Brita was going to accompany the children to Haparanda in the North, and then return to Mustaniemi, where we were going to complete our Lotta orders. Thereafter, she planned to look for a steady job with the Lotta volunteers in town.

All of this took place in Pulle's room, which was blacked out. All the paintings had been taken down and the room felt different. I sat in the sofa, relieved that I did not have to send Pi and Trolle to strangers in a foreign land. I had been worried especially about

Trolle. At the same time, I was wondering what I would have done in Mustaniemi all by myself. Suddenly I felt abandoned. Brita had promised to return for a while, but I did not even dare to hope for that.

As I sat there, lost in my thoughts, I came to think about Stina Serck. Maybe she would come out to Mustaniemi with her nine-year-old boy Gunnar? I could always ask her. Stina agreed to come, she said that she really was happy to come. It was nice that I did not have to be alone.

The next day I felt sick. I dragged myself around on errands with Brita. It was very difficult to get anything done when everything was closed for Independence Day. We went into the stores through the back door. That afternoon we traveled back to the country, and on December the 7th Brita left with her children. The same evening Stina and Gunnar arrived.

Out on the front the troops were doing well, and there was great enthusiasm and patriotism. In our world in the countryside there was hardly anything going on. Each day was the same, like a string of grey beads on a rosary. It was getting colder and the kids trudged off to Tillola to fetch the food packages. They pulled their sleds behind them through the snow which became more and more difficult with every passing day as the snow cover became thicker and thicker. The milk truck only came every other day and the bus was generally overcrowded. We often took turns standing by the roadside, waiting in the freezing cold.

Any time we heard an airplane, we crawled under some tree or bush, or into a ditch, so we would not be detected and possibly be hit by machine gun fire. One day I met Mrs. Tolppala, who could not stop crying, she asked how long the war was going to last and how it was going to end. She must have thought I was an oracle. I tried to console her the best I could, but insisted I did not know anything more than anyone else.

"Now I am calm," Mrs. Tolppala said. "The baroness would know. And this I say; I would give away everything I own for our country, if that is what it takes!"

The conversation did me a lot of good.

We listened to the radio every day, but our reception was getting worse and it was difficult to hear Stockholm. We were able to hear the Lahtis broadcast just fine, even though the Russians tried to disturb the transmissions. Stina and I did a lot of needlework. We knitted gloves for the soldiers, knee warmers, and throat protectors, which were called "mama's darling".

The girls participated with great interest in the work for our brave soldiers. The kids got

along well. Kurt-Eric and Ebba were so adorable in their devotion to each other. It was remarkable that the kids, at that age, never cried for their mother who had to remain in town. Tytti, our neighbor, often came by with her sweet little girls.

Our life in the country seemed idyllic. But out there in the cold the Russian bombs were blasting. When the ground shook and it echoed through the hills we knew Kouvola or Koria was getting bombarded. If the muted sounds came from the west it was Lahtis. And when the quakes came out of the east our throats closed up. Was it Kymmene?

Strangely, Kymmene was spared. It was hit only twice, and even then, just the outskirts of the community. Voikka was also bombarded. And this past summer I had not been able to imagine that these peaceful places would be destroyed by the enemy.

It got colder and colder, the sun would shine all day, and at night we were often able to see the moonshine. If it had been a blizzard, the enemy planes would have left us alone.

Stina and I agreed we would take turns going to Kymmene. I went home in the middle of December and met Brita who had returned from her trip. It had gone well apart from a few hardships. Willy had been called to duty. She admired him for his decision. She had started working at the cafeteria with Mi. In addition, she had become a chauffeur for the shelters. Every time there was an alarm she went to the same cave, the one that was simply called "Luolan" (The Cave), which is where Pulle also had his staff. She wore a yellow arm bandage on her coat.

The first evening at home all five of us sat together and talked. Brita, Mi and I were knitting as usual. Finnish women had gotten into a knitting frenzy. They were knitting everywhere, in the cafeteria, the shelters, and in the homes.

The telephone rang, it was the call center informing us that the first warning for an alarm had been given. We continued our conversation. Pulle did not have to give the order for the actual alarm anymore, as it was decided that it would be better if both Kymmene and Kouvola got the alarm at the same time.

The phone soon rang again: "The alarm has been cancelled". Thereafter a "Quiet Alarm" was issued. This was a "2nd Degree Warning" which meant Pulle and Brita had to leave for the Cave. Willy also went along so Mi and I were alone. They had barely made it out the door when a full alarm sounded. I got up quickly, put on my coat, and went down into the cellar. It wasn't a real bomb shelter but at least it protected against shrapnel. Mi was stalling. I was wondering why she didn't hurry, she answered that she had had enough of this rushing back and forth. I realized I had now become just like everyone else.

We sat in the cellar for an hour and a half before the all-clear came. Once we finally got home a "Warning" went off again. And we were on our way down into the cellar a second time.

Afterward we sat down and talked about our current life. Pulle was unhappy to be chief of the shelter system, he wanted to be out on the front. We were trying to tell him that he was needed more here. No one could take care of all his duties and simultaneously be in charge of the company. But Pulle remained just as worried. He had three brothers at the front, Lasse as a physician, Dulle as a platoon commander in the foremost lines, and Nisse as a veterinarian. Pulle was sitting in the Cave with "15 meters (50 feet) of rock above my head", as he would put it.

The company president, Karl-Erik Ekholm, had been ordered to Stockholm where he, in his way, served his country as a government representative.

Willy could not wait for his next orders. He was a soul on fire, full of enthusiasm and patriotism. Brita was happy to have a job, even though she was not very fond of the cafeteria. She would have preferred a more demanding job than pouring coffee for a myriad of soldiers. That is why she was pleased to also function as a chauffeur. She did not want to sit in the Cave, you couldn't see anything there, and it was too confined for her temperament.

Mi was alright, the running about in the cafeteria suited her. There were many situations that she laughed at, whole heartedly, with her sense of humor. She also decided to become an active Lotta member.

I sat quietly and listened to their conversation. It was awful to just be sitting on the sidelines all the time. It was true that someone had to take care of the children, and by taking care of the Rhen children as well, I did help Eine to perform her duties as a Lotta.

Pulle tried to confirm this. But even though I agreed, in principle, that he was right, I still regretted I was not able to participate like the others. I had the feeling my Lotta sisters were looking down on me, just as they did with some of the evacuated mothers who did not have little children. Maybe it was wrong of me to think that. One should not pay attention to the words or thoughts of unfriendly people. I had been a Lotta since 1921, except during the period between 1931-1935 when I was absent due to poor health. To sit in the bushes, like a hare, made me desperate. When I saw Brita in a uniform, my eyes started to tear up. But I had no choice. I had to travel to Mustaniemi again, I could not leave Stina to bear the responsibility of the children by herself for too long.

THE FIRST WARTIME CHRISTMAS

Christmas came, at least according to the calendar, but there was no Christmas spirit.

It was impossible for Pulle to leave town and Stina's husband could not come to visit us, so we decided, despite the danger of the bombardments, to take the kids into Kymmene. We couldn't use our own cars due to the gas restriction, however, we were able to hire a taxi. But since all of us couldn't fit into the car, I had to leave by bus.

I waited two hours at the Tillola junction and was frozen stiff when the bus finally arrived. The bus was overcrowded. People were sitting in each other's laps and standing in the aisle. I managed to squeeze into the backseat and took a poor little girl into my lap who was feeling sick.

The trip was not particularly pleasant, but I did my best to cheer up the somber mood by talking to complete strangers left and right. But one always had to watch out not to say anything inappropriate.

On Christmas Eve, I had arranged for dinner at six o'clock, and I had also managed to get a few presents for the kids. We had to work hard but we managed to make it feel a little like Christmas. It was very sweet and considerate of Willy to get us a Christmas tree through one of the workers at the cellulose plant. I was eternally grateful to him for doing that.

It was a strange Christmas. We tried to keep smiling, but Pi was thoughtful. Trolle whispered, asking why it looked so strange at home, why the paintings had been taken down and the rugs removed. It was heartbreaking to have to explain that the paintings could fall down and break if a bomb were to hit us and the rugs could be damaged from broken glass.

Trolle had also gotten a splinter under a nail, so everything was quite different from our usual Christmases.

Brita and Willy sat in the sofa holding hands. They were probably thinking about their children in Sweden and the separation from them. Brita cried a few bitter tears, unfortunately we were not able to console her.

I realized that I had it good. Both my husband and my children were with me. Most of the others had their husbands and sons out on the front.

The moon shone brightly outside and it was very light, yet not a single alarm sounded. Even so, I couldn't relax until noon on Christmas Day when the children left with Stina. Soon after the sirens went off, but at that point they were far away from town.

We spent a lot of time in the cellar on that Christmas day. But after the first alarm Mi announced: "Well, that was a short and pleasant alarm." It was a refreshing and liberating quote.

The same day I wrote to Eva Horelli. She had offered to take Trolle and Pi to stay with her sister, the Baroness Anne-Marie Hermelin at the Stjernarp Estate in Halland, Sweden. I wanted to thank her for the offer and let her know we had decided to keep the children in Finland for as long as possible. And as well as things were going out on the front, there was no reason to believe that we were not going to be able to keep them with us all through the war.

Mrs. Hermelin was fully occupied with helping children who had been evacuated to Sweden during the Winter War. She made a great sacrifice for our country. She was born in Finland, her maiden name was Sourander. She wanted to do everything possible for her countrymen in need.

The following day Willy started active duty. He traveled to Helsinki and joined the Marines, with whom he had done his basic training several years earlier. We wished him all the best luck on his journey.

I went back to the country. There, I was met by a sparkling open fire, and the little Christmas tree, which had been cut the day before Christmas Eve on our own property. It now stood neatly decorated in the living room.

On New Year's Eve, I asked Tytti to come and join us. It was the saddest, most ceremonious New Year's Eve I have ever experienced. Pulle and Mi were certainly not very far away, but they were not with us. Stina's husband, Vicky Serck, was at the mill, Tytti's husband, Fredrik af Forselles, was at the front. She was pale but calm. When the clock struck midnight, she got up and wished us a happy New Year.

It was not only our own personal joy and sadness that we were thinking of. Our thoughts were with the whole future of Finland. What would happen to it?

God willing all was going to be alright, that our land was going to be happy, that this coming year was going to be better than this past year, this we hoped, and millions of others with us.

1940

The Russians have their eyes on Finland as the Winter War rages on. Germany invades Denmark and Norway. Sweden remains neutral but continues to supply Hitler with much needed iron ore to keep his war machine going, which now was advancing into Western Europe including the invasion of Paris.

The Baltic nations are forced to surrender completely and to join the Soviet Union after a rigged election. Estonian leaders are arrested and deported to Siberia.

The Battle of Britain begins. While the Luftwaffe and the Royal Air Force are dropping bombs on London and Berlin respectively, President Roosevelt is asking congress to start war preparations, and in October the U.S. draft registration begins. President Roosevelt wins a third term and promises not to send “our boys” into war.

The Tripartite Pact is formed between Germany, Italy, and Japan, the original three “Axis” powers. Even the Russians are invited to join them, but Stalin wants new territories, including Finland. Hitler is reluctant to let the Soviet Union expand any further into the west, and so Finland ends up between a rock and a hard place, and all it really wants is to maintain its still young independence.

COLD AND CALAMITY CLAIMS ITS VICTIMS

The temperature continued to drop and it snowed relentlessly. The snow mounds were huge, at least in our area. We had constant sparkling sunshine, which made it easy for the hated Russian pilots to find their targets.

There was no word from Dulle for three weeks, and we all started to get worried. I was thinking about his words last summer and dark thoughts entered my mind. But we did not have to wait long for some signs of life. He was doing well and in good spirits. We were immensely relieved.

Then one day we heard that Ernst-Adolf Biese had been killed on Christmas Eve. He was the son of one of the engineers at the mill. He'd grown up here and went to the little Swedish school. Mi had often been to their home, as she was friends with his sister, Ruth. We were deeply shaken.

When Pi, January 5th, turned thirteen, we celebrated with coffee for the elder and juice for the young. And as usual, when lots of kids get together, there was plenty of noise. Tytti had come with her three girls, so there are a total of eight children.

Pi had gotten a nasty eczema. The cold was probably to blame, it always got worse when she was outside, so she decided to stay inside, which was both boring and unhealthy.

To keep the cold out, we had covered both the hallway and the veranda doors. We hung wall rugs and fur hides in front of doors and only used the door to the kitchen to get in and out. After two hours of heating in the boiler, the temperature in Pi's room was just 8 Celsius (46 Fahrenheit), and she was the hardiest one of us all. This further worsened her eczema. It was a little bit warmer in the other rooms.

But one got used to it. When I got up, the thermometer was usually around 12 C (53 F), and I stood almost naked washing up. If it was any colder than that it felt pretty torturous. All the corners of the room were covered in thick frost. And in one of the corners, where the radio stood, it wasn't just drafty, it was actually windy. The temperature outside was unbelievable. One evening we had -38 C (-36 F). I was worried the pipes for the heaters would freeze overnight, so we were forced to keep the fire going in the boiler at three in the morning, even though we had just added wood around one o'clock. This continued for as long as the temperature dropped below -30 C (-22 F). Unfortunately, the wood supply was starting to run out and it was almost impossible to get it replenished. We were not able to use the fireplace anymore, though we surely could have used it.

Every evening we left the faucets running for fear the cistern in the attic would freeze and break. We were able to save our pluming with all these measures.

In Tillola the temperature had reached a record low -44 C (-47 F). In some areas, including at the front, -50 C (-58 F) had been measured. Many soldiers had their fingers and toes amputated. My brother-in-law, Dulle had frostbite on his toes but not bad enough to send him to a hospital.

From the home front, countless packages were sent to the "unknown soldier" containing warm knitted clothing, cough drops, tobacco, etc. In all communities, the shelter organization and the Lotta volunteers were collecting both new and old clothes to be sent to the soldiers. The desire to give to charity was high. Blankets, shoes, furs, and other useful things were donated. Even so, the warriors, as well as the civilian population, froze more than ever before in their lives that winter.

We were able to stay essentially healthy, despite the cold. However, Pulle, did come down with influenza. He remained in bed and did not go to the office. But as soon as the sirens went off, even just a "Quiet Warning", he got up, put his clothes on, including his enormous felt boots, and left for the Cave. But, strange enough, he recovered quickly, thanks to the "horse-remedy" prescribed by Dr. Lalla Köhler.

Mi once had frostbite on her ear, and, Trolle, frequently on his cheeks. Pi's eczema got worse, but I, the family's black sheep, remained strangely healthy. If you really have to fight to survive, you just do it.

Tytti lived close by in a small one bedroom cottage. She stayed there with the maid and three kids. The room was filled with beds, the corners covered in frost. In order for Tytti to get to the kitchen, she had to walk through a foyer, which was not heated. To help relieve her misery, I ordered the boys to shovel snow against the walls, which did help to stop the draft from the floors somewhat. I offered Tytti to move in with us, but she wanted to hold out in the cottage. Eva, her older daughter, stayed with us when she had a bad cough, she became our girl for a couple of nights.

The cottage Tytti stayed in was owned by our neighbors the Mynttinens and rented out for the summer, it was by no means intended as a winter lodging. But Tytti, with her happy and calm disposition, never complained. And when the children were ailing, she took care of them the best she could. She did not have happy days.

Our sauna was in such bad shape, we had to wash up in the kitchen. The kids had a large basin where they could splash around. Gunnar, Kurt-Erik, and Trolle all fit into it wonderfully. It was more difficult with Ebba and her long legs, and Pi, as overweight as she was in those days.

We also had another problem. The electric light went out now and then. The lines were damaged during the bombardments, and we had to sit in the dark or by candlelight. In most cases the problem was quickly fixed, but sometimes we worried that the power plant in Voikka had taken a direct hit. At the same time as the light went out, the radio was also silenced.

The war became more and more terrifying. It had already claimed many victims on the front and among the civilian population. The Russians were intruding into the Isthmus of Karelia, but so far, the Mannerheim Line was still holding. Daily, the radio reported the attacks had been warded off.

Marshal Mannerheim
Commander-in-Chief

The refugee caravans from Karelia marched on along the roadways. These people were always so remarkably calm. One of the families was from Muolaa. Among them older and younger men, and women. They were wrapped in blankets and shawls. They carried bundles of all sizes. In general, it was a tired horse pulling the load. A colt or foal ran behind. I rarely saw any children. They, along with the elderly, were allowed to travel by train. Even the cows were evacuated the same way. At many stations they stood in their cattle wagons and bellowed, until they were milked by women who had been called in by the authorities.

The refugees came from all communities along the entire eastern border, but the only ones to pass through our area were those evacuating from the Isthmus of Karelia.

All over the country people were taking in these suffering countrymen. The Mynttinens, among many others, especially deserve mentioning in this regard. One evening they took in a caravan which was housed in their large cottage. The refugees got food and lodging along with provisions for the road for themselves, as well as for the horses, and they did not have to pay a penny for any of it.

The alarm signals in town and all over the country became more and more frequent, and people had to spend more and more time in the shelters.

We were shocked to hear the news that Marga Österman, Pulle's sister, was injured in a bombing of Mänttä. Why her? She had been frail all her life and now this happened. We did not know how badly she was hurt. One was not able to make long distance calls, except in extraordinary circumstances. At that point, we only knew that she had been sent to the Seinäjoki hospital.

My sister, Greta Gustafsson, wrote frequently. She was staying with our sister, Caja Mandelin, up in Varkaus. Greta's husband Verner Gustafsson, general and supply chief for the army, was located in a safe place and their son, Paul, as well. Their daughter, Margaretha, called Tippan, worked in an office in St. Michel, an area precariously located, but lost her job when her workplace was destroyed in one of the severe bombardments. Greta was so sad, it made me very unhappy. I compared her letter with my brother-in-law, Lasse's, which was full of optimism and, therefore, comforting and wonderful to read. The letters from my sisters-in-laws were peaceful, sensible, and full of confidence.

What was I going to do with Greta? I suggested she come and stay with me, and I wrote to try to calm her down, but nothing helped. She traveled to a small cottage close to Tavastehus and took her children with her. But the letters did not get any more cheerful even though she now was with Tippan and Paul, who she had missed so much while in Varkaus.

It was sometime at the end of January that we heard that Holger's son, Werner, had been wounded. He had suffered a serious wound in his back, but with no long-term consequences.

One day, out in the country, I told the others that I was going to go into town the next morning as long as it wasn't too cold. When I looked at the thermometer it said -18 C (0 F), which I did not think was all that cold. It actually was -28 C (-18 F), I had misread the thermometer. But your imagination can have a big influence on you, and I did not feel cold at all, we had, after all, not had such "mild" conditions in a long time.

I started my trip as usual. I had laundry with me and tied it to the sled, tied a cloth over my fur hat and neck, put the gas mask in my pocket, turned up the collar on my fur coat, and trudged off. I had Pulle's gray hunting socks on my feet, and Mi's felt boots.

It was still pretty dark. The forest stood still, not a sound except when snow fell to the ground from a tree branch. It was as if I was wandering in a fairyland. A bird cried out, then everything was quiet again. I only heard my own feet squeaking in the snow and the bobbing sled as I pulled it through the uneven track where no one had trampled the snow cover yet. There was so much snow that one could only walk to Tillola. A horse would have had a hard time moving forward, not to mention a car. When it started to get light, I noticed fresh moose tracks, they had been out during the night. There were also tracks from foxes and hares, who had been jumping around. Just the owls were missing. I had not heard their cries all winter.

As usual, I had to wait for the bus for a long time and it got terribly cold to stand in the snow. I walked back and forth, back and forth, but when the cold became unbearable I went to a forest ranger, who had his house close by, to warm up. When I finally arrived at home in Kymmene it was one o'clock. Pulle sat in the small sitting room, drinking coffee, he had already had lunch. I had to change my footwear, and have a tall glass of cognac, before I got reasonably warm again. It was very time consuming, during the war, to make the 22 km (13 mi) trip from Mustaniemi to Kymmene.

Only Pulle was home. Mi was at the cafeteria, and Brita, who had lived with us since Willy left, had a new job. She was now in charge of one of the Lotta sick wards. She had to take care of a lot of pneumonias and stomach flues. In her usual brisk way, she was not afraid of work. The fact that she was not a nurse and lacked any healthcare experience, did not bother her at all. The soldiers were grateful and well behaved, she got along well with them, however, she was critical of the doctor. He seemed to have minimal knowledge of medicine and a keen interest in alcohol. Brita did not lose her spirit very easily, but one time she did cry, she was so unhappy about this doctor's irresponsible behavior. It even happened that he ignored patients with pneumonia and a high fever. And it is our absolute conviction that at least one of the patients recovered thanks to Brita's help. She had a job where she could be useful and show her worth.

Myself, I felt doubly pitiful. Was I doomed to just sit in the countryside for the entire war? Pulle noticed how distressed I was and suggested I come to an agreement with Stina to stay in town for longer periods at a time and not just a few days as we were doing now. We could take turns and I might be able to get some kind of temporary job. I called Stina, who enjoyed being out in the country by herself for a while taking care of the children. She agreed that I could stay as long as I wanted. She was not a Lotta and did not really want to spend more than a few days at a time in town.

The next morning, I immediately called Eine and asked if she had some sort of job for me. I was afraid the cafeteria job would be too strenuous for me, but I was happy to take some other job where I was needed. I was pretty upset when I talked to her, as I had started to suffer from an inferiority complex. Eine right away suggested I should start working at the Lotta sewing center. She promised to talk to the manager and suggest that I could come and go as I wanted, so that I could go back to the kids as needed. As this could be arranged I became extremely happy. I felt like a different person.

I became a Lotta seamstress. We worked in a school. A needlework teacher from the Kymmene factory's Vocational School, Ms. Ignatius, was in charge of the work. She had several helpers to do the cutting. Her sister, Mrs. Niinivaara, was married to the headmaster of the school and lived in the same building. This lively and cheerful lady, from Karelia, was incredibly energetic and made loads of socks, shirts, and underwear for the soldiers, and she also helped to distribute some of the work into the community. Most of the seamstresses were workers at the factory who had been laid off. There were also some wives of company executives. Among them was Inge Kyrklund who was married to Pulle's old classmate, engineer Gunnar Kyrklund. They were new to the area. She had to be evacuated from their home north of Lake Ladoga. Gunnar was employed by a subsidiary company that was part of the Kymmene Group. It was with this group of people that I was to sew countless pieces of clothing.

We were never able to sew undisturbed. Every day we were interrupted by alarms. There were so many sewing machines buzzing at the same time that we did not always hear the sirens, so Mrs. Niinivaara had taken it upon herself to listen for them. Countless times she ran in shouting, “Alarm, alarm!” and all we could do was to hurry to the shelter.

The same school was also lodging for a company of soldiers. Mrs. Niinivaara took care of them in the most loving way. If their clothes were torn, or something else was the matter, they would come to us. It was always Mrs. Niinivaara who talked to them and made sure the holes were patched. And if the boys were sick, she would give them hot tea and a powder and other medicine. She would wash and patch their socks. There were always soldiers‘ clothes hanging out to dry in her kitchen. She was adorable in her concern. She was very nice to me as well. Many times, she would come to me while I was working and bring me coffee.

It was an eventful time for me. All these people, from such different backgrounds, had their own personal joys and sorrows. But we shared the most important thing of all– our homeland.

February the 2nd Gunnar turned ten. Stina had gotten a nice cake on her last trip to Helsinki, which we enjoyed with coffee before noon. We had wonderful canned fruit after dinner. Our menus were, in general, very simple, but plentiful. It was not until the middle of February that the food shortage in our community was beginning to be noticeable in earnest.

The boys did a lot of cross country skiing this winter in the hilly terrain around Mustaniemi. All three of them became really good. They went up and down, between trees and bushes at hair-raising speed.

They cleared an area on the frozen lake for ice-skating. Pi and Ebba also took part in this job. But the children were told to keep their ears open for any sound of airplanes. Countless times, when they heard the noise, they ran up and threw themselves into the snow piles behind the sauna.

Since we constantly had planes flying above, I became concerned that one would eventually make an emergency landing on the ice of Lake Urajärvi. This had happened frequently in other areas, and we heard rumors that the Bolshevik pilots would force themselves into isolated civilian houses and demand food. Most of the time they were arrested before they were able to do any more damage than just scaring people.

In February Pulle was ordered to go to nearby Kausala for Defense Corps training. He came to stay with us one evening, and the next morning he skied back with a full load. After the assignment, he again came to spend the night in Mustaniemi. I was happy he was able to visit with us so that Pi and Trolle were able to see their father.

Pi's eczema was becoming more and more troublesome. We decided to take her to Kymmene, despite the danger of the bombardments. There we had a Dermatologist, a Dr. Johanson from Viborg's regional hospital. He had come along when the hospital had to be evacuated to Kymmene, and now worked at the War Hospital #13 in Kuusankoski.

It was unthinkable to have the girl walk the long way to Tillola and wait for the bus, possibly for hours, so we waited for an opportunity to get a lift. This came on February 17th, when the grocer Heinonen came to visit his villa. That evening we walked to the Mynttinens, where Heinonen had driven his car. It was impossible to reach our place because of the snow.

Pi was very excited. She was happy to go back home, but it felt different as she had to be prepared to spend countless hours a day in the shelters.

Our trip started like an adventure. The car stalled in the middle of Salpausselkä Road. It was not easy to make the repairs in the moonlight with the help of a dim flashlight. It was scary to stand there and wait, horribly cold as well. Luckily the problem was fixable and we were able to continue our journey. But we only got as far as the Kuusankoski Church before we were stopped by two men from the population shelter. They told us that an alarm was ongoing. We were allowed to continue as long as we turned off the lights and did not drive farther than Heinonen's store. Meter by meter we slowly continued and finally arrived safe, thanks to the moonlight.

The grocer Heinonen was very thoughtful. First, he took us into his office, then he went outside to listen if there was any danger before leading us to a cellar under a wooden house. Soldiers and knitting girls kept us company. The atmosphere was warm. The Russian airplanes we heard humming above us were headed for Kouvola where they dropped their deadly load. I was thinking about my girl sitting beside me. She looked serious, but lit up when a soldier approached and offered us some cough drops.

An hour later we were allowed to continue to Kymmene. There was a thick fog over the river that night. It was very difficult to see the road, despite the moonshine.

Apart from the doctor's appointment, Pi stayed home. And every time the alarm went off she rushed down into the cellar. Without her needlework for the soldiers' mufflers, it would have been very boring for her, I thought, as she had to be by herself most of the day. I had resumed my sewing duties at the needle workshop and Mi was at the cafeteria. But Pi enjoyed being at home by herself.

At the workshop, I met the elementary school teacher Ms. Korpinen, who nervously told us that her sister-in-law, during the evacuation from Terijoki, had to rush out of the train into the woods when the alarm went off, and had to spend hours in the cold with her little girl. Her sister-in-law had then become seriously ill and was taken to St. Michel. There she was placed in the same hospital as her wounded husband. The hospital later took a direct hit in a bombardment, but both miraculously survived.

One day we were visited by two officers who were on leave and on the way back to the front. I had not met Major Bahne before, but I knew Captain Tötterman. He didn't recognize me at first as I was wearing my Lotta uniform.

The men had arrived from the west by train. Just as they stepped off the train in Kouvola the alarm went off. They rushed to the nearest shrapnel cover, which took a direct hit. They were in an area that was not damaged by the bomb and were not hurt. But they were very shaken as several people were killed. They insisted to avoid Kouvola station on the way to the front. People were beginning to be terrified of the town.

PI AND TROLLE TO SWEDEN?

Pulle and I had, numerous times, returned to the question of evacuating the children to Sweden. The fear that the front was going to collapse was always present. We did all we could to keep a bright outlook, but we still kept thinking about taking the trip out west. I also started to think about what clothes would be most suitable to send along with Pi and Trolle. They needed to be every day clothes, practical and durable. Their wardrobe also needed to be expanded. I took some time off from my Lotta job and sewed two shirts for Pi, mended and above all marked their clothing.

The radio broadcast from Lahtis had been silenced when a bomb had damaged the station. Instead of listening to our main station we had to listen to the horrible Russian propaganda. It was like living in a bubble. It was probably a little better in Kymmene, there were more of us there and we were able to talk to each other, but in Mustaniemi, it was awful not to get any information about anything.

At the end of February, we were again able to hear the Lahtis broadcast, but the news was much more serious. The Mannerheim Line was close to failing and the Summa-breakthrough was becoming reality. There was also bad news from the home front. Every day a myriad of locations were bombarded, people died and were wounded and large amounts of property was destroyed.

We had constant alarms. Kouvola was burning. The sky was completely red in the East. The firemen from Kymmene were sent there as Kouvola's fire department could not handle it by themselves. The men were exhausted fighting the fire. It wasn't just on the frontline where you could find heroes, there were many on the home front as well.

One day, when the explosions again were heard near Kouvola, Pulle called the county fire department from his quarters and asked if they needed help. A tired voice answered: “Yes, I am all alone out here.”

Old men, pristine young boys, and men unable to serve in the military were now acting as firemen. Their strength had been exhausted. When these men had a night off they went to Kymmene to get some sleep. There they were able to at least get a few hours of rest.

Around this time something very strange happened. The Russians dropped light bombs with timers as they flew over us during the day. At night these lit up like a lighthouse and led the pilots to their targets. Because of this clever arrangement we were never left in peace. How all the people around the Kouvola area, which was hit the worst, were able to get up night after night, sometimes several times a night to seek shelter, I do not understand.

Pulle was very tired as his sleep was interrupted constantly and he had to get dressed and rush to the Cave. There were people who never got undressed in order to immediately be ready, and they only dozed lightly between the alarms. But it really wasn’t necessary to stay indoors, ready to rush to a shelter, all day either. Kymmene had been spared from the bombardments, but on the other hand, we did not know when it would be our turn.

At this time, at the end of February, I still tried to hang on to the principle of going down into a shelter every time an alarm sounded. The girls were tired of always having to get up at night and, in the long run, we were not able to continue with it. Throughout the war, most people actually did seek shelter during the alarms. We did not have the strength anymore, we slept, except Pulle who had to go to the Cave.

Pulle kept many people's spirits up in Kymmene. People were generally optimistic, even though the alarm signals were tearing at our nerves and temper. But there were also hopeless pessimists. I met some of them.

I noticed Pulle was also beginning to look more serious with each day, but I didn't want to believe that the worst was still to come. If the front was breached, we would have a swarm of Russians over us. What would become of our country and our people? Death and misery? In this country we knew what Bolshevism really was, we were not living in a light blue fantasy.

The terrible cold was also beating upon us. The Gulf of Finland was frozen, as well as all the lakes and ponds. And now the Russians were invading from the south, through the archipelago outside Fredrikshamn and further east. Pulle was ordered to be able to leave the shelter job at any time and be deployed with the Defense Corps. As a lieutenant in the reserves he was to become a company chief. Now he thought Pi and Trolle should go to Sweden. Even though I had thought about it, it still hurt me badly when he said it. I knew he did not want to send the children away if not absolutely necessary. Since he had now made that decision, he obviously thought the situation was very serious.

I thought about some words Willy had once said: "If a person is very unhappy, it is as if she had a wall in front of her, but one day she will surely get through this wall, and then her frustration will have subsided."

I was now standing in front of such a wall. And it was going to be a long time before I was going to get through it. The next day I went back to the country to start getting the children's clothes ready for the journey to Sweden. When I told Stina about our plans, she said she would also leave with Gunnar. As a Norwegian subject, she was allowed to leave the country. No Finnish woman between the ages of 16-60 was allowed to pass the border unless she had a child under the age of 3. This was because of mandatory work orders. Despite this, many still left for some of the most unbelievable reasons. Stina promised to take care of our children during the trip. We decided I would come along as far as I was allowed to travel.

I went to Tytti to talk about it. She got upset. "But you, aren't you going to leave with them?" she asked.

"No, why should I do that, my kids are older."

"Many leave despite that, and Trolle is just eight years old," she said.

"That is true, but both Trolle and Pi can get along without me."

"If you were given permission to leave the country, would you go?"

"No," I answered.

"Don't you want to?"

"No, I am staying. I want to work. And remember: how could I leave my oldest girl, Mi, and just take off? I couldn't do that. Pi and Trolle have to manage, there is nothing we can do about it. And by the way, maybe they don't even have to go away."

All this took place in Tytti's little cottage where she was leaning against a post in the doorway. She had tears in her eyes.

Poor, dear Tytti, I thought. What is to become of you and your little ones, aren't you going to leave as well? I was too scared to ask, I did not want to worry her more than I already had.

Stina and I wondered if Tytti shouldn't leave with The Finland Help. Mothers and small children were well taken care of by this blessed organization. We, on the other hand, had children that were too old and had to travel privately.

Eine had come to Mustaniemi to celebrate Kurt-Erik's birthday. She did not say anything about mine and Stina's plans. I had the feeling I was abandoning her and her children in this dire situation. But I did not want to take the responsibility of taking Ebba and Kurt-Erik all the way through our country up north to Torneå and Haparanda. The trains were regularly bombarded, how we were going to get there no one knew. We still thought this was the only accessible route. The children could possible fly from Vasa to Sundsvall, but we were not likely to get tickets for them.

I was pretty desperate. With my own two kids, I could maybe make it. But with four kids, it would get complicated. I also thought their own mother should be able get a few days leave to take them herself. There were no guaranties I was going to be able to travel all the way up to Torneå, and I could not promise that Stina would take care of Ebba and Kurt-Erik for the rest of the trip in Sweden, that was not my place to do. But it still ate at me that I could not at least take them to the border.

I explained to Eine that her children could stay in Mustaniemi for as long as she wanted. I would keep the household going and let Brita's maid take care of it. But Eine said the children were going to move as soon as she was able to arrange it. Well, of course, she was going to do what she thought best.

I only stayed one day. When I got back into town Stina and Gunnar came along. When I got home, I got the message that there was no return at this point, the children had to leave as soon as possible. The Sercks came to us in the evening to plan how all this was going to be organized.

As both telegram and phone connections had been destroyed we did not have any contact to the west. We were completely cut off. Brita was able to get leave to visit with Willy in

Helsinki. She assumed it was the last time she was going to be able to travel.

The night of March 2nd, she was supposed to take the train to Kouvola. She agreed to buy tickets for us in Helsinki, as we had decided we were going to travel that way. We did not think it would be possible for us to get tickets if we tried to travel through Riihimäki. Besides, the town was constantly bombed, so it would be terrifying to change trains there. Helsinki, on the other hand, had been pretty calm lately. I went to the police station to get passports. The children would be allowed to travel to Sweden, and I was told that I could use my old passport and travel as far as Oulu, but not any farther. In order to go all the way to Torneå, I would have to get permission from the Lappland governor, which would take three weeks. It was impossible to wait that long so I had to settle with going only as far as Oulu. From there I would return home.

Where our kids would end up in Sweden we had no clue. They would first be sent to the Swedish Paper Industry Association in Stockholm. But the future would tell where they would end up somewhere between Ystad in the South and Haparanda in the North.

We also did not know if they would stay together or be separated.

March 1st, early in the morning, Stina went to Mustaniemi by horse to pick up Trolle and a few things. It was not easy to get away, just as she sat in the sled the alarm went off, so she was delayed.

At about five in the afternoon she was back with Trolle all bundled up in daddy's hunting fur. One could only see a little head peak out with two keen eyes searching the surroundings. For the eight-year-old the trip had been an adventure. It had been wonderful for him to travel by horse, even though Russian planes were frequently hovering above his head. Aunty Stina had just pushed him deeper into the sled hides. Now he was home in Kymmene, where he was going to hear the alarms howl and sit in the cellar, and then travel to Sweden. What adventures!

To be scared, or to miss home, was something that was not going to happen to Sten Knutson Samuel Werner von Troil (Trolle). A man of eight years was going to manage, especially since he was going to Sweden with his big sister. Delighted, he climbed out of the sled and rushed inside.

Big sister was not as eager to go. The whole winter she had said that she did not want to travel anywhere. However, now she immediately resigned. “Mom and Dad have to decide,” she said. But I was afraid she cried a few tears in silence by herself. Pi was very mature for her age. She understood how serious the situation was, although we did try our best to hide it from her. Thirteen is a sensitive age. One is neither an adult nor just a little one. And what Pi had to experience that March undoubtedly matured her beyond her years. It was a terrible time for our Pi.

Trolle had not been home many minutes before we had another alarm. He climbed down into the cellar with unmeasurable enthusiasm, where he then sat like a lit candle until it got too boring. Then he started to explore the cellar. There were lots of things to see. We sat in the part where ice would normally be stored. We had placed Koskulls’ coconut rug on the floor to keep it a little bit warmer. In the middle of the floor was a table with a tablecloth, a candle, a bowl with sugar cubes, and a bottle of camphor drops. There were lots of chairs along the walls. Brita's floor light completed the cozy atmosphere. It was surely one of the coziest shrapnel covers.

On the food shelves, we had all kinds of things. We had "evacuated" Pulle's chandelier which he got from father-in-law Uno when he passed away, and suitcases with various things that belonged to several families. In one corner was Trolle's pipe cabinet, which he had inherited from his grandfather and once belonged to his great-grandfather. On the walls, we had hung clothes in paper bags. Outside the door we had piled up bales of cellulose as protection against bomb shrapnel.

All this amazed and interested Trolle. But in the long run it still got boring, and suddenly he informed me that he had a tooth ache. I really was terrified. It was already Friday, and we were supposed to travel Saturday night. What was I going to do?

As soon as the "all clear" signal came, I rushed to the phone and made an appointment with the dentist Mrs. Stålhammar. She had promised her daughter, Brita Köhler, to accompany her and her little children to Tavastehus by car. From there they were going to take the train up north and evacuate to Sweden. She agreed with us, that the situation was critical and it was time to take the kids out of harm's way. Despite this, Dr. Stålhammar agreed to see Trolle that same evening at 7:30. I had to pack the children's clothes. In the last minute, I managed to get Pi a new dress. Our seamstress Aino made it. When she was interrupted by an alarm, she continued working in the cellar. Even "snow gowns", the white capes that helped us hide in the snow, were finished in the last minute. They were made out of old sheets.

Mi made sure Trolle got to the dentist. Trolle couldn't possibly be sent by himself in total darkness. It was as if I was walking on needles, afraid there was going to be another alarm and Trolle would be delayed. And that is exactly what happened. He had to be a good boy and trudge back into the cellar. But Mrs. Stålhammar promised to see him later, and luckily there was nothing wrong with his teeth. He had probably just gotten cold during the long sled ride from Mustaniemi.

The night became restless. Pulle and I had decided the children had to sleep through all the alarms. It was a big risk to stay inside a wooden house, especially on the second floor, where the girls had their bedroom, but it was probably a bigger risk to wear out Pi and Trolle before the journey, which could turn out to be very strenuous.

At 11 pm the first alarm went off, Mi and Pi had not fallen asleep yet, but Trolle had fallen into deep sleep and did not hear anything. The whole situation was horrible with airplanes roaring above our roof. Was it wrong to let the kids stay in bed, and without their clothes? But the bombers flew over us without doing us any harm, they saved their load for Kouvola; a short while later we heard the blast out of the southeast. When the alarm was over I went to bed and hoped I was going to be able to sleep. But no, the same alarm all over, and we heard the thunder from the same heavy bombers above us. Pulle got up and dashed over to his post. He rarely got there before the planes were already above us. He often had to jump into some pit or lie flat on the road.

I was so exhausted I did not even wake up when Pulle came home. I did not wake up until there was another alarm and Pulle had to leave again. In the morning when the sirens finally woke Trolle, he sat up in bed, startled, and asked if there had been an alarm during the night. When I told him yes, he was annoyed that we did not wake him up, he wanted to make another trip to the cellar. I was grateful he was so unafraid. It would have been horrible to have a frightened, out of his mind, crying child in the house.

We all sat around the tea table, except for Mi, who was at the cafeteria, when Brita called at 9 am from Kouvola. She had, despite the alarms, left Kymmene by horse and sled at 2:30 in the middle of the night. But the train for Helsinki had still not left Kouvola due to the constant alarms and had been moved to a side track. Before that, she had waited for hours in the shelter, out on the platform, or in an overcrowded station, where the restaurant had been bombed and burned down.

When I heard about this I was determined to avoid traveling through Kouvola with the children. To be there in the middle of bombardments was impossible, I thought. Even Pulle thought we had to rule out this travel plan. We talked to Stina and tried to get a hold of a taxi, which could take us to Elimäki parish. From there we would continue to Lovisa and on to Helsinki. But it was impossible to get a hold of a taxi. They all said they did not have enough gas, except for the trips they had already agreed to. We had to wait and see. The company had one car left, the military had taken the other one, but Pulle did not think it was appropriate for him to use it for his own family.

Saturday wasn't any better. I was unhappy about the constant howling from the sirens and sitting in the cellar, especially since I had not finished packing the children's clothes yet. The bombers were getting closer and we heard the rattle from machine gun fire. We assumed our own fighter pilots had gone up to face the enemy this time as in so many times before. Our young heroic warriors only had two paltry fighter planes to split the enemy squadron of forty planes. May history never forget this.

And so the bombs came crashing down. The cellar door flew up and slammed again from the pressure wave. I tried to shut the door but was called back by everyone in the cellar. Trolle sat far away from me, astonishment showed in his child's face. Pi sat deep in her chair, tired, resigned. Mi was on the other side of the river, where I did not know, probably in the nearest shrapnel cover that she was able to rush to from the cafeteria. Fear took over me.

"Come here Trolle!"

"Why?"

"Come quickly, run run, I have to hide your head!"

He came, although protesting. I took the boy next to me and wrapped my arms around his head. He was sitting next to the wall and I tried to protect him the best I could. I was thinking if bomb shrapnel flew inside, I would try to protect his head and face.

The door slammed over and over again, and it continued to howl, blast and crack outside. But all was well in the end. Later we heard that the water power plant in Keltti had been bombarded. This night became just as restless as the previous. In the morning, there was still uncertainty about our trip. I had to be ready to go any time if an opportunity should arise.

When there was another alarm I stayed inside. Pi and Trolle were sent to the cellar. Mi, who was off from the cafeteria, was patrolling outside and announced when the bombers were getting close, and then we rushed into the cellar. When it calmed down, I went up again and continued to pack. Taina followed me to make something to eat. We ate in the cellar. Many times Taina cooked during the alarms. The help, Rauha, and I walked around the house with our ears up, and often had to drop everything and run back to the cellar head over heels.

Under such conditions it was difficult to take care of the cooking, cleaning, and above all, the heating. It had been cold all winter, colder than ever before. Taina and Rauha were supposed to keep the fire going in our eleven tile stoves and also heat the Koskull villa every other day to keep the temperature above freezing. It was often impossible to heat during the day, due to the danger from the air raids, so the girls had to use the nights as well. They were magnificent.

This Sunday an alarm lasted five hours. Trolle became tired and fidgety. Despite our little stove it got cold and uncomfortable to sit under ground for hours, so I let Pi and Trolle get out briefly and walk about when no danger could be heard.

In the evening Pulle had to go to a telegraph station to send several telegrams for the company. We were completely cut off toward the west and had neither phone nor telegraph connections. The telegrams would have to be sent from some other telegraph station that was still operational. He, therefore, decided he could send us with the company car to Elimäki, so I could make sure the telegrams were sent off.

Monday morning everything was ready; the children's packing, my little travel bag, and the most important thing: the food basket. The snow gowns were gathered, the passports, the money, Pulle's telegrams, everything was ready to go.

I had given Pi an ornament, a pair of earrings in platinum, and some small diamonds which I had gotten from Pulle. I told her to sell them if she and Trolle got into trouble. No one knew what the future would hold.

We ate a sturdy breakfast, although it was hard for me and Pi to get it down. Trolle, on the other hand, had a good appetite. At half past ten Stina and Gunnar Serck arrived with their maid Berta, who Stina wanted to take along as far as Oulu.

While the Sercks and I had coffee Pulle came from the office. He had a revolver in his hand and I immediately saw that something had happened. “I have to go to the coast, the Russians are pushing their way in, and we have orders to leave in two hours.”

I kept silent. What was I to say in a moment like this?

“You have to hurry up,” he continued. Yes, of course, we could have another alarm any minute. It sure wasn’t very easy to get out of Kymmene.

Then he asked to speak with Pi in private. What did he have to tell her? When they came back she was completely calm. Much later I heard that he gave her his ring with the family crest and told her to give it to Trolle in case something happened to him. But she was not to tell me about it as it would just get me worried.

It was almost one o’clock. It was time to say goodbye. It was the most difficult thing I’d ever had to do. But I was not allowed to show it. I couldn’t refuse to go, or break out in an uncontrolled crying spell, even though that is what I wanted to do. We got into the car and started heading west. I did not know if I would ever see Pulle and Mi again, or if I would ever return home.

Stina sat quietly and composed in her corner of the car. She had also left her husband and her home and was on the way to Sweden. When was she going to be allowed to return, maybe never? I tried to wipe off a few tears without being noticed.

We had to pass Koria. Koria Bridge was bombarded several times a day. Just as we were to cross the railroad tracks, the beams were lowered. It was like sitting on glass. Were we going to get through without trouble, or were we going to have to seek shelter somewhere? The waiting felt like an eternity, but finally the beams were lifted and we were allowed to pass without incident.

When we arrived at the Mustila Estate in Elimäki, we knocked on the door of the house where Mr. and Mrs. Tigerstedt had lived the previous spring, and where Pulle and I had dinner with them and the Koskulls. We were told that the Tigerstedts had moved to the main building. I knocked on the first door we came upon. A young girl opened the door and when I asked to talk to Mrs. Tigerstedt she disappeared. While we were waiting, the chauffeur put all the luggage on the porch. He wished us good luck on our journey. I thanked him and pointed out I would be back soon. It was important to say that so he would understand not all executive wives from Kymmene were just taking off.

An older woman asked us to step inside. Both the estate owner Mr. Tigerstedt and his wife Elisabeth met us in the doorway, surprised that we came through the kitchen door, and asked us to step into the large living room. I told them why we had come and where we were going. Our host and hostess were very understanding and friendly. Mrs. Tigerstedt hugged me. At that point my self-control broke down, I cried uncontrollably in her arms. Stina stood next to me, completely calm, somewhat absent, and Pi had the same resigned expression that she had had lately.

"Times are hard," said the estate owner. He took my hand and asked us to step into the spacious living room.

Two ladies and a gentleman entered the room. The gentleman, who had lived on a property just outside Viborg, had to leave his home without warning and was unable to save much more than his dog. The two ladies, one a colonel's wife, the other the governor's wife, lived as evacuees in Mustila.

The conversation, of course, covered the same topic that plagued all mothers. Should one take the children away to Sweden or not? Mrs. Tigerstedt's younger son was three years old, but so far, she had stayed home with him and her older son. She said that she might send the children away with the nanny, but she herself couldn't possibly leave because of the people living in the estate. I respected her for her decision.

I sat and watched the two elegant, now evacuated ladies, and tried not to be noticed. I must have looked strange in this company, wearing a skirt that was too large as I had lost weight, Pulle's old sweater, his enormous cross-country ski boots, and gray socks. My hair was straight as an arrow, but it did not embarrass me a bit. What was crazy was that I had embarked on such a trip in a skirt. Neither Stina nor I owned a pair of skiing pants. I had not been able to do any sports in years due to my weak heart, so there had not been any time, nor any reason, to get a pair of pants and ski boots.

Pi did not go with the boys to the children's room, but sat with us adults. Mrs. Tigerstedt turned to her once and called her Miss. "Please Mrs. Tigerstedt, do not call her Miss, Britta is only thirteen years old."

"Thirteen? I thought she was sixteen."

It came to me as a little shock, and it turned out Mrs. Tigerstedt was not the only one who thought Pi was several years older than she was. She was treated like an adult, something I could not protect her from anymore.

Stina and I were able to call Brita in Helsinki, the phone lines in Elimäki had not been destroyed. We explained why we had not arrived yet and that we were going to travel to Helsinki by bus. We asked her to get tickets for the night train going north from Helsinki that same night. The train was to leave at 8 pm, and we were to arrive by bus at 7:30. She was going to try to meet us at the bus station with a car. If we missed the train, we were supposed to go to the Society House Hotel.

As I sat down in the sofa again I must have looked awful, because Mrs. Tigerstedt insisted that I should lie down for a few minutes. I thought that would be terribly rude but my protest had no effect. I had to go and get some rest until it was time to go.

Before long we said goodbye and thanked our hosts for their kindness. To get to the bus stop we had to travel by horse and sled. Berta and the luggage were towed by one horse and the rest of us by another. Stina and I sat with our boys in our laps and Pi in the driver's seat with the coachman. The wind was blowing pretty hard across the fields. Pi turned around, and for once her face lit up with a child's delighted smile.

"This is fun," she said.

Thank God, I thought.

We had to wait quite a while for the bus. And when it came it was full of people dressed in white. The bus, as all other vehicles, was painted white, and now all that white felt a bit scary. A few people got off but more were about to get on. The chauffeur explained that he could take us along but absolutely no luggage. But there was no way we could even consider traveling without it. The kids could not arrive at a stranger's place without anything. No matter how we tried, nothing seemed to change his mind. He was going to get more passengers and the luggage would be in the way.

I was close to giving up, but Stina continued to force him to change his mind with relentless energy. In the end, I had the idea to ask him if we could tie the suitcases to a grid on the backside of the bus. There was only a barrel there at this time. Stina and I said that we could hold the boys in our lap all the way. That seemed to turn him around. We were able to step inside, dressed in white snow gowns like everyone else. Stina and I sat next to each other on the first seat next to the door, Pi and Berta further back, each on a separate seat. Stina looked very tiered. The previous night she had taken a sleeping powder around 2 am, but she was awakened by an alarm twice that night and her husband had forced her to go to the shelter with sleep medication in her body.

Pi sat next to a young woman with two little girls. This poor mother was very edgy and started talking about her experiences from the last 24 hours. Pi looked so grown up that she talked to her as if they were the same age.

The woman lived with her husband and two girls in Virolahti, east of Fredrikshamn. They had been awakened the night before and were told to flee immediately, as the Russians were intruding over the ice. She had then in great haste packed the most important things, her four-year-old had to get dressed by herself. After having said farewell to her husband, who was going to stay and fight the intruding enemy, she left by horse and sled. When they were already on the way she noticed that her four-year-old was wearing her overalls but had forgotten her coat. There wasn't time to go back, the Russians could already be seen over the ice. Now she sat in the bus on her way west. She had taken out a little pink morning gown that she put on her daughter.

There were other mothers with children in the bus, big and small. The little ones in swaddling-cloths cried and the older ones were sick. More passengers got on board at every community. It had started to get dark as we approached Borgå. The trip had gone well, no enemy planes were heard.

We drove into the town where every other house had either been destroyed by bombs or burned down. Ruin after ruin. It was depressing.

More people got on board. They stood like canned sardines in the aisle. I thought my legs were going to be squashed, and if that wasn't enough, Trolle was sitting in my lap and a woman in his lap. It was amazing that the shock absorbers of the bus held and that the chauffeur was able to drive.

We got to Helsinki more than a half an hour late, so our train had already left. The streetlights had been turned off. If we met a car, it had dimmed lights and they were painted blue. I could not even see my hand in front of me when we stepped off the bus. I had forgotten my flashlight and after unloading the luggage we groped about until we got to a sidewalk. We did not know what to do, there was no car, and no sign of Brita. Even if she was there, we would not have found each other in the dark.

We headed to the Society House Hotel carrying our things. At first, I just followed the others like a blind woman. How Stina could find it was a miracle to me. When my eyes had gotten used to the dark, I was able to walk with Gunnar and Trolle on each side. Once we got to "Socis" I asked a hotel boy to help Stina with the luggage, which she and the others were guarding.

In the hotel lobby, I ran straight into the arms of my sister-in-law Ebba and Tor Aschan. Brita had come as she had promised, and Willy was with her, he was on leave for the evening. Oh, how wonderful it was to again be surrounded by these dear friends! The hotel was booked but we did manage to get two rooms. Our room was unnecessarily nice and big, with a bath, which we were not able to use, as warm water usage was forbidden in Helsinki, due to the fuel shortage.

After a very necessary clean up, we went down into the dining room, where the Aschans and Koskulls were waiting for us. It felt good to be able to eat something. The dining room was filled with people.

It is hard to explain what it felt like, to come from a bus, overcrowded with people dressed in white snow gowns who had fled their homes in the dark, afraid Russian planes would appear over the horizon, to suddenly sit in a lit hotel dining room, surrounded by seemingly calm people, eating, drinking, and smoking. My first impression of Helsinki was that the city's inhabitants had been spared a lot of what others had been forced to endure. They had no clue what was going on in the East.

A "war fashion" had developed. Most ladies were dressed in ski pants, which was very sensible, but many were wearing thin, very tight, horse riding pants with rubber boots, as well as skirts with sports boots with silk stockings and other not so warm clothing. The fur that covered the neck and ears left the top of the head bare. The next day, I was able to conclude that this fashion did not only represent those who could afford to stay at "Socis", but rather every young and middle-aged woman in Helsinki. Again, I felt like a sparrow dancing among the cranes.

Brita told me about her trip to Helsinki, a trip that in peace time took less than three hours now took eighteen. Five times they had to get out of the train and wade through the snow to the nearest wooded area when enemy planes were approaching.

That evening she was supposed to return home. I asked her to send my regards to Pulle if, against all odds, she happened to run into him. And I also asked her to send my regards to Mi. I knew Brita would do anything to help my girl. Mi would need some support if it got to the point where she had to leave the house in a hurry, she was only seventeen after all.

"We will stick together. You can just relax." She tried to reassure me.

I did not sleep much that night. It was by no means because of any sirens going off, none were sounded that night. What a strange city, a whole night without an alarm! There were two beds right next to each other, and I had thought a third bed wasn't necessary. It was expensive enough as it was, so Pi, Trolle, and I, lay next to each other, I was in the middle. But the little man was very restless, twisting and turning, so Pi and I couldn't get any sleep. On top of that, heavy thoughts were grinding in my tired brain.

At eleven o'clock, the next day, the first and only alarm sounded during our visit to Helsinki. We went down into the lobby where a Lotta volunteer asked us to hurry up. A hotel boy showed us the way to the closest shelter. While we were walking we heard mortar fire from the air defense artillery. The cellar was surely very typical for a city. A narrow hallway under a house, the ceiling supported with thick wooden beams. We moved forward in the hallway. People were standing closely packed together all over. Most of the women were knitting, that was the same here as elsewhere in the country. While we were waiting for the all-clear signal, I was thinking about what would happen in this crowded area if panic broke out, I was terrified.

We did not have to be locked up for very long. The hotel porter agreed to get us tickets for the night train heading north, but was only able to get them for the following night. Since we had to stay in Helsinki that long, Stina and I decided to make the best of it. We walked around in the city, which appeared somewhat different. The snow was piled up high on pavements and all the shopping windows were boarded up. At the top, the names of the stores were painted on in clumsy letters.

There were a lot of people out in the streets, and the stores were by no means empty. My sister Greta told me about an old lady who, every day, when her husband went into town to work, would go along and spend the day at Stockmann's department store. The couple would have lunch at Royal, after which the lady would again go shopping at Stockman's and wait for her husband to finish work. The old lady did not want to be by herself, and besides, Stockmann had a good shelter where you were able to sit in comfortable chairs and do your needlework.

She was not the only one to have her day structured in such a peculiar way. This was not unusual for older, well off Helsinki residents. There were many who had not evacuated, and many who had returned from the country because of uncomfortable circumstances. Helsinki had been spared from bombardments lately.

We ate at Stockman's where we were to meet my sister-in-law, Maj-Lis. When we walked into the restaurant we ran into an old friend, Mrs. Lydia Backman, who had lived in Kymmene. When she heard about our travel plans abroad, she told us about a terrible accident near Tavastehus where two trains had collided. It happened at night earlier in the week. One of the trains had been packed with children on their way up north to Sweden with the Finland Help Organization. My first thought was that Mrs. Backman could have spared us this news. But I understood that she was upset about it, especially since a good friend of hers was on the train coming from the north, and she had gotten hurt. Mrs. Backman may also have wanted to warn us about making a dangerous trip. The conversation just made me feel even more anxious.

Later I heard more about the accident. During the collision children had been tossed all over the place. My cousin, the singer Annikki Forström-Arni, had been on that same train. She had been sitting in an overcrowded compartment with soldiers, a few civilians, and a three-year-old girl. Suddenly there was an unbelievable crash and in the same instant chaos broke out.

"Out, out, we are being bombarded!" people were screaming in chorus.

Annikki saw the little girl and took her into her arms without a second thought so she would not be trampled on. When she got outside she tumbled down a steep embankment onto a barbwire fence. She climbed over it and ran as fast as she could in the deep snow with the crying child in her arms. She finally came upon a cottage. The whole time there was a thunderous cracking sound, Annikki was sure it was Russian airplanes shooting at the train.

She sat in the cottage for hours. She was not alone with the child, it was full of adults and children around her. The soldiers were adorable with the kids, took them into their laps and tried to console them the best they could.

When Annikki was back on a train again to continue her journey to Helsinki, a soldier came up to her with a suitcase.

"Doesn't this suitcase belong to the lady?"

Yes, it really was her bag. The man had been sitting opposite her before the accident and saved her suitcase after the collision. What thoughtfulness, what a kind deed from such a young soldier!

For us it felt very strange to hear about the accident. My thoughts went back to 1924, when Pulle and I tried very hard to get tickets for the night train from Genoa to Berlin. We did not succeed, and we were forced to take the day train over the Alps. This turned out to be our salvation. The night train had an accident in Bellinzona! The coach to Berlin, which we would have traveled in, burned down.

But now we had to pull ourselves together. I ordered some food and started to talk to Maj-Lis whose husband, Dulle, was at the front. She had stayed at the Aschan sea side cottage west of Helsinki, with Uncle Otto Ehrström. And even though she was evacuated she was happy.

We also met Irmelin von Troil, Gösta's wife. She said that they were close to sending Christiane and Gustaf to Sweden, but Christiane did not want to go. She was working with a few others of the same age at the Red Cross needlework shop. I asked her why she had to go, she was already a big girl. But Irmelin said that it was Gösta that wanted it and there was nothing she could do about it.

The same afternoon, my childhood friend, Birgit Söderlund, "Bibbi", born Emeleus, came to the hotel. As she was divorced she alone had the responsibility for her thirteen-year-old daughter, Gunvor. Bibbi had, after long deliberation, sent her to Sweden to a family in Uddevalla, where she was welcome and treated like one of the children in the house. Bibbi was in a good mood and I was happy she had looked me up, though I was rather depressed and definitely not very good company.

Even my brother-in-law, Holger, came up to visit us. Every Sunday he traveled to visit his son Werner, who had been wounded in the war and was recovering. In the afternoon, I spent some time with Ebba, just the two of us, and took the opportunity to talk to her about what had been eating me all day, that is, Pi's conversation in the bus with the woman who had fled from the Russians in the middle of the night. "All this, had been tearing at me like a nightmare, so I had a hard time sleeping," I said.

Ebba got upset and reacted in a way I had not expected. She told me that what I had told her just could not be true. That people just talked a bunch of nonsense.

I was surprised. Of course, I could not guarantee that it was true and I had not talked about it to anyone else, either. I certainly did not want to say things that could scare others. I only wanted to be sure I could speak openly with Ebba. She would not believe that it wasn't as calm in Kymmene as it was here in Helsinki. I also explained to her that we, at any time, could be forced to evacuate. Pulle thought I could go along with the Lotta volunteers, as Mi, of course, was going to do that. But I was worried I would not have the strength to work and that I could become a liability to others.

Then Ebba reacted strongly and said that I should absolutely not sign up for anything.

"You must understand that those who have to take care of the wounded, or cook, must be able to do so without someone tying them down. You should travel to Märtha in Åbo," she continued. "And Harry will give you a doctor's note with which you can travel to Sweden, you with your weak heart."

I jerked.

"No, no, under no circumstances. I absolutely don't want to travel to Sweden. It would have to get completely out of hand here in this country before I would consider crossing the border."

Did Ebba think I was scared? Did she think I would go to Sweden and leave Mi here to take care of her Lotta duties while I would just sneak out? I was deeply annoyed, one minute she did not believe me and the next she was urging me to run off to Sweden. Why did I talk to her at all? She did not know what was going on. She did not know anything about what I had seen. What did I actually know? Not much. But I still knew more than Ebba since I came from the East. I did not see the war through rose-colored glasses.

"Don't think I am a pessimist, or Pulle," I said. "We do try to see things as lightly as possible. Of course, we still believe and hope everything will be alright. But you have to understand that I am apprehensive since I left Pulle, and don't know where he is, since I left Mi, and don't know when I will see her again, and since I don't know if I can ever go back home again. If I do go back, I probably will be forced to evacuate. You can understand that I could use some good advice if that were to happen."

"Yes, of course, things are a bit stale for you right now."

Ebba never contradicted herself. Stale, what an expression, in such a serious moment.

The same night there was a radio broadcast stating the Russians had reached the islands outside Fredrikshamn. I was thinking about Ebba and the story I'd told her that she claimed wasn't true.

The next morning Stina called from her room. She was worried, Gunnar was sick. He had looked tired the day before and now he was complaining about a headache and malaise. I went up to Stina and offered to call Ebba. She was very understanding. She talked to her husband, Tor, a physician, and he prescribed a powder. He later also came to see Gunnar. Since his temperature was only barely above 37 C (99 F) we were able to travel. The boy had caught a cold on the bus.

THE MOST DIFFICULT MOMENT

It was getting dark when we walked to the railway station on March 6th. We were worried about the beginning of the journey. Would we be able to get out of Helsinki without being stopped by Russian planes?

But everything went smoothly, and we headed north. We had good seats. Two sleeping compartments next to each other. It was lovely.

Stina asked the conductor and the cleaning lady if it was safe to go to sleep or would it be too risky. The conductor apparently thought a nervous mother needed to calm down and go to sleep. The cleaning lady, on the other hand, was anything but calm, she thought we could at the most sleep until dawn, no longer. She walked back and forth in the corridor and started chatting nervously with anyone she ran into.

We went into our compartments. Stina and I decided that whoever woke up first had to wake up the other one. Pi took the upper bunk bed, Trolle stayed with me in the lower bunk. We were fully dressed including our boots and all, Trolle in sports pants. The overcoats and hats were hanging on hooks and Pi and I kept our purses with the straps around our necks. That is where we kept the most important things, the money and the passports.

It did not take long for Trolle to fall asleep. Pi was wide awake. We heard a conversation outside our door. It was the cleaning lady who was speaking to someone we did not know. Again, the same thing happened as with Stina. She was hoping the trip would end well, but anxiously she talked about how horrible some of the previous trips had been. Children had been screaming and mothers crying. She was hoping everything would be alright on this trip, but at the same time she heightened the fear by going on and on about how terrible it could be once we got around Riihimäki.

I just lay still and heard everything, and I was not the only one, Pi had also heard every word.

"Try to get some sleep, Pi," I said.

"I can't," she said.

"How stupid of the cleaning lady to talk like that right outside our door," I said.

Trolle turned around and I almost fell to the floor. The night went slowly, time seemed to stand still. I dozed off briefly only to wake up again. Pi continued to be wide awake.

The train stopped in Riihimäki and stood there for quite a while. A lot of people got on when we stopped in Tavastehus, as well as in Tammerfors. I wondered if we would have to give up our compartment, but we were left alone.

I dozed off as dawn broke but woke up startled. I got up and woke up Stina. Then went back to lie down.

"Did you sleep, Pi?"

"Not a wink."

"But my dear child, you have to be deadly tired, try to sleep

" I said.

"I can't."

I was desperate, it wasn't normal for a thirteen-year-old girl not to sleep at all through the night, even if she was in a very stressful situation. My eyelids felt heavy as I was staring out the window at the snow-covered landscape.

"Try to sleep, mamma, I will stay awake."

She was adorable, my little girl. Everything continued to go remarkably smoothly. We couldn't believe we had traveled all the way from Helsinki and not a single time had we been attacked by enemy planes.

In Ylivieska we had to change trains and ended up in third class which was packed. We were getting close to Oulu, my patience was running out, the tears were running down my face, no one seemed to notice, people crying was not an unusual sight in these times.

We arrived in Oulu and I had to say good bye to my children. It was awful. I was about to send them to a different country and had no idea what would become of them and if I would ever see them again. I only knew that they were first to travel to Stockholm, Stina had promised to take them. There, they were supposed to be taken care of by Mrs. Rosenblad, who Brita had sent a telegraph to from Helsinki. From there she was supposed to send the children to their final destination.

Pi and Trolle had their address tags sewn into their overcoats with their names and the address of the Swedish Paper Industry Association in Stockholm. This was all I had to go by. Now I was going to be separated from them, and I did not know when I would see them again and under what conditions.

Was I actually ever going to see them again?

Pi was crying silently, but desperately.

"God be with you," I whispered and hugged my girl.

I said the same thing to Trolle when I hugged him as well.

"What did you say, mamma?" he asked.

My voice got stuck and I couldn't say another word.

"You have to leave them now, the train is leaving," Stina said, and asked her maid Berta to take good care of me on the journey back to Helsinki.

I stepped out of the wagon and stood on the platform until the train had left. For as long I could see, even just a glimpse of it, I stood there. I was overwhelmed with such desperation that I wanted to run after the train. But after a while I managed to calm down. I was standing at a station with people all around me and could not let my emotions get the better of me. Then, a wonderful peaceful feeling came over me. Two in our family were now safe, I thought. And that was a great relief.

GOING HOME AGAIN

I stood on the pavement for a long time and watched the train tracks on which the train, with my children, had just rolled away. I promptly went into the station to find out when we could go back south. The next train was to leave at 11:30 pm. It was now 5:30 pm. Bibbi had told me in Helsinki that our mutual friend, Ruth Frank, born Grotenfelt, who had been evacuated to Sweden, now was in Oulu. I asked Berta to wait for me in the restaurant and went out to look up Ruth.

It was strange to walk in the streets of my childhood town. Or to be more accurate, one of my childhood towns. My parents had moved around frequently. I was born close to Kotka, but had lived in Oulu, St. Petersburg, and Helsinki. I was only nine years old when I moved from Oulu, but I still remembered a lot. It now seemed as if the town had shrunk.

When I got to the hotel where Ruth lived I only met her husband Martin. She had gone to Stockholm two days ago as it was her daughter's nineteenth birthday. I thought it was a peculiar reason to travel, but here in the North there was almost peace.

I continued my walk and got to my old school, and looked into the yard. The church looked like it had before, I remembered the enormous spruce tree that stood outside at Christmas. I remembered the addresses of my friends I used to play with. This one used to live here, and that one there. I felt like going out to the brothers Åström's factory to see the house where we had lived, but it was already getting late, and I was afraid I would not find my way back. I also thought about the risk that there could be an alarm.

Once back at the station I wrote a letter. There were a lot of Danish soldiers there. It was nice to follow their efforts to try to master a few Finnish words from a dictionary.

It was almost dark when we stepped onto the train. I went to bed immediately and slept like a log until 6:30. Half an hour later we were in Seinäjoki, and I wanted to go to visit sister-in-law, Marga, and her daughter Margaretha.

We were met by a station destroyed by bombs. We walked to a hotel. I left Berta there and then drove to the military hospital where Marga was treated after being wounded in an air raid. I asked for her room, knocked on the door, and heard a weak "step inside."

Marga had heard from Ebba that I was on my way up north, but she had not dared to hope that I would have the time to come and visit her. I hugged her carefully, for her arm was broken. Poor Marga, she had never been strong and well, but now she had turned into a little frail old lady. Ebba had warned me that Marga looked awful, but I had never imagined that she was so changed.

The arm was in a sling, there was also a bandage over one foot. It had a big cut from a piece of shrapnel which had cut her boot as well. Several ribs were broken. But the worst of all was not noticed by the doctors at first, her skull and one of her vertebras was fractured, too.

I heard Marga's entire story about her suffering. She had, during the air raid in Mänttä, sought cover under a wooden house. There were two cellars in the house. The closest cellar had an open fire she did not have a good feeling about, so she continued toward the other cellar as the Russian bombers hovered above the industrial town. A bomb hit the cellar she had just left where two children and their caretaker were killed. The house was on fire, but Marga had been knocked down by the blast. Wounded, she remained on the ground until firefighters found her.

Because of all this her psyche was not at its best. I arrived at an inopportune time, she was just about to take a bath and eat. My train was supposed to leave at 2:20 pm, so I did not have much time, and I was unhappy that I could not stay longer. I wanted to get home as soon as possible for Mi. I was not sure at all if I could make it home before Kuusankoski had mandatory evacuations. But I couldn't possibly tell Marga all this in her poor condition. Here up north I almost felt like there was peace. It was only the destroyed railroad station, a few pits here and there, and "Population Shelter" signs that bore witness to the war. I had not experienced a single alarm since my stay in Helsinki. It, therefore, felt much different than in the capital or further east. But I couldn't tell her that.

Margaretha was forced to leave her job in order to take care of her mother. I went with her to the hospital dining room and had lunch with doctors and nurses. There were even some Swedish nurses and one doctor. It was tremendous of these Swedes to come here from their safe country to Finland to help us.

When we got back to Marga's room she asked me if I thought she looked bad. I answered that she did not. I think I was able to make a face that actually made her believe it.

"But I will never be well again," she said.

"You will definitely be well again," I tried to console her.

"Yes, maybe. It is true that I have been very sick many times and that I have always recovered." And now she lit up and said: "But think what luck it was that it was I who got hurt by a bomb, I, who after all, cannot be of any use anyway."

That cut deep through my heart. I wanted to cry. Poor little Marga, will she ever really be whole again? But I could not allow myself to show what I was thinking. It was hard to break up. Marga was crying. Margaretha accompanied me outside.

"I have to go, the situation is such that I cannot stay," I said.

"Of course, mother will calm down eventually."

"I would really want to stay if only I could."

I did not want to tell Margaretha about the whole sad predicament of those who had their homes in the East. The Russian steamroller could at this moment be making its way up the coast. I had not seen any newspapers, but I did hear the news on the radio at the hotel. There were battles in Säkkijärvi and Virolahti, and the islands outside Fredrikshamn were doing poorly. But the enemy had not been able to get much farther into the country away from the borders.

I met the hotel manager.

"Where are you going?" he asked.

"Kouvola," I answered.

"Kouvola?" he just about yelled. "You can't go there. Don't go to Kouvola, no one can get there anymore."

The man was upset, he thought it was crazy for two women to try to travel to this destination.

Despite all, I could not help but smile a little.

"We will be allowed to travel there, we live close to Kouvola, by the Kymmene factory."

The man, troubled, shook his head. The hostess, who heard the conversation, looked troubled as well. We said good bye to them and went back to the station to take the train back south. I was on the way home again. It was a strange feeling, to travel toward something so familiar, yet, something so totally uncertain. I sat there and thought about my children, about Pi and Trolle, and wondered how they were doing. But I was calm where they were concerned, they were probably on the other side of the border by now.

But if I really don't make it to Kouvola, what am I going to do? I looked at my bag and realized that I did not have much clothing with me. First it bothered me a little, but a moment later I had a feeling of freedom and thought about the gypsies who only owned what they were wearing. For the hundredth time during the war, I was thinking we had too many worldly possessions to worry about.

I curled up in my corner. Brita will take care of Mi, the girl is grown up, after all, and she is strong, she will be alright. And where Pulle is concerned, there is nothing I can do. There is no point in being worried. I had resigned. I was suddenly free of all concern and restlessness. Maybe I was going to face the world with my little handbag. I pushed the melancholy aside, I would probably endure as so many others, and I was hoping that some merciful people would take care of my family if needed.

I looked out at the landscape that was rushing by. It was unbelievably beautiful; the snow was sparkling in the sunlight. It was nice to not have to listen out for possible alarms.

I was soon drastically taken out of my fantasies. When we got to Haapamäki, around 5 pm, there were lots of people waiting for the train. Mainly women and children, but among them also elderly men and young boys. They had been evacuated to the west from Karelia.

Berta and I had gone out to get some warm food while the train stood at the station. But it was difficult to move and it turned out the restaurant was overcrowded. I realized it was pointless to try to join the food line, but the line for coffee wasn't quite as bad. I poured down the scalding hot coffee and rushed back to our train compartment. It was now totally packed. Every seat was taken, the aisle was filled with suitcases and bundles, and people were sitting on them.

After a two hour wait the train finally left Haapamäki. It was a dreadful trip. Opposite me was a mother sitting with her little two-year-old girl in her lap. She also had a four-year- old son hanging onto the helm of her skirt. The girl was crying all the time and the boy was whining with fatigue. A young woman next to me offered to take the young boy into her lap, so he would be able to sleep. I also wanted to help. The boy could lie in her lap and stretch his legs over my knees. This is how he fell asleep.

The mother looked very distressed and tried to comfort her daughter by telling her the place they were going to would not have howling sirens. Then daddy would come back, the war would end, and they would all move back home.

It was adorable to listen to her. But I was wondering what that home would look like. It would probably be burnt down and leveled to the ground.

The boy in my lap was still sleeping and his little sister had finally calmed down and fallen asleep as well. The mood became more and more depressing. A tear was wiped here and there, and a suppressed sigh was heard off and on. The talk had quieted down. It was impossible to read, as the "war lighting" was miserable, there were only a few lights and they were painted blue. Fatigue took over. I dozed off for a while. Woke up and fell asleep again. The next time I woke out of my half-slumber, I saw that the clock was approaching midnight. This trip was an absolute nightmare, wasn't it ever going to end?

When the conductor walked through the compartment I asked him if we were going to arrive in Tammerfors on time to make our connection to Riihimäki. His answer was no. I asked him when we could continue, and that would not be until 6 am. This answer upset everyone in the compartment, we had all hoped to continue immediately.

I was exhausted. What was I going to do? All one could do was to follow the stream. When we finally got to the Tammerfors station it was 2:30 am. Berta took a steady hold of my arm and led me to the station house. She had realized how poor my vision was in the dark.

Once we got there we wondered how we were going to find any room for ourselves. The floors were filled with soldiers who were sleeping with their backpacks under their heads. We resolutely climbed over the men. The ladies' room was almost empty. There were a few chairs and a table, but one could also sit on the floor.

The table was not taken so I sat on it. In front of me sat a woman. I placed my bag on the backrest of her chair, folded my arms over the bag and leaned my head on top of them. I was very pleased with the arrangement, since I did not have a backrest, this was the least tiring position.

A moment later the room was filled with women and children. Some lay down on the floor to sleep, others pulled out their provisions. Berta went out to explore, hoping, like many others, that she could find an open restaurant so we could get something warm to eat, but unfortunately it was closed. A man got lost and came into the ladies' room, it was a soldier on leave. He was nearly sober, talking uninterruptedly and making acquaintances with those sitting close by. He really wasn't a nuisance but quite good humored. His speech became so monotonous, it put me to sleep. I promptly dozed off and slept pretty long and well. At four a clock I was awakened by Berta telling me that the restaurant had opened and that she had reserved seats for us. She took me to one of the tables and went to get some coffee for me. She took care of me as if I was a little child. I felt pretty silly, but I was grateful. It was nice to be able to hang onto someone, as tired as I was.

Across me sat a petite young woman with something so sad about her. She looked at me off and on, and in the end, she asked me where I was headed. I told her that we were on the way to Kouvola and gestured toward Berta.

The woman lit up and told us she was on her way to Lahtis. No one else was on the way to the East, so she was glad to be in our company. Poor little one! I understood her well. Of course, we would let her come along with us.

It was warm inside the restaurant and it was wonderful to get something to eat. I studied the people around me. They were of different ages, soldiers with full gear, mothers and children, old men and women. And all were wearing their dirty snow gowns.

The clock was nearing 6 am. The three of us went out on the platform in good time and hoped we would get seats on the train, which we managed to get. Now we were on the way south again. It was dreadfully cold this morning and I curled up in my fur coat.

Day was dawning as we stopped at the Parola station. A completely exhausted conductor walked through the compartment. We asked him when we would be in Riihimäki and when we would be able to continue to Kouvola. According to the conductor we were going to arrive at about 9 am and continue at 11:10 am. I was very happy about this answer. It certainly was a gamble to travel on the route between Riihmäki and Kouvola in the middle of the day, but it wasn't any safer to sit at the station in Riihimäki. We stopped in Ryttylä. In the distance we could hear that there was an alarm in Riihimäki. The train stood still, but so far, we did not have to go outside. I looked out through the window and saw a wooded area just next to the station house and thought that this is where we will have to run. I was not going to go to any shrapnel cover at the station.

Berta interrupted my thoughts and asked me if I was afraid.

"Yes, of course," I answered, as I was not in the mood to pretend I was any tougher than I was.

Finally, the all-clear sounded and we were able to continue. At about 9:30 am we rolled into the Riihimäki station.

What a sight this place was! One house next to the other, some completely burned down, others half way. There were houses where one wall was missing and, on the upper floor, a bed was hanging over the edge out in the open. Blown out windows gaped with torn curtains fluttering in the wind. The station house was also damaged.

We got off the train and saw a large sign with the departure times for the trains. The 11:10 train was crossed out. I got scared, turned to the station inspector who, with his red hat, happened to be coming toward us. Everyone was asking him when the next train was going to leave. He said the next one was leaving at 11:30 pm. In other words, we would have to wait fourteen hours in this place with Russian planes always in the air. But what could you do? We went into the restaurant to eat and thereafter out on the platform.

While we were walking back and forth the little woman told us about her worries. Her husband, an elementary school teacher, was out on the front, and she had at the start of the war left Lahtis with her little child and traveled in an overcrowded train to Seinäjoki to stay with her parents. Now she was on her way back to Lahtis to try to save what she could from their home. She thought the war would go on for a long time and that she may never be able to go back to Lahtis.

She thought, as I did, that we may have to leave our house and home, like the people of Karelia before us. It got cold to walk so we went inside and sat in silence, our spirits low, when we suddenly heard a voice on the loud speaker informing us that all passengers traveling east could take a train at 1:30. An extra train was to leave for Kouvola.

There was blinding sunshine when we stepped on board the train. The wagon we sat in was almost empty. Another was full of workers. The train started moving and on the way, we were met by one station after the other destroyed by bombs.

In Lahtis, we were separated from our little travel companion. The trip had gone well, we had not seen or heard a single Russian plane.

We were lucky to arrive in Kausala, a station close to Mustaniemi, without any problems. There, I went to the station inspector to send a telegram to Pulle so he would know we were on our way, but I had little hope it would go through. After leaving Kausala I dreaded passing Koria Bridge and walking through Kouvola. And all this in broad daylight.

It was a devastating sight that met us at the bridge. The bridge itself was only slightly damaged, but the beautiful beach south of it now had huge bomb craters. Some of the wooden houses on the west bank were partly burned down, on others only the foundation remained. Most of the trees on the east side were snapped in half, with bomb holes everywhere. But the barracks remained.

Everything went well all the way to Kouvola, which was unbelievable. We started to walk through the town to take the shortest way to Kymmene. It was a very dreary Kouvola. The burnt down restaurant at the station was still smoking, as were many other houses. Here and there were still flares of fire among blackened logs. This town, that in times of peace was so vibrant, now seemed dead and abandoned. Only a few tired resigned people were standing around talking. A few lonely souls on foot passed us now and then, but there were no cars or horses.

I suddenly imagined an obituary that only read: KOUVOLA. I hastened my steps, wanting to get out of this ghost town.

When we got to the market place I saw, to my great pleasure, that the house of the Defense Corps, called "The Lock of Kymmene", was undamaged. Pulle had for years been the president of the Kymmene River Valley Defense Corps' district support group, he had been the one to get the money from the industries in the valley for the district. He could rightly call himself the father of the Lock of Kymmene as he had worked hard to collect money for this stately building. At the inauguration of the building he was ceremoniously thanked for it. It was mainly for him that I was happy to see the building intact. But most of all it was pure malicious joy that the Bolsheviks had missed the target.

No one had asked for our passports, we were able to continue toward Kymmene without hindrance. In other words, nothing special had happened, at least Kuusankoski had not had mandatory evacuations. The pressure was beginning to diminish. But I was still burning to hear if Pulle really had left Kymmene only two hours after we had. I was convinced, that sooner or later, he was going to go out to war, which I welcomed for his sake out of the bottom of my heart. The whole winter, as the director of the shelters, he had suffered from just sitting with "15 feet of rock above my head," as he used to say. I wanted so much to see him just one more time. If he had already left it was possible I would never see him again. The war had taken its toll on the soldiers and officers alike, and every day there were more casualties. And the way it looked in this month of March, with the Russians advancing, and with our men who did not have the benefit of the Mannerheim Line to protect them anymore, no one could have any illusions any longer.

Out of the blue, I saw a horse and sled coming toward us. It was the factory's horse and the Swedish speaking coachman Öhman.

I was thoroughly surprised.

"Where in the world is Öhman going?" I asked.

"I am on the way to meet the baroness," he answered.

My surprise had no limits.

"Meet me? But how could you know that I was coming just now?" The telegram must have gotten through to Pulle, I thought.

"The gentlemen at the factory know everything," he said and laughed. "The baron called me and told me the baroness was coming and to immediately ride to Kouvola."

"The baron- is the baron still at the factory?"

"Yes, he is."

I was indescribably happy. We stepped into the sled and rode home. On the way I asked Öhman about all he knew. I wanted to know if anything special had happened in town while I was gone and got the answer that everything stood in its old place, nothing had been destroyed by bombs. What wonderful luck!

It was a feeling of gratitude I felt for our Lord as I was riding home to Pulle and Mi. Pi and Trolle were well across the border in Sweden. And our home was still there.

Brita stood in full Lotta uniform on the porch. "Musti- already home?"

She was on her way to work, but came back inside, she wanted to hear about the trip.

THE BLACK DAY

The first thing I asked was why Pulle was still at home. The answer was he received a contra-order the same day we had left, just as he was lining up his company outside his office to inspect them. As the company existed of elderly men and boys, what happened was best, Brita thought.

Brita, Pulle, and Mi had been healthy and had had an unusually calm period while I was gone. There had been only a few alarms and no bombardments.

"But now you have to see to it that your backpack is ready," Brita said. "Pulle's is still sitting fully packed in the dining room, mine is done and Mi's is almost done."

"Yes - but I really don't want to think about that now," I answered.

"Really?" Brita said. "Don't be as unhurried as Mi. She is never going to be done. She is too apathetic. We don't know how soon there will be an order to leave town, and then we may only have a few hours to get ready, maybe less."

"Yes, yes, but first I have to go to Mustaniemi, I want to take some things there," I answered. "And I will not go tomorrow. I want to rest, I will absolutely not leave until Monday at the earliest," I said.

"No, I understand, but you have to go on Monday," Brita said.

As Brita left for the sick ward, I followed her out to the porch where I noticed Mi's skis and Pi's chair sleigh. We had no hope of getting on a train or bus if we were evacuated. Everyone who could walk had to give up their seat to the elderly and sick, mothers, and children, and I was thinking I could use the sleigh so we wouldn't have to carry anything.

A little later Mi came home. How happy I was to be able to hug my girl! And Pulle came for dinner. The joy of the reunion was mutual. That evening we sat in Pulle's office and talked in peace and quiet. We naturally realized that we only had a few days to be together until he probably had to head south and the other three of us toward the northwest.

Brita told me that she had a little revolver in her backpack.

"Maybe, I should also have one," I said.

"Yes, dear, you will get my small one. I have another bigger one to carry," Pulle answered.

I had never been able to shoot and did not know anything about guns but in these times, even I had to learn to deal with such things. Later that evening Pulle gave me the revolver.

"Do you think you have the strength to use it, if it was necessary?" he asked.

"I don't know," I answered.

Pulle and I both knew that there was no way I was going to be able to defend Mi or myself against any Russians. But that wasn't the point. The revolver was only meant as a last bullet for each one of us should it be necessary. But would I ever be able to do something so horrible?"

I looked at the gun in Pulle's hand. He showed me how it was loaded. Then he handed it to me.

"Put it there," I asked him, without touching it. I did not want to think about having to do something so atrocious. But I had fully realized it was better to die than end up alive in the hands of the Bolsheviks. I was terrified mainly for Mi. God help us.

Monday, March 11th, was dawning in brilliant sunshine and clear skies. I was supposed to travel to Mustaniemi by bus at one o'clock and had packed a bunch of things, which I had to take there, among them my mother's wooden box with a Russian pattern, packed with some family letters, as well as other memorabilia. I also wanted to take with me the

Venetian little glass fish and the blanket for the grand piano. All this may have been childish, but I wanted to do what I could to try to save something from our home in Kymmene. I was hoping to be able to keep Mustaniemi, which was located west of the river.

It turned out to be impossible to get out of town. One alarm followed the other. The bombers rumbled above us, lowered themselves over Kouvola and dropped explosives and firebombs over this city so tormented by war. But it wasn't only Kouvola that had been sought out, Voikka Bridge and the settlements between Voikka and Kymmene were also hit. But the bridge was never damaged despite the rain of bombs.

I found myself in one bomb shelter after the other. During one of the alarms I rushed to the Cave. It was crowded outside. A Russian machine gun could have caused a lot of devastation here. But that did not happen. Everyone got inside all right. I headed for the uncompleted part of the Cave. In the finished part there were floors and heating. But here the floor consisted of loose pebbles. As usual it got crowded. A bunch of soldiers sat down on the benches in the back while the rest of us sat where there was room. The atmosphere was strange. The soldiers sang one patriotic song after another.

Here and there small electric lights hung on the damp walls. Suddenly there was a powerful rumble. The blast was so strong our ears locked up and the lights went off.

The Finnish people have good nerves. There was no panic, no crying, and no complaining. Surely everyone knew that when we stepped outside again everything would lie in ruins. Many were temporary visitors to the bomb shelters. It was known that there were people who came from Kouvola and other parts of Kymmene to visit friends, and they sat in their outer wear the whole day waiting for alarm signals.

Many of them had tired and tortured expressions, especially the mothers with small children.

We sat in the dark as the bombs fell and listened to the soldiers sing “The Marching Song” with the lyrics by our Nobel Prize Winner E. M. Sillanpää. It was as if we were part of a Finnish film. Burning torches were brought in which gave a strange, slightly flickering light and made the atmosphere even more eerie.

When we were allowed to go outside again we saw that the houses were still standing. The bombs had hit a few kilometers away, but the blast could be felt inside the Cave. Kymmene factories had, yet again, been spared from devastation. When would it be our turn? Around us Kouvola, Voikka, and Keltti had all been hit hard while we only had some hits near the railroad station, in Kolarinmäki, and in the subdivision Star. The factories were still standing.

Voikka Paper Mill owned by Kymmene
5 km (3 mi) North of Kuusankoski

Our troops were fighting a heroic battle along the border. In some areas they were doing well.

February 29th the Russian 34th tank division was destroyed at Lemmetti, north of Lake Ladoga and the Taipale front was still holding.

But the Mannerheim Line at Summa had been broken through on the 12th of February. The battle of Viborg started February 26th. The situation was very serious. On March 12th there was a blizzard, a real fine snowstorm, so that we, for once, could feel completely safe. Not even the devil could have flown in that kind of wild weather.

That day I traveled to Mustaniemi.

I sat in an overcrowded bus that was about to burst. I was pretty nervous as the chauffeur, because of the weather, had a hard time getting through. Just outside Kuusankoski church we almost ended up in a ditch. On Salpausselkä Road we were met by an endless column of Red Cross vehicles. The meter-high (3 ft) snow piles made the road unrecognizably narrow, which resulted in our bus having to stop and let the Red Cross cars go by. The chauffeurs were nervous and there was a lot of shouting and swearing. But we got to Tillola and I was able to step out. The walk to Mustaniemi was strenuous in the snow, the road had completely filled in from the snow blowing around. I literally had to plow myself through.

There were strangers staying in Mustaniemi. Two ladies from the Kymmene factories, Mrs. Roos and Mrs. Waalamo, had moved in with their children. Mrs. Roos had earlier been evacuated from Utti to our friends Gunnel and Bibi Ehrnrooth. Bibi was out in the war, and Gunnel stayed with the children in Haukkasuo. It had gotten very restless in the East and Pulle suggested they should move into Mustaniemi.

Mrs. Waalamo had been a nurse at the Kymmene war hospital and both her boys were placed in Liikkala village, close to Fredrikshamn. But the area had been thoroughly bombarded and was now within the zone that had mandatory evacuations.

That is why she had come to us with the kids. Finally, Tytti had abandoned her cold cottage and moved into Mustaniemi for the remaining time until she was to leave for Sweden with Eva and Mita as well as little Pirkko Halme. Even Mrs. Roos and Mrs. Waalamo were contemplating sending their children to Sweden.

It felt a bit sad to come to our own little place which now felt unfamiliar. Tytti had moved into the master bedroom, but when I arrived, she said she was going to move out again. It was a bit awkward, we went back and forth, and finally Tytti won.

Forester Roos had been wounded in the war, but was now almost back to health. He had a job at the war hospital.

In the evening Tytti, Mrs. Waalamo, and I were sitting together, listening to the radio and talking about their husbands who both were at the front. Tytti tried to talk me into staying another day in Mustaniemi, but I didn't want to do that. I wanted to leave the next day in order to get everything ready to evacuate Kymmene with Mi and Brita. On top of that, I felt annoyed being in my own home. I believe it was one of the ladies that jokingly said:

"Who is actually the hostess in this house?"

I felt as though I didn't belong and wanted to leave as soon as possible. In the evening, we listened to the radio, there were rumors going around about a possible peace. But we couldn't believe that.

The next morning, March the 13th, there was a radio announcement saying there was peace and that the fighting was to stop by 11 am. Cabinet member Tanner was going to speak at noon. What was going to happen now? How were we able to get a peace agreement when the Russian invasion had reached far inside of our borders?

I went to the Mynttinens to pay our bill. As usual, I was met with kindness and soon the conversation went to what was on all our minds. Was this peace talked about even possible? We did not have a single Russian bomber above us all day and that appeared strange. We usually had those dreadful vultures above us, unless the weather was unbearable as it had been the day before.

At noon I sat at home with Tytti and Mrs. Waalamo listening to the radio. There was peace! Quiet and shocked we listened to the terrible peace terms. Yes, there was peace, but Karelia, including Viborg, and the Hangö Peninsula were to be given over to the Russians.

Author: Central Intelligence Agency Employee
Modified by Stella von Troil
Map of Finland 1996
REPOSITORY Library of Congress
Geography and Maps
Washington, DC, Unite States
http://hdl.loc.gov/loc.gmd/6960.ct001018
CIA released the image into PUBLIC DOMAIN
Areas Ceded to Russia 1940
North to South:

Rybachi Peninsula
Salla
Karelia
Islands in the Gulf of Finland
Hangö Peninsula

March the 13th, 1940, was a black day in the history of Finland. If the Russians believed they had broken us, they were mistaken. Exhausted, torn apart, and, for now, defeated the Finnish army pulled out beyond the new border. The people clinched their teeth. Our country had been mutilated. We had always been poor and now we were poorer. But we were not broken, we still had our freedom.

That afternoon we traveled into town by bus, all three of us. The doors to our, as well as the Koskull's house, stood wide open. It looked so strange that I went into Brita's place. The furniture had been cleared out of the empty rooms. Some men were picking up things and Brita, in her very resolute way, was giving orders. When I came in she stopped and walked with me to one of the empty rooms. She was crying her eyes out.

"It's unbelievable, the peace terms. And wherever you go people are crying; the nurses at the hospital, the office staff, everyone. And Viborg, and Hangö...lost to the Russians."

Brita was struck with grief.

I asked her why she was clearing her home. It was because of the hospital that needed housing for volunteer nurses from Norway and Denmark to help care for the wounded.

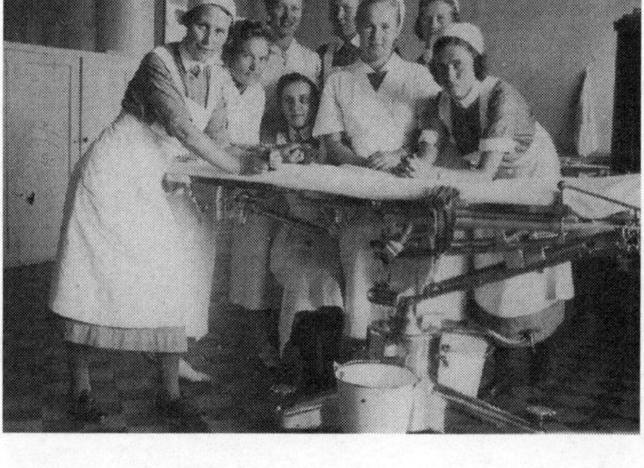

Kuusankoski Regional Hospital

I went home and saw that Trolle's room had been arranged for three persons, using some of the Koskull's furniture. All of Pulle's and my things had been moved out of our bedroom. Pulle had given the order as he thought it would be best for the five ladies coming to stay with us to use the two rooms with the bathroom between them.

I organized our things into the guest room and Brita moved into the girls' room. In the evening the five nurses arrived, one of which was sick. She was bedridden. It was worrisome as the doctors did not know what was wrong with her. Later we found out that she had salmonella. I was unhappy that I was not able to offer her proper sick bed food, as getting food was becoming more and more difficult. Eggs and fish were not available. I managed to get veal a few times, never chicken. I was only able to get soup meat, and even that was becoming scarce. Brita was nice to let me use her cellar as if it had been my own. From there I was able to get cauliflower and water-glass eggs (eggs preserved in a sodium silicate solution). I was already out of my own preserved vegetables.

I had not had a very big household to support anymore, but by the end of February I had to feed fourteen people and that did, at times, become a problem. At least we had bread and butter. The food supply in Kymmene was becoming catastrophic, but there were also other problems of a local nature.

Pulle, as chief of the Defense Corps, tried to stop people from returning to town all at once after the peace agreement. The evacuees wanted to come home, which was only natural.

There were many upsetting tragedies unfolding. The newspapers front pages were full of obituaries of the fallen. The end of the war had been bloodier than the beginning. Countless brave heroes never returned to their homes.

New patients were constantly arriving at the hospital. The number of wounded rose above two thousand. There was no way to get all of them treated and placed in beds right away. They lay waiting on the floor in the entrance hall, in the stairways, in the hallways, everywhere. Pulle saw all of this and it upset him deeply. Doctors and nurses worked day and night trying to help and relieve the wounded. Quietly, and without complaining, they lay and waited for their turn.

I would have been glad to help, but Pulle knew how limited my strength was and thought I had no business in the hospital. I went to the needle workshop and asked if they had any work for me there. And soon even I was needed. Kilometers of fabric was sewn into shirts and underwear for the wounded. At that point, the most common flannel fabric for shirts had already run out, but there was still pink, purple, and green flannel available with enormous yellow flowers, sky blue and fire red roses, or tulips and chrysanthemums of various colors. In the middle of all this misery, we had to laugh at these bright fabrics.

We were bitter about the peace agreement, and here so close to the front we did not yet realize this peace was a necessary evil. If it had not happened when it did, no one knows how horrible things could have gotten for us.

Mannerheim's Order of the Day was to be read over the radio. Quietly and troubled we sat and listened:

"Soldiers of the Glorious Finnish army!

Peace has been concluded between our country and the Soviet Union, an exacting peace which has ceded to Soviet Russia nearly every battlefield on which you have shed your blood on behalf of everything we hold dear and sacred.

You did not want war; you loved peace, work and progress; but you were forced into a struggle in which you have done great deeds, deeds that will shine for centuries in pages of history. More than fifteen thousand of you who took the field will never again see your homes, and there are many who have lost forever their ability to work. But you have also dealt hard blows, and if two hundred thousand of our enemies now lie on the frozen snowdrifts, gazing with broken eyes at our starry sky, the fault is not yours. You did not hate them or wish them evil; you merely followed the stern law of war; kill or be killed.

Soldiers: I have fought on many battlefields, but never have I seen your like of warriors. I am as proud of you as though you were my own children; I am as proud of the man from the northern fells as of the son of Ostrobothnia's plains, of the Karelian forests, the hills of Savo, the fertile fields of Häme and Satakunta, the leafy copses of Uusimaa and Varsinais-Suomi. I am as proud of the sacrifice tendered by the factory worker and the child of a lowly cottage as of those of the wealthy.

I thank all of you, officers, non-commissioned officers and men, but I wish specially to stress the self-sacrificing valor of our officers of the reserves, their sense of duty and the cleverness with which they fulfilled a task that was not originally theirs. Thus, theirs has been the greatest sacrifice in this war in proportion to their numbers, but it was made joyfully with an unflinching devotion to duty.

I thank the Staff Officers for their skill and untiring labors, and finally I thank my own closest assistants, my Chief Commanders, my Army Corps Commanders, and the Divisional Commanders who have often transformed the impossible into the possible.

I thank the Finnish Army in all its branches, which in noble competition have done heroic deeds since the first day of war. I thank the Army for the courage with which it has faced an overwhelming superior enemy equipped in part with hitherto unknown weapons, and for the stubbornness with which it held on to every inch of our soil. The destruction of over fifteen hundred Russian tanks, and over seven hundred enemy aircraft speaks of deeds of heroism that were often carried out by single individuals.

With joy and pride my thoughts dwell on the Lottas of Finland - their spirit of self-sacrifice and untiring work in many fields, work which has liberated thousands of men for the fighting line. Their high spirit has spurred on and supported the Army, whose undivided gratitude and respect they have achieved. Posts of honor have also been those of thousands of workers who, often as volunteers and during air-raids, have worked beside their machine for the Army's needs, or labored unflinchingly under fire, strengthening our positions. On behalf of the Fatherland, I thank them.

In spite of all bravery and spirit of sacrifice, the Government has been compelled to conclude a peace on severe terms, which however are explicable. Our Army was small and its reserves and cadres inadequate. We were not prepared for war with a Great Power. While our brave soldiers were defending our frontiers we had, by insuperable efforts, to procure what we lacked. We had to construct lines of defense where there were none. We had to try to obtain help, which failed to come. We had to find arms and equipment at a time when all the nations were feverishly arming against the storm which sweeps over the world. Your heroic deeds have aroused the admiration of the world, but after three and a half months of war we are still almost one. We have not obtained more foreign help than two reinforced battalions equipped with artillery and aircraft for our fronts, where our own men, fighting day and night without the possibility of being relieved, have had to meet the attacks of ever fresh enemy forces, straining their physical and moral powers beyond all limits.

When someday the history of this war is written, the world will learn of your efforts.

Without the ready help in arms and equipment which Sweden and the western powers have given us, our struggle up to this date would have been inconceivable against the countless guns, tanks and aircraft of the enemy.

Unfortunately, the valuable promise of assistance which the western powers have given us, could not be realized when our neighbors, concerned for their own security, refused the right of transit for troops.

After sixteen weeks of bloody battle with no rest by day or night, our Army still stands unconquered before an enemy which in spite of terrible losses has grown in numbers; nor has our home front, where countless air-raids have spread death and terror among women and children, ever wavered. Burned cities, and ruined villages far behind the front, as far even as our western border, are visible proof of the nation's suffering during the past month. Our fate is hard, now that we are compelled to give up to an alien race, a race with a life philosophy and moral values different from ours, land which for centuries we have cultivated in sweat and labor. Yet, we must put our soldiers to the wheel, in order that we may prepare on the soil left to us a home for those rendered homeless and an improved livelihood for all, and as before we must be ready to defend our diminished Fatherland with the same resolution and the same fire with which we defended our undivided Fatherland.

We are proudly conscious of the historic duty that we shall continue to fulfill; that defense of that Western civilization which has been our heritage for centuries, but we know also that we have paid to the very last penny any debt we may have owed the West."

When the man had finished reading the order of the day we quietly returned to our work. All of us felt the same immense grief.

There came a time when I more than ever wished I had double the strength that I really had. I was often terribly tired, but I was not allowed to be, I had to work, and so I clinched my teeth and continued pedaling my sewing machine. A bright light came in the form of the message that Pi and Trolle had arrived safely at the paper mill in Vargö. It was not until now that we found out that it was Mr. and Mrs. Levan that had taken care of the children.

We had peace, so their journey had been pointless, but there was no way we could have known that before they left. We were eternally grateful to these people who had helped us in our time of need. I wrote to Mrs. Levan, that despite the peace we were thankful the children were able to stay in their home for a while. The situation was such that there was no way we could arrange for their return immediately. It was even said on the radio that those who had evacuated to Sweden should stay there, as all the trains were now needed for more important matters. Mrs. Levan answered that the children were welcome to stay.

The Russians had demanded certain areas be cleared by a certain time. A terrible unrest broke out wherever people lived on "Russian soil." People had to leave abruptly and were only able to take with them the bare necessities. People who had been evacuated from places like Viborg and Sordavala were allowed to go to their homes and save what they could, although most of them were not able to do so due to the lack of travel options. Many tried to assist these people with use of their own cars and horses but the military had requisitioned most of these. The few trains that did run were overcrowded.

In some places, like Sordavala, the Russians arrived before the agreed upon date, and many residents did not have time to take all their belongings with them. Some destroyed their furniture and household equipment in their desperation. A young physician, Dr. Rauramo, immediately left, by truck, for his parents' home in Viborg when he heard about the peace in order to save his parents possessions. He never got that far as in this part of town the Russians were already ravaging. But he did not return empty handed. He took a few wheat sacks and all the sewing machines from the closest house he could get into. Their owner was most definitely very appreciative.

There were caravans of people and cattle that moved toward the west. Many animals did not make it, they were slaughtered in all haste. There were massive amounts of dead animal corpses along the roadways.

This migration was something unheard of in world history. Never before had a conquered area been left to the enemy completely void of its people. But all these people left their beloved Karelia, with the utmost courage. And all had the same belief of a bright future. They said they only gave Karelia to the Russians as a loan. "When the lilacs are in bloom, Karelia will be ours again," they said.

On Sunday the 17th, we were visited by the young physician mentioned above and his parents. His father was also a physician and employed at the Kymmene war hospital. The son worked at a war hospital in Sippola and lived close to Henrik and Pia Gripenberg's home. One of the coachmen at the hospital called this home the "Rippentrop Villa", which amused us thoroughly, as the man obviously thought that Gripenberg had the same name as Germany's secretary of state von Rippentrop.

We sat and talked about the future, about how all these homeless were going to arrange their lives. Dr. Rauramo, Sr., said he only owned one suit, which he was wearing. Everything, the entire home, clothes and paintings were left in Viborg. It had not occurred to him to evacuate anything from there earlier. No one had been able to believe that Viborg would be lost under the claws of the Russians.

One afternoon while we were having coffee we received a phone call, Pulle's brother, Dulle, had fallen March 11th in Karelia. Just as he had predicted he would not survive. Even as a boy he had foreseen that he would die young like his namesake who was born in 1803, a hundred years before him, and died in 1839. Dulle predicted he would fall victim to the same fate when the war broke out in 1939. Dulle had been right about his fate but got the year wrong, 1940 instead of 1939. He had been the fifth chief of his company, three previous chiefs had died and one had been seriously injured, and only thirteen of the original soldiers remained.

Dulle had received the order to recapture an island in Lake Karstilanjarvi. He succeeded, but was injured, his soldiers had carried him to the nearest first aid station where he died twenty minutes later after he had asked the doctor to send greetings to his wife and sister. The Russians went on attack again and the company had to retreat. They were only able to carry the injured and had to leave the fallen behind. Later, an officer asked to go back to retrieve the bodies under parliamentary flag, but this was not allowed.

Among his fellow warriors Dulle had been known as a good and happy friend. Once, however, he had become very serious. This was when his friends were planning to take their wives out for a night of fun after the war was over.

"At that point, I won't be around", Dulle had said.

When he was on leave for the last time, which had been in January, he had arranged many practical things for Maj-Lis, for it was possible, after all, that he was not going to return. In his last letters to his wife, one could clearly read between the lines that he did not think they would ever see each other again.

Dulle's memorial was held in the Helsinki Crematory Chapel, but the earth of Karelia had become his grave.

Dulle

The death of Pulle's brother had shaken him thoroughly. I could see how deeply he was grieving. He, as the rest of us, had been very worried about Dulle. Now Pulle said that he, as the elder, should have been at the front to help his brother.

"But my dear, what could you have done?" I said.

"No, of course, nothing," he answered.

But it was an agonizing pain of sorrow that was eating at him. He went to his work, quietly, and I to mine.

One day I met a woman who had evacuated to Tillola with her children. Now she was back in town. I had often talked to her in the village and on the bus, and now she stopped me. She was happy and pleased that there was peace. I said that the peace agreement was too horrible to be able to feel happy, but I was too tired to try to explain to her how a patriotic person reasons.

There were young factory girls who sewed new dresses, for now they were going out to dance. It made me sick. But these were the exceptions. Most thought differently. And it was very difficult for the soldiers to follow orders and leave the areas the Russians had conquered.

The country was in mourning. But life went on.

Easter was approaching. I had not been able to buy any eggs so I was very happy when Mrs. Niinivaara gave me a few. They came in handy when I wanted to invite a few Danish and Norwegian nurses for tea on Easter Eve. They were part of those tremendous people who left their safe havens and came here to help us. Now I wanted to make it nice for them.

I was happy we were all going to be able to get a bit of a rest during Easter. That is why I was so disappointed and felt exploited when Mrs. Roos called Thursday night and said that she wanted to leave Mustaniemi with her girl and Mrs. Vaalamo with her boys. She told us that Tytti had already moved out. I told Mrs. Roos that I would not like to travel to Mustaniemi during Easter, but if they absolutely wanted to move, then I would have to do it. The heating units would have to be emptied, as well as the water pipes if no one was heating the villa. She suggested that kids from Tillola could do it, a suggestion that was completely unacceptable. The heating units in Mustaniemi were no toys, I pointed out.

Mi and I had to travel to the country and do some major cleaning, among other things, put rugs and blankets in naphthalene, tidy up after the evacuees, clean up after the Roos' and the Vaalamo's maids etc. And all this on Good Friday. Mrs. Roos had suggested to send one of my own or Brita's maids out there, but I could not accept that. How could you send someone else to do major cleaning on Good Friday?

We returned to Kymmene the next day after we had pushed hard to finish the job. I was very upset with Mrs. Roos as we had tried to be compassionate by opening up our home for her, as if it was her own, but she did not have any consideration for us. I could understand Mrs. Vaalamo better, as her husband had just gotten back from the front and he obviously wanted to see his boys.

In such times, there will undoubtedly be disagreements, people's nerves are strained, and it can also be difficult for strangers to be forced to have too much to do with each other.

The night before Good Friday something funny happened. We went to bed as usual, I was in a bad mood thinking about the trip the following day with the Roos family. At 1 am I was awakened by a male voice, brother-in-law Lasse. He had come from Mänttä by train to Kouvola. There he got off to visit with us and spend the night. The next day he was supposed to continue to his old troops who had been forced to withdraw behind the new border. There they had fought successfully and had been able to defend their post during the entire war. When Lasse arrived, he knocked on our door. The maid opened. She was surprised to see him, so he felt compelled to say who he was and asked if he could have a bed for the night. She asked him to step inside after which she disappeared. He decided to wake us up and went into the master bedroom, but there lay two complete strangers, the Norwegian nurses! Startled he went to Trolle's room, only to find another three girls. That was too much for Lasse, so he went upstairs, where Brita had just woken up. She was waiting for Willy who was on leave. When she heard the steps in the stairway she rushed into the hallway, just as she was, dressed in a very thin night gown.

"Have I come to the wrong place?" Lasse asked confused, as he now thought he was at the Koskull's place.

"Yes, you sure have," Brita said and turned around and went back into her room.

She did not recognize Lasse and could not understand what this complete stranger in uniform, a major in the Medical Corps, was doing here, in the middle of the night!

"Who is there?" I yelled from the guest room. I thought I had recognized Lasse's voice.

He was pretty tired as he had recently been taken ill with salmonella. In the morning, I noticed that his coat had two bullet holes. When I said I would patch them Lasse got all wound up. The bullet holes were to stay there forever, they were never to be sewn up. The coat had been pierced by the bullets as it hung on the wall in his quarters. He had experienced hails of lead and furious bombardments, but had only sustained an abrasion on his nose during the whole war when a window frame fell on him.

I was happy I had a good bottle of beer to serve him and a few cigars to take with him. When he left he forgot half his things, his bag with maps and the cigars among others.

After the Easter holidays, I returned to the needlework shop. Pulle and Brita had worked almost as usual during the holiday, but Mi and I were allowed to be lazy after our trip to Mustaniemi.

One day, five French nurses and a female doctor arrived at the hospital. They lived in the emptied Koskull house. But the poor little Norwegian was still bedridden. She was taken to the regional hospital.

GREETINGS FROM SWEDEN

We received a letter from both Pi and Trolle. Small little letters in which they said that they were not missing home. Pi understood that they could not come home immediately after the peace. But between the lines it was clear that they did miss home.

I could not even think about bringing them back as the peace wasn't a real peace. The new border was even closer to us. Our town was now a border community, which was also pointed out at the Lotta meetings. But we could not rely on the hospitality of the Levan family forever.

Shortly after the children had been sent away, we received a very nice letter from the sales manager Levan. The letter was dated March 13th.

"Baron Knut von Troil
Kymmene Factory

I thank you for your letter. The children arrived here late at night between Sunday and Monday in good health, apart from the fatigue from the trip.

I understand that you probably would like to know something about us. I am forty-nine and my wife is twelve years younger. Our kids are Olle fifteen, Gunnel eleven, Agneta almost nine, and Henric four-years-old. Your children are almost of equal age and we hope they will be happy, which they already seem to be. We are living in one of the company's villas in a park district. The children are allowed to do whatever we do from day to day. They have been very nice and well behaved, a true joy to have them among us. It seems they are beginning to enjoy themselves and feel at home. Pi told me that they would be happy if they were allowed to go to school. The schools are currently closed due to the lack of coals to burn, but should start again after Easter. Gunnel is in first grade at the Vänersborg Girls' School. My wife has talked to the headmistress, there should be no problem for Britta to join a class of her age and skill level. I believe 2nd or 3rd grade. Formally some authority will have to agree to this, but you can count on it. When it comes to Sten, he is just about the same age as our daughter Agneta, who is in the 2nd grade in our elementary school. My wife talked to the teacher in charge, who promised that he can join Agneta when the classes resume. That my wife and I wanted to do something for Finland, and take in a pair of children, was only natural, as we whole heartedly sympathize with you. My own great-grandfather moved to Sweden from Finland as a young boy in 1809, where his ancestors had lived mainly as priests.

I have just heard the news about the peace on the radio, which certainly came as a surprise, and which both of us have a hard time understanding. The future will tell how serious it was meant to be, and how long it will last.

Britta and Sten are doing well. I see, they have also written themselves. We will take good care of them as if they were our own, so you do not have to worry.

With the warmest greetings from Your children as well as from my wife.

Sincerely yours,
Uno Levan"

We were very happy to get the letter. Pi did start school in Vänersborg in the 3rd grade. She became good friends with her classmates who apparently thought she was interesting. They thought it was strange that she could speak Swedish and that she had gone to a Swedish school and also spoke Finnish. She was given the task to help three other girls evacuated from Finland. They did not speak a word of Swedish, so Pi had to jump in to translate. She also had to translate their homework.

At home she became good friends with all the Levan children, especially with Olle who was about the same age. Trolle went to the elementary school with Ninna. The first day a whole wall of kids gathered around him. They looked at this strange creature who had seen thirty-six Russian bombers, flying low, all at the same time. At the end Trolle felt so embarrassed about all the attention he pushed one of the kids aside and broke through the wall. The questions hailed over him as well as over Pi.

All around Sweden, so called "Finland parties" were organized. The program was comprised of speeches about the country and the war, declamation, songs and so on. In Vargö a similar party was held, to which the Levan family went. The film Private Stal was shown (based on the Songs of Ensign Stal) after which everyone sang the Suomi Song (the Finland Song). When Pi knew the words by heart, she caught a lot of attention.

A little episode happened one day, not unusual for that time. In Vargö, as all over Sweden, a population bomb shelter was built just in case. The rules were written by the chief of the population shelters on signs attached to telephone posts. Pi read the rules and saw they were pretty complicated. During an alarm, the windows were to be closed, the doors locked, and the keys were to be placed in a certain place. Pi shook her head.

"That won't work in reality. One does not have the time for all that."

Mr. and Mrs. Levan were looking at each other in dismay. Was it really possible?

"If it is cloudy, or some other reason for the alarm to be late, the planes can just appear out of the blue. At that point, all you can do is just drop everything and run. You can't be thinking about keys, windows or anything else, as it can blow any moment."

Pi had experience. It was a child who informed the adults about the realities of war.

Pi read the letter that Dulle had fallen. She thought it was horrible but remained resigned and calm even though she had been very close to Uncle Dulle. Our girl, from a mental standpoint, was not a 13-year-old, she had seen too much.

One beautiful April day brother-in-law Nisse came to visit. His regiment was not much farther east from where we were, so Nisse took the opportunity to come to Kymmene. At the same time, a fellow officer, Lieutenant Jutte Ahlbom, came to visit his wife and mother in town. Nisse was himself. He was annoyed that he had been in the war as a veterinarian and not in the artillery. He was allowed to fire only one bullet, and that was when he had to euthanize a horse.

Lieutenant Ahlbom's arrival became somewhat legendary in Kymmene because he brought with him a heap of his fellow soldiers' dirty laundry! Nisse had not mentioned a word about it, so I did not know anything about it until I met Jutte's mother, Mrs. Ingrid Ahlbom, who told me she had received over 400 kg (880 lb) of clothes to take care of. She had spoken to laundry attendants and reserved a wash house. The problem was that a great deal of the clothing was torn. I had never seen anything like it. Mrs. Ahlbom stood there with her daughter-in-law ironing and then started patching everything.

It seemed impossible, but Mrs. Ahlbom thought it was feasible to sort it all out.

I admired her resolve but realized it was going to be too much for her so I ordered our domestic help, Rauha, to assist, and did part of the patch work myself, as well as ironing, and sewed some new things. I delegated some of the work to a seamstress. Even Clara Ekholm, who was in town, was informed of the work load and she brought her maid to help. Slowly the clean and mended laundry could be sent back to the regiment.

Pulle and I traveled to Helsinki at the beginning of April, for Pulle it was a business trip for the Kymmene Company. I went to visit family. We also visited Marga, who had been transferred from Seinäjoki and was now resting in her home. Her condition continued to be dreadful.

We were in the capital on the historic day when the Germans marched into Denmark and Norway. We were wondering how our nurses were going to react to the news. The next day we met one of the nurses at the Stockman department store. She had immediately left Kymmene and was going to continue by plane to Stockholm, together with her sick colleague, and from there try to get to Norway somehow.

When we went back to Kymmene we met three Danish girls who also were very upset by the news. On April the 14th, they went back home. Before they left we had a glass of wine together and had one last chat and thanked them for all they had done for our people. They gave us a flower as a farewell present.

We decided Pi and Trolle should return home. They were going to come to Helsinki with Stina and Gunnar who also were on their way home. Somebody had to go and meet them, I sent Mi a few days ahead of time, so she could get some rest from running around in the cafeteria, and to have some fun after a long and dreary winter.

I expected all three of them to come home on April the 17th at 8:30 in the evening. They arrived at

10 o'clock. The bus that was supposed to take them to Kymmene was full. They had to wait outside, as there was no room inside the station house either, people were jammed packed. It was cold and all three were freezing, especially Mi who did not feel well. She was dressed in a spring coat and silk stockings to look nice on her Helsinki trip.

I embraced the kids and the questions were hailing down over Pi and Trolle about what it had been like. They were pleased. They had been led to the Herrljunga train station by Mr. Levan and they had continued by themselves to Stockholm, where Stina came to meet them. In Stockholm they went sight-seeing, went to the movies and bought a pair of shoes for Pi.

Mi looked pitiful.

"I am really sick," she said.

Mi was never squeamish, so I knew she had to be put to bed as soon as possible. I checked her temperature. She had a high fever.

It was a stressful period in our house as Mi really was seriously ill. Unfortunately, Dr. Forss was not able to figure out what was wrong with her. In the end, the diagnosis was stomach flu. But at times I suspected pneumonia, and at other times salmonella.

While Mi was sick, Pi and Trolle came down with the stomach flu. They had barely recovered when they got sick again, this time with strep throat. Luckily my job at the needlework shop had already ended, otherwise it would have been impossible to work and take care of all three children.

When Mi was allowed to get up the first time she refused. The next day she dragged herself to a sofa where she fell asleep. After that it took a long time before she made any new attempts. Once she was getting better she had an X-ray and it turned out she did have pneumonia.

In early May, Trolle looked totally worn out. His cheeks had flared up and his eyes were glassy. The same evening, he became violently ill. I had, myself, had a nasty cough for several days and was so hoarse I could only produce a faint whisper. Pulle wanted me to stay in bed. I agreed only if I could have Trolle in the same room. When Pulle came home for dinner Trolle and I had a high fever. Pulle called for Dr. Köhler who told me I had pneumonia. The next day I could not take care of Trolle anymore, so the nurse, Ms. Holmgren, came to us.

Not even the new strong medicine B.396 was able to control our fever. Trolle was playing in bed, when he did not have his legs wrapped to cool him, but I was so weak I was not able to do anything. Despite that my brain was very active. Mainly trivial household problems were bothering me, especially the gardens in Kymmene and Mustaniemi. I explained to Taina, in fine detail, exactly how she should sow the seeds. It was at this time grain products were rationed. One had to report what type and how much grain one had in the house. Taina, of course, made notes about this, but I wanted to check the list myself and sign it. And then there was the storing in naphthalene that worried me... All this worrying was unnecessary, but I was too tired to think clearly.

Brita had moved back to her place, but since she did not have a radio, she came over several times a day to hear the news from the big world. A lot was happening, and all this was reported to me at my bedside by Pulle, Brita, and even Dr. Köhler. Sometimes I became desperate. "Close the door, I can't listen to that radio!" I thought I was going to go crazy, couldn't they leave me alone and stop telling me about how the Germans were marching into Belgium and Holland, what Hitler had said and so on.

At times, I thought I was maybe not going to get up anymore. Once I told Brita so. She thought I was childish, I should not look at the situation so grimly. But I was so tired. I asked her anyway to go through all my things if I died. She promised she would and that calmed me down a lot, it would have been a nightmare if my sisters-in-law came here and poked around in my stuff. Nobody knew me as well as Brita, she did not care if everything wasn't in perfect order.

I tried to think about happier things and remembered Pulle's and my trip abroad exactly a year ago. I thought about how we flew from Stockholm to Berlin and from there to Munich. There we saw a wonderful ballet with modern music by Lathe. Then we traveled to Merano, where we had two incredible weeks. There was a trip to Gardone by car, a boat trip over Lake Garda, the channels of Venice, and the sights of Rome, the memories cheered me up now that I needed comforting.

May the 18th a vigil was held for Dulle. Pulle went to Helsinki, but I was still in bed. Slowly Trolle and I got better. Ms. Holmgren was able to leave us and Mi became our nurse.

At the beginning of June, I was able to get out of my sick bed. Trolle was already outside playing.

GENERAL UNREST

We were living in a strange uncertain situation. There were all kinds of rumors, people were nervous, and one did not really know what to believe. The inspections on the railroads became more intense, the passports were constantly checked. One could not travel to certain areas without permission from the local police authorities. Pulle and I traveled to Helsinki on June 22nd. For Pulle it was a business trip. I went to congratulate brother-in-law Verner Gustafsson on his 50th birthday. We had to have certain papers with us, including one to be able to travel through Kouvola, as well as our regular proof of identification.

The mood became so tense, that Hilde Bygden, who was supposed to come and visit from Ingerois, called and said she couldn't even leave for a few hours in the morning, as anything could happen at any time.

In the end, even I was affected by this general unrest. Brita and I decided to organize the children's clothes, to make it easier to pack up our things in case we needed to leave quickly. If there was war again, Kuusankoski would have mandatory evacuations. Would we yet again have a storm blow over us from the east? Was everything that had been built and repaired since the peace on that disastrous day, March 13th, going to be wiped out again? And were we, after a bloody war, going to be able to reconcile with our neighbor - now, that we had such a rough border? I was freezing in the summer heat.

No, we have to hope that we are going to be left alone. Fate cannot be so cruel to, yet again, throw us into war after just three months.

There was a terrible heatwave at the beginning of summer. It was the time of year when the apple trees were supposed to bloom, but they were bare and dead after the cold winter. I met with Eine and looked at the devastation. "It says in the Bible, that when the trees are bare, when they really should be in bloom, that humanity will encounter the worst of times," she said.

The Karelians thought they would have Karelia back when the lilacs were in bloom. But the bushes only had leaves and a few abandoned buds.

Tytti af Forselles had visited me in April before I got ill, and now I wanted to return the favor. A few days after our visit she got sick and was taken to the Tuberculosis hospital, where she remained. It was a result of the gruesome winter cold, the hardship, and unrest in the little cottage in Tillola. Poor Tytti, it was a difficult time for her.

We moved out to Mustaniemi the last day of June. There were many reasons why we moved out to the country so late in the season, among others, Dr. Köhler thought it would be too risky for my lungs to leave earlier. However, he was not worried about Mi or Trolle.

I did not have a good time in Mustaniemi. Everything reminded me of the evacuation in the winter. Therefore, I was happy when I got a reason to go away. This came in the form of invitations to two weddings. One of them was the wedding of Bubi, Caja's son, who was getting married on July 18th at the Järvikylä Estate, Bubi was going to marry the step-daughter of the estate owner, Aune Lamminpää. The other, was the wedding of Caja's daughter, Dorrit, and engineer Fjalar Holmberg. It was to be celebrated at the home of Caja and Rainer in Varkaus.

Trolle, Pi, Mi, Pulle

It seemed unreal, after the experiences in the winter and spring, to dress up in an evening gown and a fur cape, the latter just in case due to my long illness. And it was wonderful to sit at a table, in good company, eating and drinking like in good old times.

Willy came back home from his military assignment the last days of July. Ulla and Peter rushed into his arms, the family was reunited.

Willy had been promoted to master sergeant, but was a little disappointed when he ended up spending most of the war in the classroom. He wanted to do more. Pulle had felt the same.

Whenever a country has been at war, it needs a lot of money. This was also the case with Finland. There were all kinds of new taxes in the summer. Sales taxes were charged for all goods, except for the most essential food items, at 10 %.

In addition there was a gold collection. A large portion of the population considered it their duty to donate a piece of gold jewelry to the state; rings, brooches, and watches, etc. For a wedding ring one received a smooth iron ring with a heraldry rose, and for other gold pieces one received the pilot ring, an iron ring with ornaments.

Pulle and I gave up our wedding rings and a few other pieces. A great example of this was Dr. Tauno Relander and his Danish wife. They had lived in Viborg and lost their home. They donated every piece of gold they had, even though they had to start all over again, starting with buying six children's beds for their very large family. Such is the love for the fatherland.

The first of August Pi was supposed to start school in Helsinki. The previous fall I had signed her up for the New Swedish School. She was not able to continue her education in Kymmene as she had already passed all the grades offered there. The school year started earlier than usual because of the many school days lost during the war.

When Pi made her entree in the capital, I went with her to Holger, where Pi and Mi were going to live during the upcoming school year. It was exciting for our girl to go to a big school. It did not take long before she had a lot of friends.

At first, she went to the 5th grade where she had a try out until September 20th. She did extremely well and was moved up to 6th grade.

One day, Pulle's brother-in-law, Hugo Österman, sent us a telegram asking us to come with him to Bäckisviken in Kyrkslätt. His wife, Marga, was there in a small villa that the Östermans were renting. Hugo was going to take the car and we could take the empty car back. I warned Pi about Marga, that she was in bad shape, so the girl would not be too upset. Marga had been in the hospital during the summer with skull and spine fractures.

In the car we met Hugo and Mary Tallberg, a second cousin of Pulle. We had not seen each other since our early childhood. When we arrived, Marga met us at the door. I hugged her carefully and so did Pi, but at that point Marga had used up all her strength. She wobbled and we had to lead her to the sofa where she would stay during the daytime. She was able to sit at the dinner table, but she hardly ate anything. Her sense of smell had been damaged, and everything smelled bad. The smell of boiled potatoes tormented her, and the scent of strawberries was abominable. Later she was given a nose pincher, which she thought saved her life, because of it she was able to start eating again.

While I was gone Mi had taken care of my household chores in Mustaniemi. She had also stepped in to be Trolle's substitute mother. Marga's daughter, Margaretha, visited us for a short while in the country, and Mi enjoyed having someone to play tennis with. She certainly needed that after the long winter, the way she had been confined to the cafeteria and the cellar. The pneumonia had also taken its toll on her.

In mid-August, we moved back into town from the country. We made jams and juices until we ran out of sugar, the rest was left sour. All the berries we had picked were used and the vegetables were preserved in sealed jars that were cooked. We collected the preserved foods in the barn to prepare for a bitter winter.

I had bought a 3 kg (6.6 lb) smoked, boneless, ham in Helsinki. We could not have gotten that here, and we were not going to take it out until all the other food was about gone. It was becoming more difficult to make up a good menu with the food available.

A dark August night when we were already in bed, but not yet asleep, Pulle heard strange noises from the veranda. He got out of bed and saw a man fiddling with the lock of the glass door. Pulle got furious and yelled in Finnish: “Go to hell!”

The man answered: “Why don’t you go there yourself!” And he made a move as if he was about to break the glass.

Pulle called the police, but when they arrived the thief was already gone. In the morning the ham, the juices, all the preserved foods, the eggs and butter, where all gone from the cellar. I was desperate and Taina cried furiously.

Pulle was a little abashed that he did not think about taking the revolver and going outside through the back door, then around to the front to stop the thief on the veranda. The man was later caught and admitted that he was hiding under the bushes while the police were patrolling outside. After that, he went into the cellar. This episode caused Pulle to sleep with the revolver next to him every night. As soon as we heard the slightest noise we thought it was a thief.

Sometime later Pulle caught a man who came to the Koskulls to beg. He appeared suspicious. Pulle tried to take him to the police station, but he started twisting and turning and got away. Pulle threatened to shoot, fired a shot into the wall of the factory, but the man did not stop.

Pulle did not have any luck as a detective and we were joking with him that he needed to take a police course. It was as if we had suddenly moved to the Wild West. And I have to admit it was not a very pleasant time until the thief was caught, he had committed several home invasions. We were constantly living in fear of not being safe. When Pulle was not at home I was afraid to sleep alone with Trolle downstairs.

At the beginning of August, the members of “The Organization for Promoting Peace and Friendship between the Soviet Union and Finland” caused an uproar and held demonstrations in the whole country, mainly in Helsinki. It was unbelievable that there could be people so irresponsible, so cruel, real traitors to one's country. And this after the Winter War we had endured!

The demonstrations in Helsinki were held on August 1st-8th, in Sörnäs, east of the center of Helsinki, and, therefore, Pi and I did not see any of it.

There was something to be happy about as well, reconstruction work was going on all over the place. Kouvola, which was completely devastated when I was there on March 9th, was now cleaned up and looking pretty again. The evil of war had been cleared away, and out of the charred ruins there was new growth.

Usually Mi did not have the opportunity to celebrate her birthday at home on September 2nd, she would typically be in school. We, therefore, used to celebrate the day of Märtha, her name, which is August 26th. This was also my deceased father's birthday. This year, however, she was able to celebrate at home.

The 4th of September, Mi and I traveled to Helsinki. She had always been interested in young children and now she wanted to become a kindergarten teacher. We went to the head mistress at the Ebenezer Kindergarten Seminar. With a loving smile she explained an applicant, first of all, had to be at least nineteen, and secondly, Mi's middle school report card was too weak. She was especially concerned about her writing. I tried to point out that while in high school at Klostret, her report card was much better and she had almost all nines (10 is the highest score). To Mi, this whole thing was so unpleasant she never wanted to study at Ebenezer.

In the end, we decided she should start sewing at the Helsinki Cutter Academy. It was difficult to get fabric for her assignments, but with the help of the rest of the family's ration cards we were able to manage.

Mi and Pi stayed with their Uncle Holger, as mentioned, where they shared a room. They were on their own for breakfast, but for dinner Holger was home. Sometimes he got home early and took a nap on the big sofa in the living room. During dinner the radio was turned on at a low volume. Thereafter he would read the paper and disappear. If he ever stayed home, he would write poems.

The household was taken care of by Mrs. Gerda Facius, who Pulle jokingly called Bonifacius. The girls started to call her Boni. It was not easy to get enough food for everyone, and it only got worse when Holger, who was very hospitable, invited one guest after the other. He would also give up his home for guests overnight, one could for good reason call his house Hotel Troil.

The bread rations were small, 300 g (10.5 oz) per person per day, and butter rations were 250g (8.8 oz) for ten days. Out of that only half was actual butter, the rest was margarine or lard. Later in the fall, there were ration cards for cheese as well. One could choose between cheese, margarine, or lard if all three were available. On the children's milk cards, one could get 100 g (3.5 oz) of extra cheese or margarine, sometimes for 15 days, sometimes for a month. Before meat was rationed, one could use hog's lard or suet for frying, but these were not always available. Guests who came to visit from areas with larger rations did not understand the lack of food in the cities. It happened that a guest would take a knife and dig into Mi's little pat of rationed butter in her butter cup that was supposed to last 10 days. Poor Gerda did not know how to manage the bread rations. The girls came home for Christmas with almost empty ration cards and it was difficult to keep them home for three weeks with practically no cards. Our bread economy suffered for several months. The only one who understood the situation was Holger's daughter Jeanne-Marie. She always brought food when she came to visit her father with her husband and children from Salais Estate.

You were still able to buy fish in Helsinki. Starting in November meat was rationed; about 250 g (8.8 oz) per person per month. Sugar rations were reduced from 1 kg (2.2 lb) to 750 g (1.5 lb) and later to 500 g (1.1 lb) a month. It was difficult for Gerda since Holger did not understand it and kept pouring sugar on his food. Soon there was a recipe in the newspaper how to make syrup out of potato flour. All the potato flour was immediately gone from the shelves, and subsequently it was also rationed, and in December one could only get 250 g (8.8 oz) per person per six months. Milk rations were 2 dl (0.8 cup) plus one portion cream (low fat) per adult per day, and 6 dl (2.5 cup) per child under 16 years old.

When meat was rationed one was allowed to keep it in storage up to 5 kg (11 lb) per person. If one had more than that, one had to cut the corresponding amount of coupons from the cards.

Gerda had nothing in storage, she lived day by day. When even sausage, with the exception of mixed- and grain sausage, was included in the meat rations, things really got bad. She often served strange vegetables and fish that she bought at the pork butcher's.

In Kymmene things were worse. Fish was no longer available, and we only got hold of meat after great efforts. I often had to stand in long, discouraging lines. The Helsinki residents complained about their miserable conditions, but they had been spoiled with good grocery stores during peace time, no wonder it now felt bitter. But they should come to the industrial towns and see what it can be like when it really gets bad.

As for us, I did not complain since we had a good cellar in Kymmene in which we could store roots, preserved vegetables in glass jars, and meat from the time when it still wasn't rationed. In December we were only able to get meat in cans. I stored those for a long time in case things got even worse.

Pulle did not hunt as often as he used to. His hunting party had a permit to shoot one moose, but Pulle got sick so it was killed by someone else. However, he was allowed to share in the bounty. Several kilos were left over even after we gave away more than half of our share. The moose meat was sure to be needed during the upcoming winter.

In the fall, one was still able to buy canned foods like Portuguese sardines. But they were soon sold out. The hoarders unscrupulously bought up everything they could get their hands on. Especially in Helsinki they had been ravaging for a long time. They had started at the beginning of the war in September 1939. The black market for coffee, butter, bacon, and grain was flourishing. People would buy coupons for food and clothing, and even whole ration cards. If someone did not want to use their card they should have been able to do with it what they wanted, but it was forbidden to give it to someone else. The population supply minister made inexcusable mistakes, people became angry and ignored the regulations, and their morals were deteriorating to say the least. One could have expected a bit more loyalty toward the authorities as well as one's fellow man, especially from the educated class.

Pulle still held on to his principles. There was no secret business in our house. A few persons who lived on estates, and were better off than we were, gave us a few things, sometimes butter or flour. We still had the freedom to give away and receive gifts in this country.

One of the worst mistakes the population supply ministers made was the mess with the soap supply. Strange enough it was not rationed in the summer and the hoarders bought up everything. Suddenly the regulations hit like a bomb; we were only entitled to 125 g of soap per person per two months. Unless the market had not been saturated with a bunch of cleaning products with less than 4 % fat content, that were not on the ration cards, the situation would have been catastrophic.

Washing clothes had to be reduced significantly. I put away all white table cloths and we started using small placemats. Most people bought wax-tablecloths as long as they were available, after that one had to get by with paper tablecloths. Paper towels also became very popular.

It went without saying that the people of Karelia would get land, through the so-called rapid colonization, to make up for their lost land, but terrible mistakes were made. One of the estates that was confiscated by the state was Multamäki, a Kymmene Paper Industry property. Generally, the large estates where the ones who delivered the food supply, including Multamäki, it had a hundred cows standing in its barn. They had to be sold when the people of Karelia were to get the property including the barn. Only eight cows were moved into this enormous barn after that. In the past, Multamäki had been able to supply milk for the town, after this not a drop. This was not the only case, there were many such mistakes.

The rapid colonization gave Pulle a lot of work. He tried to convince the authorities to be reasonable as they took away company property piece by piece. Some companies gave up parts of their properties willingly. Pulle tried to influence how much was payed out for the confiscated lands and buildings, hoping for a fair market place value. He brought forth experts of all kinds. But it happened that the company only received a fraction of what the property really was worth. This was not a pleasant or easy job to do.

LET'S WALK!

Despite the lack of food and other problems people started socializing again. For a few years we had lived a fairly quiet life because of Pulle's heavy work load, for the most part, it was only I who had kept up with my little circle of ladies.

We started going out for walks again in the evening with Willy and Brita. Shortly after seven o'clock they came to us and Willy would say the infamous words: "Let's Walk," and at the same time he would do the Hitler greeting. Maybe the words could have been preceded by "Heil."

Once outside, the babbling started. We never ran out of things to talk about. Politics was discussed endlessly. Willy's sympathies with the Germans and Pulle's more sober-minded view of both Germans and Englishmen gave fuel to high-tempered discussions, especially when I joined in expressing my anger with the Germans. This view point was based on the unbelievably poor treatment we got from the Germans during our Winter War, a view I changed later as they became our best supporters.

We did not only talk about politics but also discussed morals, sports, theater and literature. In the last subject Willy was the expert. He read everything and had an incredible memory. Willy and I also got deep into music, which Pulle and Brita often joked about. It was the fancy way Rachmaninoff played, Rubinstein's genuine performances of whatever he played, or Orloff's elegance. Willy's dislike of Chopin's monotonous sound was something I supported, and he did not like Schumann either. In the beginning of our friendship he could not understand my fondness of Albenitz, de Falla and other modernists, but once he said: "Now I know how you listen to music." After that we were "einverstanden" (in agreement).

But most of all we were gorging in the symphonies of Sibelius. It was an experience to listen to Willy lay out all his feelings about these grand works. Countless times we listened to recordings of the greatest orchestras in the world on his fine gramophone. His own music studies were limited to a few piano lessons. Therefore, it was even more respectable that he was so in tune with everything. He would have been able to defend himself in any conversation with educated professors or professionals.

I will never forget these moments.

Unfortunately, I did not have enough time for my own music. When it comes to my favorite hobby, composing, things were even worse. I missed the moments at the grand piano, but I did not have the strength for all my interests. Rather, I had thrown myself into my social work for as far as my ability could take me.

The towns Kymmene and Voikka are located in Kuusankoski County with a current population of about sixteen thousand. Since the community is small, in terms of surface area, and the farming population is a minority, most of the population is employed at the paper mills.

Kymmene Company has always done good social work. Many elementary schools have been supported by the company, partly to be able to select the teachers. It was important that they were patriotic and good citizens. Some of the elementary schools were united to the big "Central Elementary School", which the community built on land donated by the company. In addition, a vocational school was built for 500 boys and just as many girls.

The Vocational School
War Hospital #13

The subjects for the boys were divided into metal and carpentry classes, plus theoretical subjects. For girls kitchen and needlework. They also had classes for infant care, plus theoretical subjects. The courses took two years, except for especially strong students who were able to add a third year. After completing the third year, the boys were automatically employed by the company. The courses are free and mainly intended for the children of the company workers.

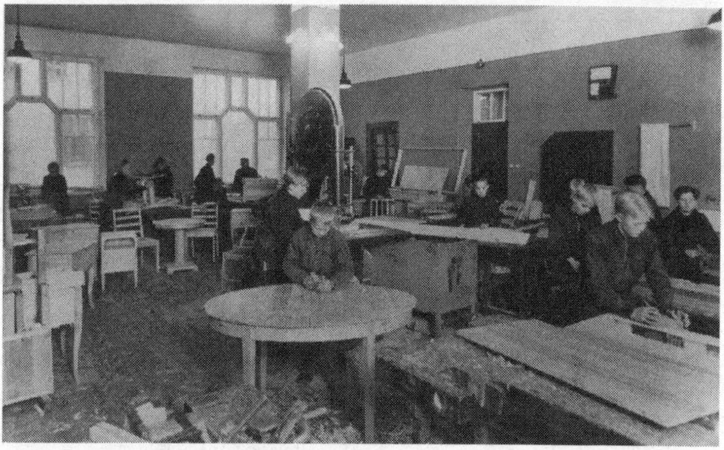

The institution surely has the most beautiful banquet hall in the country. The walls are decorated with the portraits of President Svinhuvud and Field Marshal Mannerheim, painted by Eero Järnefelt. Outside the banquet hall is a hallway with paintings of Finland's battles for freedom in 1918, with the intention to impress pure thoughts into the students and bring them up to be reliable and able citizens. Pulle has for several years been the chairman of the schools governing board.

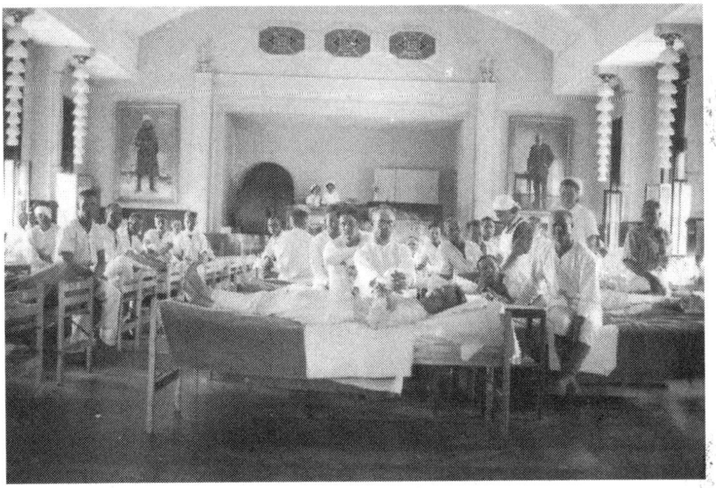

The Vocational School Banquet Hall
Ward #3 at the War Hospital #13

Despite the fact that the company has done a lot for its workers, there is still a lot of poverty. To help the needy, the "Association for Organizing Charity" (AOC), was founded, which is run with voluntary contributions by the company and its executives. Two daycare centers were established at company locations where women working at the factory are able to drop off their kids before seven o'clock and pick them up after 4 pm. The children are cared for and fed for 1 mark a day, which essentially is free.

The executives' wives' needle work shop is a subdivision of the AOC, which to some extent is a subdivision of the Mannerheim's Children's Foundation. The purpose of the association is to hand out clothing every Christmas to the needy, usually worker's families, and also to hand out money for food.

It isn't always easy to collect the money, especially as the association is small. There are about forty members, but there are actually not that many active members. All kinds of things are sewn on demand, sometimes bazaars are organized. The children's parties are the most profitable ones. The kids are happy and the parents are proud to stand in the glow of their children.

In October the work at the needle shop was resumed after a lengthy pause due to the war. My first task was to report that the 1939 Christmas gifts which were handed out despite the difficulties. Just before evacuating to Mustaniemi, Stina had bought the last handouts and sent them and the money to the diaconate to help distribute them.

When I visited Marga in August, she told me about a car trip she had made to Suomussalmi and Kuhmo in the summer. She had seen people cook their food and bake their bread under an open sky. The only thing left of their home was their stove. Marga, among others, founded the "Rebuilding Bureau" under the organization for "The Friends of the Border Communities". These people performed great deeds.

I walked around at home plagued by the fact that I wasn't able to do anything for these devastated border communities. At least I helped Brita receive wool deliveries from the Swedish association of "Save the Children of Finland." Out of this wool, Brita got loads of pretty garments by giving it to knitting friends. Mi knitted mittens all summer. And even Pi got into it.

In the end, I asked Glory if she could take care of shipments of old clothes. The result was two large storage containers with good garments sent to Kuhmo. Glory suggested some ladies should make baby clothes and send them to the border. We gathered at her place and she was then able to send off eight complete sets of baby clothes to Kuhmo.

Mary Tallberg told us how people had taken it upon themselves to take care of some of the families in the border communities. It was the same idea as the help for the war godchildren. Persons and associations were willing to pay a set amount of money every month for a fallen hero's child. Mary asked us to help the Polvinens, two families with a total of 16 children, in other words, a total of twenty persons, for a period of one year. The families were literally standing on bare ground. Their homes had burned down and they only had a ramshackle sauna to live in. All clothes and household goods were lost. These were decent people according to the pastor in Lentiira village close to Kuhmo. If they got some help, they would get a new start in life.

I promised to talk to friends and acquaintances and 15 families agreed to pay a certain sum every month for one year. We also decided to send sheets, outdoor clothing, household goods, and some furniture. Since the textiles were rationed, I wrote to the Rebuilding Bureau and asked for a license for fabric to make blankets, towels, sheets, thread, etc. We got the licenses. But for the outdoor clothing I wrote to the pastor in Lentiira and asked him to talk to the families, to entrust us with their own ration cards for clothing. It took a while for the cards to arrive, this was because the pastor had to travel 60 km (37 mi) to reach the Polvinen families who lived only 10 km (6 mi) from the Russian border. The cards came with a very sweet letter, which was difficult to decipher, but at least I could understand that they were grateful for the help. Sadly, one of the children had died.

We decided to divide the children among us, so that each of us had either one older child or two small children to send packages to. I got Tauno Hermanni, who was fifteen. For Christmas we will send more clothes to the children under our protection.

Brita organized "Talkos" several times, a gathering of volunteers who worked for a common cause and received food and coffee on site. Her large nursery was perfect for quilting, for example. When the first shipment was ready, it was a joy to pack it up. Sometimes we received donations in boxes that were shipped just as they had arrived, as was the case with a box of china that came directly from the porcelain maker Arabia, it was donated by Brita's brother, engineer Eric Frosterus. In another box we put a washbasin, washing powder (not rationed), pots and pans, and a coffee pot, as well as one box with mattresses, pillows, blankets, etc. We also sent a children's bed and two cupboards. All this was needed, which was evident from a list we received from the Rebuilding Bureau about the possessions the Polvinen families already had. Both families owned a total of two cups, three glasses, five plates - or something like it. It was heart breaking. For Christmas we are shipping the outdoor clothes, each person receiving a specially wrapped Christmas present. All the children will receive toys and candy, the older ones will also receive some money, writing material, bags, and the younger ones toy horses, dolls, etc. The Polvinen wives will receive "Korvike" (a coffee surrogate).

Since I functioned as the Operation Polvinen secretary, all the letters went through me, with a few exceptions. When Glory heard about the family, she sent a package to the youngest one, a two-month-old girl. She received a thank you note, which also stated that their only horse had died. We were able to collect another 1,000 marks.

The letters came to me with the most unusual names. Even though I tried to spell out the sender address very carefully, I still got named “R pita von Troil, Riita Roili, Riita von Toril, Riita von Troiel, or Riita Voi Trael”, so I have to say the post office had their hands full, but most of the letters made it. They usually contained a thank you note and that things were “moving slowly” for them. Once they wrote that one of the fathers’ feet were frost-bitten.

Brita also helped a little three-year-old, fatherless boy, Unto Kääpä. The mother was living on the outskirts of Kymmene on the way to the Keltti power plant. After her husband had fallen in the war, she was left alone with her son, as well as a one-year-old, and she was expecting her third child. Brita and Willy often visited the little family. To help those who had lost parents, husbands and sons, house and home, during the war, became a true national movement. A matter of honor, for each one of us, to do whatever our ability and monetary resources allowed us to do.

TICKS

One day in September, Pulle was going out hunting. He hadn't really had time this fall to hunt like he used to, he had not even been able to make time for the yearly "brother hunt", which this year was organized by Lasse in Mänttä.

On Saturday night, he started fussing over things he wanted to take with him and walked around mumbling while looking through cartridges, socks and boots. Reku, the dog, came in waving his tail. When his master was choosing cartridges, he knew they were going out to hunt the next morning. It was also, as usual, difficult for Pulle to pick what clothes he was supposed to wear. I had to joke with him about that. "Well, this is nothing," he said. "You should see my friend Petter Forsström, he walks around for hours, picking and discarding things, but the end result, anyway, is that he is wearing the entire Stockman's sports section."

The yearly "brother hunt" was a story to be told. They hunted, played cards and quarreled, but they had fun. Once Holger and Nisse were quarreling, and Holger pinched Nisse's nose. "You don't pinch me in the nose," and he punched his brother. But Holger did not hit back, took an angry look at his little brother's enormous body, bit his lip and realized it was better to back off. Dulle was laughing with his cigar in his mouth, his belly jumping, and tears running. Pulle was yapping like a fox terrier and Lasse said "hoh, hoh." The one to take it all in stride was their brother-in-law, Hugo Österman, the general, who had been invited as well: "Hey, let's keep playing boys." A man, who witnessed the whole thing, said: "You Troil-brothers are a damn strange pack. In the evening you fight, where one has to worry one of you will pull a knife, and in the morning, you are best buddies in the woods."

Apart from an extra pair of boots for papa Uno, who sometimes took part, loads of food were packed into laundry baskets. We cooked bouillon and out of the meat we made meat balls and cabbage rolls, we made roast beef and leg of lamb, and the gentlemen could count on a few hares that they would shoot. Kilos of bread and butter, tea, coffee, juice, pickles, and lingonberry jam were packed, and then some spirits; snaps, Swedish punch, and of course beer.

This year we were only able to put together a tenth of all this wonderfulness. Early in the morning the alarm clock went off. Pulle sneaked carefully, trying not to wake me, to the dining room where the night before Taina had put out the tea pot, an empty thermos, bread and butter, as well as baking paper and an electric boiler. He would always make his own tea when he got up early, filled the thermos, made the provisions and ate his breakfast in peace and quiet. It would be quiet in the house until Reku realized Pulle was up early. At that point the whining and barking started, and despite Pulle's efforts to hush him up, the noise went on until the hunting buddies left in a hurry. The dog was too excited and Pulle had to place Reku in a sack to keep him calm during the car ride. Only the head was visible as Pulle carried the barking and fussing dog out to the car.

Trolle, Pulle, and Reku

When he returned all had been well. Only one thing was bothersome, a tick had bitten him and was now stuck on his arm. It was at this time Pulle's rash started. There was a red spot around the bite. The arm was operated on twice, but the poison just kept spreading. I cannot describe how horrible it all looked in the end. The rash spread all over his body. It itched and burned day and night, and he could not sleep despite the strongest sleep medicines. The rash also spread to his face, and his scalp was all crusty. He turned red and purple, I was worried he would get blood poisoning. There were open sores on his arms, big craters that oozed puss and fluid.

Lalla Köhler sent Pulle to bed. There he was treated with a variety of medicines. But nothing helped, so he traveled to Stockholm and spent ten days in a hospital and picked and picked at himself. In one of the wards were a few Finnish soldiers from the Winter War. Since Pulle did not have to lie in bed, he was able to visit with them from time to time. They were very happy to be visited by a fellow countryman.

When Pulle got a lot better, he was allowed to travel back home, but on the boat back the misery started again. He, therefore, went to Salu Hospital in Helsinki. Dr. Ingman cured him in one week with turpentine injections. But Dr. Ingman told him he would not get completely well until the summer, when the sun would do wonders.

Pulle got back home just before Christmas. The reason for the rash was probably not the tick bite alone, but what it was, no one could really tell for sure. He had not had any vacation since June 1939 and had worked weekdays and Sunday (Saturdays were workdays). During the war he also, in the capacity of chief of the shelters, had to get up several times each night. He was probably so exhausted, he reacted very strongly to the tick poison.

His hospital stays had been short, and, therefore, he did not neglect his duties. Even when he was in bed in Kymmene, he took care of his job by phone, and one after the other came to visit and sit by his bedside with all sorts of papers. Pulle never let go, despite the itching and suffering. His ambition was as great as always.

A commemorative medal was handed out, everyone who had either been at the front or behind the front could apply for it, as long as one had worked in the army or with the Lotta organization, had been a nurse, or something similar. Both Brita and Mi received the medal, I did not. I had not worked long enough at the needle shop, and work from home did not count.

One of Pulle's peculiarities was his dislike of these "metal pieces", badges of various kinds. Out of all the honors he had received, there was only one he really valued; the 1st Class Bravery Badge from 1918. One of the badges he called the "Dinner Party

Medal". He had lost the respect for these medals, as someone witty once pointed out, "They so often, just like grenades, hit the innocent behind the front." That is why he was so upset when he once was awarded such a medal. On top of all, it was the Freedom Cross III Class without a sword, in other words a medal for people behind the front.

President Kyösti Kallio's health had been very poor for a long time, and he finally had to resign from the presidency. This time the new president was not elected by the people, but rather by the same electorate that had voted for Kallio. They appointed the director of the Finnish Bank, Risto Ryti. Kallio fully and whole heartedly supported the appointment.

The same day, December 19th, Kallio left the presidential palace to travel to his country estate in Nivala in Ostrobothnia. An honor guard was lined up outside the palace, and under the cheers of the people the former president left for the train station, where another honor guard was waiting. While he was inspecting the honor guard, he fell dead into the arms of a man standing by.

It was a beautiful and honorable death for a father of a land. The Finnish people payed reverence to him and were in deep mourning.

Christmas was near and the girls returned from Helsinki. As a modest thank you gift, I sent a table cloth and serviettes out of linen to Mrs. Levan in Sweden, which I had weaved at home, as well as some Orimattila lace. For our own family, I had arranged a few presents. The food was "real Christmas food", as we were able to get a hold of a ham and some rice grain. I had saved plums and applesauce for better days, so we had a nice, quiet Christmas Eve.

Suddenly, in the middle of it all, the Koskulls came storming in dressed in paper hats. They had with them a fine present, a bracket-candlestick made out of cast iron.

We celebrated New Year's Eve with Koskulls according to old tradition. We played, cast tin, and jumped into the New Year from chairs, on which we stood hand in hand.

When the clock struck midnight, we wished each other a Happy New Year. It seemed as if the previous New Year celebration was ages ago, so much had happened. We hoped the New Year would bring a lot of good with it, that it would be happier than the year gone by.

1941

The Germans force all Jews to wear the yellow Star of David badge and conduct mass shootings of thousands of Jews, “one bullet, one Jew”. Their prison camps are expanding.

The US is beginning to patrol the North Atlantic. A destroyer is torpedoed by a German U-boat killing eleven sailors, the first US casualties of the war. The Tuskegee Airmen form the 99th Fighter Squadron.

The Russians start to deport thousands of prisoners from the Baltic States to Siberia while the Germans start the invasion of the Soviet Union in “Operation Barbarossa.” Finland joins the Germans in “Operation Arctic Fox”, assisting in the Leningrad siege where thousands starve to death.

Britain signs a defense agreement with the Soviet Union against Germany and later declares war on Finland. The US supports the Russian war effort with one billion dollars in a lend-lease aid package. However, the German advancement into Russian territory is hampered by the temperatures in Moscow dropping as low as -35 C (-31 F).

The US officially enters the war after the Pearl Harbor attack by Japan on December 7th and declares war on the Axis nations Germany, Italy, and Japan, but not on Finland.

THE GERMANS ARE GIVING US HOPE

It is hard to give an accurate picture of the political situation in the spring of 1941. There was chatter and discussions. The big war out in the world was vented in all directions. Even though we had peace, we were experiencing a strange feeling of uncertainty, and always thought there was the possibility that there would be war again. There were also those who were lulled into thinking comfortably, or not thinking at all, and for them it would be a huge shock if war really did break out again.

The Russians had shameless demands, but most people did not know how unashamed they were. And those who knew all the details couldn't say anything. The Soviet Union was like a big spider sitting in Moscow spinning its web further and further. I was in despair, although I tried to push the thoughts aside and focus entirely on my day-to-day chores. There were times when I realized I could not allow myself to just sink into a complacent mindset. But I couldn't stand all this worrying.

"If there is war again, how are we going to manage?" I burst out.

"We have to," Pulle said. "And I will say what the Karelians are saying, at some point we have to take back Karelia, the borders that we have now, in the long run, will not hold. Don't think the Russians are going to honor them, they will start a war as soon as it suits them!"

"But it would be terrible to again have to face all that misery..."

"You have to give up something in order to gain something, and we have to hope the Germans are going to beat up on the Russians," he said.

Yes - of course. The thoughts still went back to ourselves and the children. Kymmene, a stone's throw from Kouvola and east of the Koria Bridge, did not have an enviable location.

But there were those who had it worse, for example Fredrikshamn and Villmanstrand. But what are we going to do with the kids? This was our standing question.

"If there is war, I will take the children to Sweden at once," Brita said. And I will take Trolle with me."

Pi had said, ever since coming home from Sweden in the spring of 1940, that she would not evacuate another time. And in school her opinion had been strengthened. She told us that some of her friends had worked in hospitals or in other places when she was in Sweden, and had, therefore, looked at her with discontentment.

"My dear child," I answered. "To begin with, you were the youngest of your class. You told me there were fifteen, sixteen and seventeen-year-olds in your class. You had just turned thirteen when the war started. On top of that, your home was located in a dangerous zone. If we had lived in Tavastehus or Vasa, it would not have entered our minds to send you to Sweden. And had your friends had to experience the same thing you had to in Kymmene and Mustaniemi, under the constant threat of attack by the Russians, they would probably also have been sent away. Remember, nearby Kouvola was hit by more bombs than the entire county of Åbo and Björneborg, even though Åbo was considered to have been one of the worst hit areas on the home front."

Holger's daughter, Isa, was one of those who had been surprised at Pi's trip. Yes, but Isa had not lived in the Kouvola area. That Pi suffered I could understand, and that is why I did not want to send her away, even though I did not think it was fair to blame a thirteen-year-old for being sent to Sweden with her little brother.

I said, that if Mi wanted to follow her Lotta section, no matter what happened, then Pi should try to go to Mänttä. Under no circumstances should she come home, as Kuusankoski was immediately going to be evacuated if the war broke out. She could then come with me wherever I was going to be sent by the Kymmene Lotta organization. A 38-year-old, sickly Lotta, like me, was probably not going to be sent to the front.

Food as well as other things became extremely expensive and difficult to get. There was lack of clothing, especially made of wool, and shirt fabric was almost unavailable. And if one got a hold of tricoline, it was twice the usual price. The common cotton fabrics were not available at all. It was impossible to buy yarn. It was forbidden to make whole wool fabrics, they had to be mixed with cellulose wool, which actually did not turn out that bad at all.

When the food shortage got worse, Pulle's sister, Märtha, started sending packages from Åbo. The city had distinguished itself by being better supplied than most other areas. Märtha sent cheese, marmalade, and other little goodies. She really was sweet.

In April Brita bought a little pig that she placed in our doghouse. The pink little piggy got the name Josefina. We also had a pig, which Trolle named Sofia, but it lived very well on a farm in Mälikkälä. People in general started buying animals like sheep, pigs, rabbits, and hens. Everyone did what they could to help the food situation.

Pulle's health slowly got better and we started socializing pretty actively. We were invited to visit friends in Kymmene and had our own dinner parties that turned out very nice. There was good news from Marga. She kept getting healthier and gained strength. She also regained her bright outlook on life and her joyful disposition.

In February Eine, Brita, and a few other Kymmene Lottas from the Kymmene Valley Lotta Command held a district meeting in Kouvola. Apart from being an annual meeting, it was also the district's twenty-year anniversary. The atmosphere was great with many patriotic speeches. One of them was held by an elderly lady, Mrs. Hukan-Antti, who, on her Lotta uniform, had two Black Freedom Crosses. She wore them in memory of her two sons, both pilots, who were killed. Her speech, like her entire performance, was dignified, simple, and affectionate.

The girls had it good with Uncle Holger, but we were all longing for our own place in the capital city. Pulle and I decided we were going to buy or rent an apartment where Dulle's widow, Maj-Lis, would also live. She agreed to take care of the household. It was not easy to get a suitable apartment, but we did find one with five rooms and a kitchen on Kapten Street. It was a bit large, but we accepted that Maj-Lis was going to decorate it with all kinds of "things". Her passion for antiquities meant that she had collected lots of beautiful furniture, household items, etc. Some were useful items, others pure luxury things with which she really didn't do anything but just enjoyed their beauty. Now these items were coming out of the boxes and were going to be put to good use.

In April, Pulle and I went into the city to celebrate Lasse's engagement to Lisa Palojärvi, born Hyden. The dinner was held at the Aschan's place. They were always very hospitable and quick to arrange parties in their home. We had the opportunity to meet our new sister-in-law and welcomed her into our sisterhood.

The rapid colonization had reached Mälikkälä. Pulle had to go there and negotiate with several people who came to see the property. But no land was confiscated.

In May the national marching competition was held between Finland and Sweden. Finland won in brilliant fashion. In our family everyone took part except me. Trolle marched with young Willy von Koskull. Flushed and proud he came home with a badge on his sports shirt. Children under fifteen completed the same distance as women, 10 km (6 mi), which had to be finished in less than one hour and forty minutes. The men marched 15 km (9 mi), which had to be completed in less than two hours and twenty minutes. Children born after 1931 were not allowed to participate.

Father Willy was so excited that he walked his own distance and then walked with the boys, just to see how they would do. Their time was one hour and nineteen minutes, which was good for two nine-year-olds.

The schools had finished on May 21st, so the students were able to participate in the upcoming food campaign. The children had filled out forms where they were asked if they were willing to go out into the country and work in the farms with people they did not know, or if they were able to work at home or with relatives. Pi belonged to the middle category and was put to work in the garden in Mustaniemi.

But we had not moved out to the country yet for the summer. Pulle was planning a longer vacation, which he certainly was in need of, but there were still some uncertainties with the move to the country and the vacation.

While Pi and Mi were waiting for the gardening work, they played tennis with passion, which showed that Pulle was their daddy. He had been the tennis champion in town for many years. Pi also enjoyed herself tremendously. Apart from hanging around the tennis court, she belonged to a gang of four girls and eight boys. They danced, went to the movies, and walked the roadways. It was also around this time that Pi had her first episode of chest pain, which turned out to be harmless.

Pulle Preparing the Chalk Lines
for the Clay Tennis Court

The lilacs were in bloom. Never had their splendor been greater than now. When Pulle came home from the office on June 11th, he told me that a few people from Kuusankoski had been drafted. He said that the situation was serious. Ever since that infamous day of March 13th last year, it was as if we had been living on a volcano. I had been dreading the day when we would again be standing face to face with the war, but now I stayed completely calm. We all had to look the truth in the eye. The situation was completely different from the Winter War. Now the Germans had joined us. There were rumors that German troops had already arrived in Finland, they were somewhere up north, but to what extent we did not know, and there were, of course, no official reports. But there was whispering from man to man, and it cheered us up - and the lilacs were in bloom.

The next day the situation was even more serious. It had been said, that if there was war, Kuusankoski was going to be evacuated. The future was not filled with joy. The police chief Mr. Saastamoinen again held a speech about how the evacuation was going to be organized. I did not go. I had enough of his bombastic speeches and his predilection for scaring people. If there was war, we were going to be evacuated to Mäntsälä, about 90 km (56 mi) southwest of Kuusankoski. There we were going to be housed in elementary schools and other buildings. Those who had a bicycle were supposed to be prepared to travel 30 km (18 mi) a day. Buses were going to be available only for the sick and children. You were not allowed to take with you more than what you could carry. Outdoor clothing and sheets were packed into boxes ahead of time. The boxes were to be collected at a designated spot and from there taken to Mäntsälä by the authorities. All furniture had to be left behind. Later, if possible, other things could be transported, mainly clothing, then sewing machines and hand-looms.

I organized the children's things. The backpacks were packed, and we had decided on the provisions. If needed, all three of us were ready to leave within the hour.

Pulle was surely going to be called to duty and I would have to walk the 30 km (18 mi) a day for 3 days to Mäntsälä. Mi was hoping to join the Lotta section number 5 in Helsinki. Pi and I would stick together, as we had previously planned. And Trolle, at least for now, was going to stay with me, as Brita had changed her mind and was not going to send her kids to Sweden.

This is how things were supposed to go, but the outlook for us got better when we heard that we may be able to evacuate to Mustaniemi. The Itis community was not going to be evacuated immediately. We had received a respite.

Lasse and Lisa were going to get married in Helsinki and Pulle and I had promised to attend the wedding. The draft was taking place all over the country, everybody was talking about the war, and we were supposed to go to a wedding!

I thought it was downright grotesque. Was it right to leave the kids under such conditions? When Pulle did not see any reason not to go, I decided not to disappoint him and also not be unkind to Lasse and Lisa and the entire family. I was sure no one would have understood my motives anyway, they had never had to live close to the border. So, off we went to Helsinki.

We got on a train filled with military personnel, civilians, and mothers and children. Many were traveling west before the order for evacuation was given, very smart, I thought. I looked at our suitcase on the baggage counter. It contained a long tail tuxedo, a gala dress, a pair of golden shoes, a fur cape, some toiletries, and night gowns, that was all. All you could do was to try to shake off the awkward feeling and look at everything as optimistically as possible.

The wedding was a glamorous celebration. After the ceremony in the pastor's office, we went to the Fisherman's House restaurant. One could still get good food at the restaurants, as long as one was willing to pay the exaggerated prices. We had salmon and chicken, food that was not rationed. We sat at a huge square table with beautiful flower arrangements. There was nothing wrong with the atmosphere, no one was thinking about tomorrow. We sang, laughed, and cried in the true Troil spirit. There was a more somber moment when Marga made a toast for the only one of the siblings who was missing - Dulle.

Lasse was really sick. Influenza, with more than 39 C (102 F) fever. Despite that, he seemed to enjoy himself. Lisa was lovely in her lace dress with pink carnations in her hair. Her bouquet was made out of an enormous bundle of the same flowers. It really was a celebration, and Ethel Hyden's enthusiastic words were so fitting:

"The Troils are wonderful people to be able to enjoy themselves like this just before the fateful blow, but we can only hope it will not be a hard blow," she said.

The next day, while visiting with the Östermans before our train was supposed to leave, the newlywed bride called and said Lasse had been called to duty.

We were able to get back well to Kymmene. The children were at home, nothing had happened. But the same evening, Pulle got orders to be at the Defense Corps' Headquarters in Kouvola.

"There goes my vacation," he said.

On Monday Pulle got dressed in a field gray lieutenant's uniform and started working with the men of his company in the Defense Corps. He had, at his own request, been released from his position as the director of the population shelters. This time he was going to serve as an officer.

Brita and I started to weigh our options regarding evacuating the children. Since there was a possibility that she could get her kids placed with family on a property near Borgå, I told her to contact them as soon as possible. Her first thought had been to send them to Mustaniemi together with Pi and Trolle, but since I could not guarantee that they would get enough food, it would surely be better for them to stay with the family in question. If they did not come to Mustaniemi, I would be able to offer room for my family with children in the country. I was mainly thinking about my Winter War kids Ebba, Kurt-Erik, and Gunnar.

In the morning of the 17th, the Tigerstedts came with the milk truck from Mustila to visit with the Koskulls and chat for a while. People had the need to see each other. They tried to talk the Koskulls into "borrowing" the boys for a day. But at that time the situation was critical, and they had to stay in the country. Mrs. Tigerstedt even called me up and offered Trolle an evacuation home. I could not accept her offer since we had our Mustaniemi, and it would have been irresponsible to leave the responsibility for two children to someone else before it really was necessary.

Ulla, young Willy, and Peter never left for their family in Borgå. They stayed the entire summer with the Tigerstedts who had ten children to take care of, their own and others. The children were having a good time and did not miss home at all. Nobody had to worry that there would not be enough food. What a paradise!

Willy Sr. traveled to Helsinki to sign up as a volunteer. He did not want to wait to be called up for duty. Before he left he came by to say good bye to us. We wished him good luck.

The same day that Willy left, Pi, Trolle, Ebba, and Kurt-Erik, and the maids, Taina and Rauha, were sent to Mustaniemi. They used bicycles since none of the buses ran. I had sent food and clothing with a truck, which I had managed to get a hold of just before it was confiscated by the military.

Taina agreed to take care of the household in the country, and Rauha went out to do some major cleaning. I did not go anywhere. This time I did not want to be stuck evacuated. During the Winter War it was different, it was cold then, Trolle and Kurt-Erik were younger. Now they would manage without me, at least for now. One thing I wanted, no matter what: stick together with the Kymmene Lottas.

Mi and I stayed in Kymmene and waited to see what my role as a Lotta would be. The entire nation was holding its breath. The army was at the border, also waiting.

On June the 22nd, the first Russian bombs fell. A couple of Finnish ships were bombarded, as well as the Alskär Coast Guard station. On June the 25th, there were violent bombing raids on civilian targets. Extensive damage was reported from Åbo and Kotka.

On June the 26th, President Ryti spoke to the Finnish people on the radio. He did it, as before, calmly and objectively, convincingly, in a manly way, and patriotically. Now our second defensive war had started, he said, and talked about the difficulties Finland had had during the so-called peace, how the Russians had forced upon us all kinds of concessions. The people had not known anything about this, the President was not able to really speak out until now.

One thing we had known for a long time, we had seen it with our own eyes: how the Russians had forced us to give them the right to use their own railroad wagons to transport people and goods between Hangö and the eastern border. Every time we traveled to Helsinki, some of those disgusting red painted wagons were attached to the trains, traveling in both directions. They looked unsympathetic with their curtains drawn. The hyenas were watching their pray. We were at war again. But everyone thought it would only last a short while. "When the crop is ready to be harvested we will be back," the drafted farmers said.

The sirens began howling again as the Russian bombers swept over the town. But now we had an air defense gun which started shooting as soon as an enemy plane got close. We did have a similar gun for a short time during the Winter War, but that one was removed. There were no fleets of planes above us anymore. There were not nearly as many planes.

Pulle took his bike to Kouvola every morning just after eight. He was allowed to come home overnight. This was good as his rash had still not resolved and needed daily treatment.

When the bombs were falling Pulle would sometimes provocatively go out into the streets and shout "get down" to pedestrians passing by. He was happy not to have to sit with "15 m (50 ft) of rock on top of my head" anymore. He refused to go to any shrapnel cover. He wanted to see what was happening.

He was not happy to be placed in Kouvola, it was the same as during the Winter War, he wanted to go out to the front. "Try to get to the front then," I said. "In that case I am prepared for you to quickly end up in a field hospital."

With this I meant his rash. I was thinking about all the little creatures that follow an army in their footsteps and the misery they could cause Pulle's bad skin.

But he stayed in Kouvola where he was better fed. Willy was out at sea, Rhen out on the front, Brita's kids in Mustila, the Rhen and our kids in Mustaniemi, except Mi, who was home with me in Kymmene where we only had four left to feed; Brita, Eine, Mi and myself.

The meals were eaten at Brita's place since she had agreed to be the hostess. We enjoyed each other's company. We listened to the radio, news and music, and occasionally heard that there was an alarm, which we decided to ignore.

Our cellar was full of ice and could therefore not be used as a shelter. We were supposed to go into the hollow between the Rhen's and Koskull's villas. But we never went there, Pulle thought we might as well jump into the closest ditch and lay there instead.

One time, Brita had the radio's volume turned up high enough for us to hear into the next room where we were sitting. I thought it was careless, were we not supposed to at least try to listen if any Russian planes were approaching and if the air defense was shooting? Brita smiled. Was Musti nervous? Yes, maybe I was.

At night I sometimes sat on the porch during alarms. I felt I had to watch the house. Pulle just rolled over and fell asleep again. Mi came downstairs, if I asked her, sleepy and grumbling. But it all typically ended with: “Uh, nothing is going to come of this anyway, I’m going back to sleep.” Said and done. And we would fall asleep again.

But when the enormous German planes were above us, Pulle shot up like a rocket. He, like everyone else, was enthusiastic and wanted to see the planes with his own eyes. Low and majestically they sailed east.

“Now they are going to bomb the Russians,” Pulle said and rubbed his hands. “Now they will see what it feels like.”

We had already had war several days, but we were still lingering in Kymmene. The expected mandatory evacuations had not been started yet. The people from the border towns were walking the country roads with children, bundles of luggage, horses and cows. We were wondering when it would be our turn to do the same.

We had taken some precautions. All the furniture was marked with red ink. If we had to leave, and if later anything was salvageable, at least it was marked. I packed the family’s best wool socks, sweaters, and mittens into a little box. It was difficult to buy such things anymore. I took the silver to the office. I arranged Trolle’s room downstairs into a storage room with Mi’s help. There were rugs, paintings, suitcases with sheets, the wool box, Pulle’s suits, the girl’s and my wool dresses. I had sent the better winter gear and other things to Mustaniemi in a truck.

In the pantry I organized what little I had of sugar, grains, and flour on a shelf so it could be rescued quickly in case of fire or evacuation. Many families had large packages standing in their foyers containing anything between heaven and earth.

Brita, Eine, and I all had each other's keys in case we had to rush to help one another. We were just waiting for the evacuation order. Everyone, who could afford it, had bought a bicycle, anticipating the trip out west. Brita was among those with a brand-new bicycle, but I did not have one. As a child, I was not among the lucky ones to own one. I had learned to ride with someone else's bicycles but broke it and sustained a few bruises. It was obvious, I was better off on my own legs rather than wiggling around on a bicycle going west.

Stina and Eine offered to walk the whole way to Mustaniemi, even though both of them had their own bicycles. Of course, I protested. Nobody had to take any notice of me. But deep inside I was dreading the moment the entire Kymmene valley industrial population was going to be dragging along the country roads.

BOMBS OVER KUUSANKOSKI

Shortly before midsummer, our Mustaniemi evacuation family was expanded by Gunnar and the maid of the Serck family. Soon after that a bus started traveling between Radansuu (close to Mustaniemi), Kouvola, and Lahtis, which we were very happy about. That way the kids were not as isolated anymore, as it was now much easier for us mothers to visit with them.

Standing Left to Right:
Gunnar, Trolle, Kurt-Erik
Sitting: Pi, Ebba

I had still not gotten a Lotta job despite pestering poor Eine with constant questions about my chances. I had the opportunity to go to the country to visit the kids for a few days to see how they were doing, organize the food a little, and check on the garden. But above all I wanted to see how things were going for Pi. She had again had chest pains for several days. After two days in bed she felt better.

Pi was not able to come to Kymmene to see a doctor as she was not strong enough to bike the distance, nor could she walk the 4 km (2.5 mi) to the bus. The doctor near Kausala was available if her condition worsened.

The whole thing was bothering me; the girl had to be examined as soon as possible. She had surely overdone it while carrying water to the garden. Our usual help in those situations, Mr. Saari, hadn't had a chance to fix the pump before his sudden departure to the front.

The day Stina and I were to travel was a hopeless day. We were supposed to wait at the club gate to get on the bus. Eine, Mi, and I went in good time, but when we got to the cellulose factory the sirens went off. When the all-clear signal came we ran to the gate and barely made it to the bus, which had stopped under a tree during the alarm.

It did not take long, and the sirens sounded again. The passengers rushed out and tried to seek shelter in a ditch under the shadow of some trees. I thought it wasn't necessary to crawl into the ditch overgrown with nettles, which the others slowly realized. But the bus driver wanted to stick to his timetable, so he decided to continue the trip. It was irresponsible of him, but all went well.

In Mustaniemi the kids were doing well although it was difficult to get enough food. Pi was feeling better. The garden looked good, everything was in order. It was just as during the Winter War, the bombs were crashing all around us, both our own and the hated Russian planes were hovering above us, and the ground shook. I woke up at night from the boom coming from the surrounding hills and lay awake hour after hour worrying about Kymmene.

One evening in July I went to Mynttinen's to pay the monthly fee for supplies. I was, as usual, warmly welcomed and was sitting with the older hostess when the younger hostess came in with Mrs. Halme, who was staying in Tytti's cottage. Mrs. Halme was very distressed. She had heard that Kuusankoski had been bombarded.

I thought it must have been a mistake since neither Brita, Pulle, nor Mi had called. I called Brita from Mynttinen's and heard that the bombardment had happened that morning. Pulle had been standing in the bathroom shaving, and Brita had been studying a map in Pulle's room when it suddenly started blasting in earnest. They had ignored the alarm as usual. But Pulle did throw himself flat on his stomach on the bathroom floor, Brita and Mi had rushed to the porch and followed his example.

The closest bomb had dropped in a yard next to the railway embankment. The shrapnel had shattered several windows and flown into two of the Koskull's rooms, up onto their veranda, and finally to the far side of our veranda. There had been a shower of little bombs on the roof of the cellulose factory, shrapnel and broken glass had been scattered as far as the Rhen's house. On the other side of the river a large bomb had hit between the Henrickson's and Hessle's, it had crashed all the windows, and pushed in the walls so that both houses were now leaning. A huge bomb crater was formed outside the Wiklund's, as well as in between the Executive House and the Vocational School, which was functioning as a war hospital. Bombs had fallen along the entire Lautta Street. Strangely, all the houses were still standing. The sad thing was that two human lives had been lost.

I went home with Mrs. Halme. We were both very upset.

What was I going to do? If I was not going to get a Lotta job, it did not make any sense for me to go back to Kymmene, I thought. But I immediately changed my mind. I could not leave Pulle, someone had to cook and clean for him while Rauha was still visiting family. If anyone was going to leave Kymmene it was Mi.

Eine came out to visit us and told us more about the bombardment, which she seemed to take rather easily.

We went back to Kymmene. I asked Mi if she had been scared during the bombardment.

"No, I did not have time to be, it went so fast..." she answered.

The one who supposedly was very scared was Rauha, who had been with her parents in Kymmene. She asked me if I was going to stay in town. When I answered yes, she asked if Mi was going to stay as well. When she heard Mi was staying, she calmed down.

Our new chairwoman for the Lotta organization, Ms. Virtanen, had asked Mi if she could work in Kymmene even though she actually was a Lotta from the Helsinki region. "There is a lack of Lottas here." Mi promised to ask her closest supervisor. It worked out and Mi was happy to come home. She was also glad to not have to live by herself in the capital during the summer. She got a temporary job at a small Lotta cafeteria, but the next day she was ordered to report to the head nurse at the hospital. A telephone receptionist was needed. Mi was entered into the hospital staff records and received her "dog tags" to wear around her neck, just like the soldiers. This is how her hospital work started.

Mi with a Soldier at the Hospital

While I had been gone from Kymmene, Brita got a job as a first aid Lotta. She was supposed to apply the first bandages, help to arrange for ambulance transportation, and send the wounded to the hospital. Every time there was an alarm, she had to drop everything and get on her bike. Several times she had to get up in the middle of the night, sometimes several times a night.

Eine also had a job, which she had had during the whole war. One day, thank God, there was even a job for me. It was the same kind as during the Winter War, in other words sewing. Many women, most of them about my age, were sewing all day at the club house. We sewed shirts, underwear, map bags, backpacks, etc. Brita was also there, but not on a regular basis, she had her first aid duties which were pretty strenuous.

In the evenings, Mi worked in the garden. She irrigated and picked weeds. When I wanted to help I was promptly told to leave. "What use is it, you know this is nothing for you," I was told.

Eine came for a visit with juice bottles and preserved vegetables. How sweet of her.

Our troops were doing well in the war. Salla had been reconquered. Things were moving ahead on the entire Eastern Front, only in the South the troops were at a standstill, biding their time. On the home front many areas had been bombarded and badly damaged. Among them Åbo, where a whole block had burned down. My sister-in-law, Märtha, took the initiative for a collection for those who had lost their homes and collected a total of 90,000 marks.

Helsinki was bombed with 17 dead and 156 injured. Kotka was hit badly many times, Lovisa and especially Borgå were hit by severe air raids. But now, it wasn't like the end of the last war, now we had the Germans on our side. People from other countries were fighting the same war against the Bolsheviks along the longest front in world history.

Another thing was different than during the Winter War. Now, there are those in our country who don't understand the situation. I can mention, as an example, that during the draft, when it looked like war was going to break out, Taina was furious. She took it as a personal insult. No matter how I tried to explain that we had to be prepared to defend ourselves, she did not understand. This was regrettable, since she had been very patriotic during the Winter War. She and Rauha had knitted countless pieces of warm clothing for the soldiers. Frustrated, I concluded: "For the fatherland one may also do things that are not that pleasant."

She became quiet, but she was not convinced. And she was by no means the only one. There were workers, seamstresses, other domestic workers, and especially the wives of the workers that shared her opinion. I was upset when I told Pulle about it.

"That's a given, how could they understand," he said. "They have not been told anything, and now this war comes over them like a thunder bolt from a clear sky. They have not thought about the political situation in the same way that we have. Remember that they are uneducated people."

And I believe that many never thought about what danger there was in having such an impossible border and that the Russians could attack again. They thought there was peace, and, therefore, there was no need to think about the political situation any further.

The speech by President Ryti worked wonders on people's attitude. At least Taina was changed after that day. I told my sister Greta Gustafsson about it, without mentioning any names, but asked her to not unnecessarily speak about it.

"On the contrary," she said. "We ought to talk about it, because everyone does not get in contact with the factory workers like you."

That is when I realized that of course more information should be given out about the situation. For me just talking behind people's back, who could not defend themselves, was not going to lead anywhere. It would be something entirely different if I was able to broadcast patriotic propaganda on the radio as a counter-action to the dreadful Bolshevik propaganda. But as of now, I had not been in contact with anyone with connections that could have helped me. I hoped Greta would bring up the matter with her husband Verner Gustafsson, the general.

I never managed to get a hold of anyone to help me, but apparently there were others who shared my views as there were several well-known speakers on the radio who started appearing in a very robust way and were able to reach the common man.

Later, I heard that there were many soldiers that were pretty "red" (Bolshevik supporters) when they left for the front, but returned completely changed. This was the result of seeing what "paradise" really looked like when they crossed into Russian territory: crumbling houses, dirt, and poverty.

The food situation became precarious during the summer. The bread rations were now only 200g (7 oz) per person per day for people with light duty, whereas people with manual labor received slightly larger rations. The money we were allowed to spend on meat was 12-18 marks per person per month. Taina sometimes was able to get a hold of fresh meat in Kausala but not very much as the price had gone up to 20-30 marks per kilogram (2.2 lb) depending on the quality. If one wanted to buy eggs one could use the meat coupons. At the beginning of the summer one could not get any eggs in Kymmene. When they again appeared in the stores, we received an extra egg coupon on the meat rations, which equaled six eggs in July and three in August per person. I bought as many eggs as I could get and put just about all of it into winter storage.

Around midsummer Pulle's good friend Hugo Hornborg had saved us by sending us several kilograms of fish. I don't know what else Brita would have served her hungry family. At that time, one was only able to buy turnip and carrot "steaks" in the stores. The shelves made a sad impression gaping with emptiness. For a while there was still some rye flour, bread, sugar, coffee, coffee surrogate, and tea. Oatmeal was available only for children. Then there was a time when even the wheat flour had run out.

"When the need is at its greatest, the help is nearest," it has been said, and even we could say that. In the middle of July the un-rationed blood pudding arrived, which was available pretty often. And then we got the strange pale grain sausages, which were later transitioned into potato sausages, also not rationed.

We were certainly hungry and many of us lost a catastrophic amount of weight, but the working population surely had it even worse. What they were eating is a mystery to me. It was common for them to consume all their grain rations by the time only half the month was up. Then they went to the population supply authorities to complain and wanted more rations. And when the supply authorities were not always able to accommodate them, like a "Jack in the Box", the needy became frustrated. Most of them also did not have the right to get milk directly from the dairy farms. The wives had to stand in the daily, depressing, milk lines, and it often happened that they did not even get the little splash of milk the ration cards entitled them to. No wonder they were unhappy and could not understand many things about all the politics. When stomachs are growling, the unhappiness is not far away.

The so-called educated population split the bread rations so that it had to last until the end of the month. And maybe they also had more imagination and knowledge when it came to preparing food. One made casseroles of spinach, potatoes, and other vegetables. Later in the season one ate cauliflower, beans, and tomatoes. If one did not have one's own garden it became too expensive for many to buy these things. Especially in Helsinki, the prices at the market squares became unbelievable. For example, beans cost 60 marks per kilogram.

At the end of July, we made herring casserole with salted herring from the previous fall, but one has to wonder how many people actually had these kinds of resources. Or we ate the beloved blood pudding, spinach in a casserole or in some other form, and carrot casserole with grains. Such casseroles had to be made with barley grain, as rice was not available anymore. The barley was not available in stores either, I had to buy it directly from Hugo Hornborg's property. The estates had the right to sell milk, bread, grains, peas, etc., according to rations. Sometimes we would have a real feast with pea soup, but the peas were not from the store, I bought them from the Mynttinens. For desert we had potatoes flavored with almonds, rhubarb soup or pancakes, maybe berry porridge, but when we ran out of semolina, the porridge was cooked out of rye grain. We were not able to cook berry creams due to the lack of potato meal. We sometimes used barley meal in fruit soups. Pancakes were still made out of wheat flour and milk mixed with water.

There were families that started eating at the Club House. A lady told me that otherwise her family would have starved to death. In my mind I was wondering if it wasn't just proof that the lady was just not practical. Or maybe she really did have it that bad.

In Mustaniemi the kids were fishing with traps that Mr. Saari had left us before leaving for the front. The trap supplied the fish for the daily fish soup. The kids were all of the age when the appetite is great, there were real giant eaters among them. They could lap up three generous plates of soup, plus sour milk on top of that, and still be hungry half an hour later.

At more festive occasions the children were allowed to drink juice, as when one of the mothers came to visit and brought a gift, a cardamom roll, for instance, or some cake. This is how we celebrated Ebba's 14th birthday. People got very inventive, cakes were made out of potatoes and carrots with just a little egg, sometimes none. There was an egg surrogate, a yellow powder, which mainly resembled soda powder.

But in Mustaniemi we never had to experience flax-seed or cellulose bread, which I had made when I was very young in 1918 during the Civil War. And the children got rye grain porridge every day, something that for me and many others was an unattainable dream in 1918. As much as my stomach was screaming then, I don't think their stomachs were screaming as loudly today.

I kept to the principle that all children in Mustaniemi had the same rights and the same duties. Eine trusted me completely, I could decide whatever I wanted, and she was always pleased.

Eine had also come out to Mustaniemi. We had it good, brushed off the dust from Kymmene, and we were happy to be able to spend some time with our kids. I could spend a few days, Eine just one. We went to bed after a cozy day when everything was nice and peaceful. When I woke up the next morning and went into the living room, Trolle and Kurt-Erik were playing cards. They told me that Gunnar had left to go back into town. I could not believe my ears and asked the Serck's maid Ester if she knew where the boy was. Weak and upset she saw that his room was empty. The boy had left early in the morning and told Trolle and Kurt-Erik, who had caught him in the act, not to tell anyone until they were asked where he was.

First, I got worried, then really angry, sparking angry. Later, Stina called sounding troubled; she regretted what had happened and said that the boy had arrived at home. He had been homesick and unhappy, although she did not want to admit the latter.

The same day when Eine and I were walking to the bus, Stina returned with Gunnar. She had to come herself to get the boy to stay with us. Gunnar was forced to apologize, but he did not seem regretful at all. Later, Trolle said that his father had thought he was a brave boy when he escaped. I doubt that, but one thing is for sure, he did not get the kind of beating he deserved!

I was unhappy about what had happened, especially since Stina and I had gotten along so well during the Winter War. But, thank God, there was no harm to our friendship. Gunnar was a spoiled only child who missed his mother so much that even though he was eleven years old, he could not be happy without her.

Shortly before this incident Russian planes had dropped leaflets. The kids ran around noisily picking up the flyers. I got all worked up. They could not understand what it was all about, but I was terribly upset about seeing them run after these papers that contained Bolshevik propaganda and spread heinous lies. I asked them to burn them all in the kitchen stove. Everyone obeyed, except Gunnar, who hid the leaflets in his bedroom. He apparently thought Aunty

Brita was unbearable. My nerves were not under control. I was crying from the commotion.

Then a boom was heard from the nearby village of Kausala, we were at war, I had to calm down and get used to it. Lives were lost during the bombardment of Kausala; a mother with her child was killed.

In Kymmene everyday life continued. Eine was fully occupied with her chores, and I went to the needlework shop. Mi had a lot of work and sat at the telephone reception desk at the hospital.

In Mustaniemi Taina had been very nervous during the summer. She did not seem to understand that the situation was not very pleasant for anyone, and that one, in consideration to others, should try to keep a happy face. On top of all, she had it a lot better than most; she had no husband or fiancé at the front. Her bad mood affected the children at Mustaniemi, especially Pi suffered from this. In a way she took over hosting by taking care of the milk rationing at the breakfast table, looked after the boys, took care of the garden, went fishing, and took turns with Ebba to go to Kausala to shop for food with Taina, and went to fetch the milk with Ebba every day. Even Gunnar helped to carry the milk, and the kids took turns getting the mail from Tillola by bicycle. Pi also gave lectures in mathematics to Ebba, Trolle, and Kurt-Erik. This she did with the enthusiasm she was known for. No one was allowed to be absent from the lectures, although Trolle was grumbling about it. But he had such respect for his big sister that he did his assignments properly. When he returned to school in the fall he was better at math than ever before.

In the beginning of their stay in Mustaniemi, Pi and Ebba had frequent visits by boys from Kymmene. And when one of their girlfriends stayed close by they had a lot of fun together. They rowed, ran around on the islands and the cliffs, and enjoyed themselves wholeheartedly. But then the young boys were called to serve with a company that chased Russian intruders and were not able to visit the girls as often anymore.

In the long run, it became a bit boring for Pi. In addition, the somewhat embarrassing mood after Gunnar's escape bothered her sensitive disposition. When Stina came back with him it further strained the mood. And then Pi had the same problem that many other youngsters her age had: she felt that she was not being useful enough. I talked about it with Pulle and we decided to take her home to Kymmene.

One day Stina and her husband came to visit and let us know that they wanted to move Gunnar to Stina's sister, the Baroness von Graevenitz, who was to move into a villa on the opposite side of Lake Urajärvi. The villa was owned by her father, engineer Fredricsson from Voikka. They asked if I had any objections. How could I have any? Stina offered to leave her maid Ester with me, if I needed her, but I did not want that. I told them that Pi was moving back home, and to that Mr. Serck answered that it was even more appropriate for Gunnar to move, as Pi was the one he had gotten along with the best.

When Eine heard that Pi was going to leave Mustaniemi, she wanted to take Ebba back home as well. The family at Mustaniemi suddenly consisted of only two little boys. Taina could not imagine staying there with two nine-year-olds, only the three of them. She was worried, on a daily basis, about the Russian intruders who jumped from the Russian planes. Therefore, I sent Rauha to Mustaniemi and took care of the household in Kymmene with Pi's help. Pi made lunch while I was at the Lotta needlework shop, and we made dinner together.

PULLE, COURT-MARTIAL PROSECUTOR

The Russian intruders, or spies, were a nuisance in the whole country, but they operated mainly in the south of Finland. There were a lot of them especially in the Eastern Nyland district. Their job was to, among other things, tear up the railroad tracks. They sometimes wore civilian close, sometimes Finnish military uniforms. They worked by themselves, or sometimes in groups. They were very young, most of them just boys, who were put on the planes after a short training period and then dropped on Finnish territory. Some of them were devoted Bolsheviks, some of them had volunteered in the hope of getting asylum and getting away from the Bolshevik tyranny. The latter surrendered their guns and let themselves be captured.

At the end of August Pulle got a new job among the staff officers. He was declared general prosecutor for the court-martial, an uncomfortable assignment, which he did not like at all. He had to interrogate countless intruders. Some of them were cheeky, others humble. Many of them spoke good Finnish, especially those from the Baltic States. There were also some that spoke English or even French. Most of them listened to their death sentence with complete tranquility.

The intruders were hunted by our home bound troops that, with a few exceptions, consisted of boys, men unfit for military duty, or those who had been granted postponement of their duty.

One day Pulle came to Mustaniemi with a few other officers from his staff as Mr. Saari, who was on leave, had seen a suspicious individual on his way home from a visit with the Mynttinens. Pulle had longed to chase them all summer long. Now he had a chance to do it.

Trolle and Kurt-Erik were surprised when they suddenly saw Trolle's daddy and other men in uniform turn up with guns in little peaceful Mustaniemi.

One of the men was placed on guard inside Mynttinen's barn outside Tytti's cottage. In these times it was very unsafe for those living in remote areas as the intruders could force themselves into their cottages and demand food. But there was no trail of the strange man.

Brita decided to travel to Helsinki to visit Willy, whose leave seemed to be delayed. In his enthusiastic letters, he had written about how their boat had to perform difficult and dangerous assignments, but what they actually did, we did not know, he was not allowed to write about it. But one thing we did know: he was in the thick of it. He continued to be loyal to his optimism and never regretted signing up as a volunteer.

So Brita went to Helsinki, where Willy had his land based station.

The July nights became darker and we had to make sure the windows were covered. Pulle's room was carefully covered up, but the little sitting room was untouched as during the Winter War.

At the beginning of August, Einar Rhen returned from the front. Those who were born in 1897, and were not officers, were allowed to go home. Eine was happy, but Brita was missing her Willy.

We tried to make things as nice as possible despite the war. We invited Dr. Relander and Dr. Köhler and the Rhens for a crawfish party. Relander was a big man with a roaring bass voice, bushy eyebrows, an impressive nose, and the friendliest eyes in the world. As a surgeon at the war hospital he was overloaded with work and we were grateful he took the time to visit us. We were completely charmed by him, he was sweet, despite his booming voice, or maybe just because of it.

We chatted and philosophized. It was a typical discussion in this war summer. The troops along the southern part of the easterly border Virolahti-Joutseno had started go move on July 31st. The anticipated offensive had been started. We were not able to hear the faint canon thunder that we sometimes heard at the end of July when there was no easterly wind. The front had moved farther away.

Brita returned from Helsinki and traveled to Mustila to meet her children. The food preservation period had started. I arranged my work as a Lotta to be able to be absent for a while and traveled to Mustaniemi to relieve Taina. Rauha could not be left alone with the boys, and the increasingly nervous Taina was needed in Kymmene to help with the making of preserved foods, juices, and jams there.

On the evening of August the 8th, I was sitting by myself in Mustaniemi. The boys had gone to bed. It was almost 9 o'clock and I decided to call Pulle.

"Do you know what has happened?" he said. "Something horrible, Willy has been killed!"

"Who?" I couldn't hear.

"Willy, Willy...."

It was unbelievable.

"I will drive to Mustila and pick up Brita to stay with us," Pulle continued.

"It's awful, and I am stuck here," I said.

There were no buses running at night and Pulle was not able to arrange for me to be picked up from Mustaniemi.

"Brita will take the train to Helsinki tomorrow, so you would not be of any use here anyway," Pulle tried to console me.

It was terrible, a horrible fate had struck our poor Brita. Why Willy? He who still had so many things he wanted to do in life.

Pulle had received the death notice around 8 pm through the Southern Kymmene Valley District. While patrolling in the west, Willy's ship had been bombed and attacked with machine gun fire from enemy planes. Willy had been standing on guard on deck. A bullet struck him in the head and he had been killed instantly. Pulle had called Mustila to report what had happened and asked Mrs. Tigerstedt to give the message to Brita.

Poor Brita, her happiness has been broken.

It took Pulle almost two hours by car to get to Mustila and pick up Brita. The children were fast asleep, all three of them. She did not wake them up when they left.

She stayed at our place over night. She got to bed late, not until about 2:30 am. I am not sure if she was able to sleep at all. Her planned trip to Helsinki was postponed until Sunday. There were many practical arrangements before the funeral that Pulle was able to help with by contacting various persons.

In the morning Brita walked over to her empty home all by herself. I called Pulle.

"It is best that you come here as soon as possible," he said. "You can go with her to Helsinki and stay there with her."

I promised to take the bus. The boys could not stay in Mustaniemi alone with Rauha. I also had a bad feeling about the Russian intruders and the August nights that were getting darker. Therefore, I could not accept the brave suggestion by the girls to stay in Mustaniemi. Taina wasn't able to keep her bad mood under control, so in order to preserve the peace I told them to pack.

It was a miserable departure. The rain was pouring down when we walked to the bus, which was overcrowded, but we were at least able to get on board.

Brita was at our place. I found her in the living room surrounded by flowers from her and Willy's friends. On the table next to the window were two pictures of Willy with a beautiful little Finnish flag at half-mast. Willy had gotten it as a keepsake from his fleet brothers during the summer of 1940. Brita showed me Willy's last letter. It was so like him, in such harmony with his friendly disposition. He had been happy that the clouds of uncertainty were lifting, and that Finland was moving toward a brighter future. He was happy to be part of shaping this future. And happily he stood on deck in sunshine, or in windstorm when the waves came crashing down over the stem.

On Sunday we traveled to Helsinki. Brita was going to see Willy a last time. I wanted to go with her to the morgue, but I wanted her to decide. In the end her brother-in-law, George, her sister-in-law, Elsa, and I went with her. Willy's mother was ill and did not have the strength to come.

Willy was lying in a simple soldier's coffin with his head turned a bit, and from where I was standing it looked as if he was sleeping peacefully. Brita showed wonderful restraint.

The 13th of August Pulle and Mi came to Helsinki with Ulla, little Willy, and Peter. They still had not fully comprehended what had happened.

The funeral was held the same day. Pulle accompanied Brita and the children to the Sandudd Chapel. Even though Willy's mother was very ill and tired she was still there, as well as Willy's three brothers. Walter had been far off at the Eastern Front, but was granted leave, which his mother was happy about. Eric came directly from the front at Hangö together with Brita's brother.

It was a beautiful funeral. An honor guard and four Marine officers stood in attention next to the coffin covered with the blue and white Finnish flag. After an organ solo, a string quartet played Hayden's "Adagio" and Schumann's "Träumerei" and pastor Thure af Björksten carried out the ceremony. Among the speeches I want to mention Willy's commanding fleet officer, Lieutenant Captain Carring's tribute to his good friend. After that came Pulle's speech:

"Brother Willy! One of the hardest things a man can face is the loss of one's best friend in life. In such an unspeakable loss, we - my wife and I - stand here today in front of your open tomb, for You Willy, were that best friend to us. We never really talked about what this friendship meant to us, but I know, that you - as we - valued it as one of the most precious, most priceless things we owned. You - if anyone - were able to show your affection in an infinitely considerate way, which was so characteristic of you, and which never made the receiving party feel embarrassed. And, yet, it was always you that gave and gave with an open hand, the way only one who experiences the joy of giving and never expects anything in return can. For all this, Willy, and for all the thousands of good and loving thoughts you have had for us and our children, we thank you from the bottom of our hearts.

You, Willy, loved the archipelago and the sea. Wasn't it then, by the providence of God that you, in your hour of fate, were fighting for their protection and that they together formed the great, vast altar, upon which you sacrificed your life. I don't think we could have imagined a more beautiful death than this one, which is in such complete harmony with your

nature. But even if you fought your last battle for the protection of the archipelago and the sea, all of us who knew you, know, that you made the ultimate goal of your battle to go far beyond the fatherland's borders. Just like the great idealist you were, you wanted to see the good conquer the bad, see the light break through all the darkness in the world. It was for this that you fought to the utmost, it was for this that you gave your life, and God willing, your sacrifice will not have been in vain.

Sleep Willy, sleep well the eternal rest, for you have done your deed."

After the funeral we gathered at Willy's mother's place. Even the forester, Henrik Gripenberg, had arrived from the Eastern Front. The next day Pulle, Brita and I went to the grave site. It was raining again, but during the burial the sun did shine, something we were all grateful for.

At the burial office Pulle asked if the grave next to Willy's was for sale. It was. Pulle bought it, he wanted us, all four of us, to rest beside each other. Our friendship in life was to continue in death.

Pulle and Mi went home with Ulla, little Willy, and Peter, who were to go back to Mustila, while Brita and I stayed in Helsinki for a few days before returning to Kymmene. Later, Brita's mother came to stay with her. The children were doing well in Mustila and when the Tigerstedts suggested they stay a while longer, Brita accepted.

I returned to my Lotta duties, Brita gave up her first aid work and dedicated herself entirely to her home and her garden.

The war was going well for our troops who pushed farther and farther into the east. But war is war, and many heroes were laid to rest in mother earth. Many fathers lost their hope, many mothers their support, many wives their husbands, and thousands of children stood there with big sad, questioning eyes. They could not comprehend that their father was going to be gone forever.

On many Sundays the flags flew at half-mast over Kymmene. Then everyone knew there was going to be a hero's funeral. Every time, a Lotta, a

Defense Corps representative, a soldier, or an officer was to honor the fallen with a wreath.

Two times I participated as a Lotta. The first time, my partner in the ceremony was Lieutenant Ruben Jansson, the commander at the war hospital and a school headmaster in civilian life. He had been good friends with Dulle. We laid down our wreaths on a young private's grave. While we were standing there, next to the open grave, the private's father and siblings came to lay their flowers down. The father made a touching speech in Swedish. His son could not be buried at home in Ekenäs, which had been forced to evacuate. He, therefore, had to be put to rest in unfamiliar ground far away from his hometown. That it became Kuusankoski was due to the fact that he died at the war hospital there.

The second funeral I participated in was very large. The coffins were carried through an honor guard of men from the Defense Corps and Lottas. I was extremely tired and swayed like a flagpole in the wind. My partner tried to give me a sign to leave, but I wanted to hold on. At last I took a step back toward a wall of people.

"The Lotta is about to pass out," I heard someone say, and then I was pulled aside. I laid down flat on the ground, but soon returned to my post with knees shaking. Another Lotta soon came to take my place.

During the funeral there was an alarm. The ceremony continued, but those standing further away started to run. It was terrible to see how people were panicking. When I started to walk home, two little crying girls turned up next to me, they were half running, holding on to each other tight. I forgot my own misery and consoled the girls the best I could and took them the safest way through the woods. They calmed down and stayed close to me. When we got to the country road, we headed in opposite directions, but they insisted they would find the way. I managed to get home, but outside the gate I was only able to get the key in the lock with a last great effort.

The 30th of August was a triumphant day. Viborg was again in our hands! The day before a patrol company had hoisted the blue and white flag over the Tyrgils old castle. All over the country the flags were flying at full mast. The radio played the patriotic March of Pori.

HARVEST IN TIMES OF NEED

According to the Orders of the Day, given by the headquarters, the country's old borders had been entirely restored by September 3rd. We had taken our Karelia back. Now the Finnish army was to continue, even in those areas, where the last bits of the border had been conquered. Since 1937 the Russians had built secret, strategically important, railroad tracks all across the East Karelia wilderness toward the Finnish border. As long as this threat existed we could not be safe.

It was calmer in Kymmene since the border had moved farther away. Kotka was still bombarded off and on, but there were rarely enemy planes in the Kouvola area. Our lives started to follow a more peaceful track.

Pulle, as a war prosecutor, was inundated with work up to his ears. He usually got home around seven o'clock, but, after skimming through the newspaper, he sat at the dining room table with his papers every night. He rarely got into bed before 11:30 and sometimes not before 1 am.

The papers spoke of great efforts and there were countless heroes. The Finnish "Sisu" (spirit, strength, or effort) was phenomenal. But there were also soldiers who had seen too much during the last war, as well as this one, and were now simply run down. There were all kinds of deserters, big strong men, little scrawny ones, those who deserted knowing exactly what they were doing, and those who did it because they did not know any better.

Pulle was suffering. It was awful to be prosecutor. It had been easier to be the judge. He was losing weight and looked tired and pitiful.

We did all we could to prepare for the coming winter by collecting food for our pantries and cellars.

Even Trolle participated. He dug up dandelion roots with amazing energy. Maybe it was mainly because he was paid well. We made good coffee out of these roots. All kinds of resources were used this fall to make coffee surrogate, apart from the dandelion roots, we also used acorns, parsnip, and red beets, and even almonds. We stuck to Trolle's roots, and thought we made a terrific "coffee", especially when we added a few real coffee beans. This fall we only got 250g (9 oz) of real coffee, and the same amount of surrogate, before the December rations were handed out, which were just as small. It was also the last time real coffee was available. After that we were happy to just get the surrogate.

Tea was even more difficult. There was none left, the military was to receive all that was in storage. In order to still be able to drink this popular drink, we collected raspberry and black currant leaves that we dried and mixed with our own leftover tea. It was really good.

One day Rauha and Pi went out to Mustaniemi to collect the harvest from the garden. It turned out that our neighbor's cows had eaten the rutabaga and other turnips. They had also eaten and trampled the shoots of the red beets, carrots, and potatoes, but strange enough they had left the beans. I was hoping that we were going to be compensated by the wealthy Salminen farm, but we didn't even receive one carrot. The hostess explained that it had absolutely not been their cows that had roamed around on our property. The Mynttinens were deeply shocked when they heard how the Salminens had tried to get away with it. I believe they were embarrassed to have such neighbors.

In Kymmene our little garden gave a phenomenal harvest. The kids and I took up the potatoes and the red beets. We ate beans and red beats just about daily in August and September. And even after that, we were still able to preserve enough for twenty glass jars and two large bags of dried produce, and that does not include the beans from Mustaniemi. I also bought carrots, red beets, cabbage, and turnip roots, and of course potatoes. The potato crop had been good, and since the government took a lot of it, many farms were not able to provide any potatoes at all.

It was not only in Kymmene that we collected food, even our Helsinki cellar was to be filled.

On the 30th of September, the flags were flying high again. Petroskoi, the capital of Russian Karelia, had been conquered.

The schools had not started the school year by September 1st as so many of the teachers were on duty. In the country and in the cities the elementary schools were occupied for different purposes. Some of the schools in Kymmene housed soldiers. The Central Elementary School again housed the Viborg Regional Hospital, which during the short peace time had moved to Kotka, but now it was impossible to work there because of the frequent bombardments. The hospital was merged with War Hospital #13, which in turn was located in the Vocational School.

The Little Swedish School was empty and able to start classes October 1st. I was happy for Trolle. But Pi became more and more bored without anything to do. The garden chores were finished by now, as well as her lectures. She had actually held lectures for Trolle and Kurt-Erik. Willy and Peter were also supposed to take part, but they always had some excuse. Either they were sent to the store by Brita or they had to take feed to Josefina. Sometimes they went to Mustila. And sometimes they forgot about school altogether.

We were frustrated, but we told Pi she did not have any obligations toward the boys since not all of them took her lectures seriously. Only Kurt-Erik and Trolle always turned up at the time she had ordered. Pi had a wonderful talent for teaching but categorically denied wanting to become a teacher. She wanted to study mathematics and chemistry, possibly physics, and maybe biology as a fourth subject for undergraduate studies. Deep inside I was hoping for the day my girl would be able to revel in numbers and chemical formulas in peace and quiet.

Eine made it possible for Pi and Ebba to take care of a small stand for candy, pens, stationary, postcards, etc. It was located in one of the elementary schools, where a company of soldiers was housed. There Pi met Arne.

The young man was 19 years old, 182 cm (6 ft) tall, dark and apparently very charming in a young girl's eyes. He was a volunteer stationed in Kymmene, but soon returned to civilian life to his hometown Åbo. From there he bombarded Pi with letters. He was a Norwegian and had seen a whole lot in Norway in the spring of 1940, which made him even more interesting, although Pi had already previously been courted by number of cavaliers. Roughish Pi did not say no. If there was a chance to have fun she was going to take it.

Big sister Mi's work was of a much more serious kind. When Pulle and I one day visited her at her work place, she was in the process of informing a soldier's family that he had died at the hospital. This was nothing out of the ordinary. She had to talk to a lot of people and tell them how their sons or husbands were doing. She had to experience many things girls at her age typically knew nothing about.

There had been talk about the hospital moving eastward for a long time. As soon as the danger of the mines in Viborg had been eliminated and the electricity and the water pipes restored, the hospital was to be moved there.

Mi had been promised a Lotta assignment in Viborg. One morning at the end of October I accompanied her to the hospital, where everyone was in the process of moving. She was allowed to take the bus to the station and I went down to tell her good bye. She was full of anticipation, as she was about to embark on her life's first adventure. The compartment in the train for the Lottas was different from the others, an extra level had been built above the benches. I hugged my girl and wished her luck on her journey.

Soon she sent me a letter from Viborg (starting with the secret code for her location):

"24.X 41
2 Kpk./1636

We started moving, at a slow pace at a quarter past 10 pm. We stopped at almost every station and the whole trip took a ridiculously long time. In a few places there were many ruins, chimney after chimney, but no life. Gloomy. When we finally reached the station, the train just stood there for a long time, but no one was allowed to step outside. But what a view from the train window! Walls covered in soot and empty, gaping windows. You have read the descriptions in the newspapers, so you know about what it looks like. There were a few people in the streets, but most of all there were Russian prisoners driving two horses in front of strange-looking carts.

All the moving, shuffling and organizing is much faster here with all the Russians available to help. For now, we are still staying in the main building but will soon be moving to some smaller place. A school friend of mine from Kymmene, Siv, and I first ended up together with two strange individuals in one room, but then we walked around exploring and found a small room just for the two of us. Thanks to Siv's actions this morning we now have our own mattresses and sheets. It is only 8:30 pm, but we are both so tired, we are about to go to sleep. The Russians carried our beds, we had to hail them down ourselves and then point them to where we wanted the beds carried."

After this letter many more followed, where she told us that she had to do all kinds of other jobs since the telephone reception was not finished yet; carry mattresses, scrub down her own bed, use a calculating machine, wash bottles and organize the cork stoppers that had belonged to the Russians, which had a strong scent of perfume. When the telephone center was ready the commander was on leave, but when he returned after a week, he thought it was not appropriate for Mi to sit in the same room as the lieutenant on call. She was placed in the post office but did not like it there. Later she was moved to the commander's department and did office work.

November 3rd, she wrote that she had changed rooms and now lived with five other Lottas from the office. The furniture had been hoarded from a church, which the Russians had used as some sort of storage room. The six girls were comfortable in their room. Sometimes they had "parties" and invited the chief of economy, the cashier, and the priest. The last mentioned would court her quietly.

Siv's mother would tell me that the other girls were jealous of Mi's success with the priest, but Siv thought that one priest could not be enough for several girls. There was laughter and joking at the needle workshop. Mi was also good friends with the pharmacist. The priest would, for fun, call this gentleman the "shepherd", and Mi would call him the "lamb".

In the beginning the Lottas were still allowed to walk in the center of town without the permission of the commander, but later they had to get authorization if they wanted to go to one of the reopened stores in town. Otherwise they were able to move about without any obstacles. Everywhere she saw prisoners:

"It was funny to see prisoners all over working, trying to fix things, etc., generally one can get used to anything, including the prisoners and all the ruins. In some places there is even a lot of traffic, both cars and horses are rattling by, as well as the hordes of Russians, to and from their work places. The prisoners were often watched by some young stripling with a rifle on his shoulder, and a look on his face, as if he was the emperor of China himself. It is strange, but even the prisoners seem to have perfume, and when they walk past, one is hit by a disgusting stench."

Mi would write about the unusual habit of these prisoners to poke around in garbage piles or under windows, they were happy if they found, for instance, a cigarette butt. Sometimes they would pick up potato peals, fish heads, etc., which they would cook, but most of the time they ate directly from the garbage pile. This is unbelievable for civilized people.

She was able to visit five of the cafeterias, including the one in the Round Tower. There she met a good friend of Dulle and Nisse, Bo Grotenfelt, the tennis player. He had never seen Mi, but claimed that, based on her looks, she was "Pulle's girl." She thought that was pretty funny.

At the cafeterias one could get anything between shoe polish and headache powders, hot juice, and surrogate, and sometimes a dry biscuit that was not rationed. As far as the food was concerned, it was good but simple. The Lottas where allowed to eat with the doctors and nurses, which they were not allowed to do in Kymmene. When Mi started work at the commander's office, she got so busy, the walks came to a quick halt. She barely had enough time to eat, but did not have time for a sauna, she had to plod along from morning till evening. She also happened to get a stomach bug, which was raging at the hospital, and she had to spend two days at the women's ward.

According to the letters, Mi still enjoyed herself and did not regret volunteering to go to Viborg. We heard, indirectly, that the chief of staff physician was pleased with her and thought she was diligent and dutiful. The commander and the head nurse were also very kind to her. She got along well with her friends and got a small flag as a keepsake.

I think Mi did her best. She even gave blood once. In the whole country, giving blood was arranged for those age eighteen and above.

Pulle gave blood during the war. Brita, Taina, and Rauha also did it, but my health was so poor that I could not. Those who donated blood were given a special needle and after donating five times a special medal of honor. At home we were still living a quiet life. Pulle had too much work and sat evening after evening with his papers at the dining room table. He kept losing weight, so I was happy when he, starting on December 1st, began to eat dinner at home. The food at the headquarters wasn't all that bad, but it was very simple. At home we had our vegetables and our preservatives in glass jars. And also moose meat since Pulle had participated in the hunt. Taina and I made an effort to cook nutritious food and Pulle stopped losing weight, he actually gained a few pounds back.

Periodically I went to the needle workshop. We had a good time, talked about politics and Lotta activities, but most of all we talked about food, which was the common burning problem. We exchanged food and cake recipes. Sometimes someone had picked up something extra smart, like how to bake a cake without eggs or flower.

There had been a rag collection in the area. Out of these pitiful rags we made many neat little pieces of clothing for children who had been orphaned during the war. When Eine turned forty we had a party. The “rag studio”, which is what we called our workshop, honored her with flowers and coffee. Taina had baked the cake from ingredients we had collectively scraped together. Some brought sugar, others eggs or almonds. We did not need the flower, it was replaced by potatoes.

Trolle strolled to the school each morning. It was customary for him to complain that school was boring, but deep inside our boy actually liked it. He took care of his homework by himself and did not even want to hear about any help. His Christmas report card showed he had done well.

Due to the lack of food the children accepted that they would be denied at times. Trolle was adorable. I often saw he wanted to eat more, but didn’t. He would say, “There has to be enough for the ones in the kitchen as well,” or “You need to take some more, mamma, you are so skinny,” or “Has everyone really had enough?”

Trolle’s main dream during the fall was to be invited to some estate. Willy and Peter were invited several times to Mustila and once to the Gripenberg’s in Sippola. The boys had spoken about all the glasses of milk and all the sandwiches they’d had, and about all the animals and other things they had experienced. When Pulle went to Sippola to hunt, Pian was kind enough to invite me as well. Trolle asked if he was invited too. I had a hard time telling him no. I could see the disappointment in his young eyes. His longing for bread, butter, and milk was also evident in his desire to become a farmer, he wanted to live in the country where one can get food.

Brita came over to visit us just about every evening. She had studied agriculture in the past, but quit when she got married. Now she restarted her studies and decided she wanted to complete her Master of Arts degree. It was respectable, for a mother with three children and a big house to take care of, to throw herself back into her studies. And since September 1st, she only had one servant. Three months after her husband had been killed she passed her first exam.

Since she came to visit us frequently, she became a witness to the "sour milk quarrel". Pulle's milk ration was made into sour milk, which he was supposed to eat with his evening tea. But he had gotten this crazy idea into his head that I needed it more than he did. And so we fought about which one of us was skinnier. Pulle would win the battle and I, while grumbling, ate the sour milk.

Brita was joking with us about it, and the girls were making fun of their silly parents. If Brita did not have tea with us, we often went to her place. She would serve us something home baked. Little Ulla, now thirteen, learned to face a challenge from her practical mother and served good cakes baked from the simplest of ingredients.

Pulle hunted moose in the fall. None were shot in October, but he was happy about the days off. In the beginning of his military duty he did not have any weekends free, but since August he was given every other Sunday for his own disposition. As an outdoorsman, he was delighted to be able to breathe in fresh air after having been cooped up behind his desk from morning till evening.

His big day came in November in Sippola. He called and told me that he had shot the first moose in his life. I could tell by his voice how happy he was. Then he went to Heinola to continue the hunt. I was surprised to see him come back the next day, the Heinola hunt was a failure, but he was still ecstatic from the experience of the day before.

"It was an enormous moose, the ground was shaking when it came," he said. Pi was next to him listening with delight. I had to call Brita, even though it was already past ten o'clock, she came over and had great fun. Trolle was sleeping, but the next day, even he got to hear the same story and Mi was informed, in a letter, that her daddy had shot a moose. Despite all the work that hung over Pulle, he still wrote a four-page letter to Henrik Gripenberg who was out on the front. Henrik should have been there, it happened on his hunting grounds.

Pulle's hunting party had the permits to shoot six moose. They shot five, but Pulle only killed one. The meat had already been confiscated. The owner of the hunting permit was allowed to keep 50 kg (110 lb) per moose, but the rest had to go to the general consumption. Another possibility was to give up your ration card and keep 2.5 kg (5.5 lb) of meat per person per month, or the same regulations as for slaughtering your own pig, sheep, or other animal. Out of the 250 kg for 5 moose, Pulle was allowed to keep 50 kg, which he had to distribute among his hunting buddies.

50 kg of meat, without using up your rations, was nothing to be contemptuous about. I was happy with the result.

The price of non-rationed food was incredible. In Helsinki one had to pay 300 Marks for a wood-grouse and 100 Marks for a hare. The chicken, which saved people in Helsinki from starvation in the spring, were not available anymore, nor were the eggs. The black market was flourishing. I heard about farms that did not deliver their milk but churned it to butter and sold it on the black market for 200 Marks per kilo. I heard a story from a gentleman who had traveled to Helsinki by bus. The bus was stopped by the police close to Helsinki and they found 20 kg (44 lb) of butter in a box, unmarked and no address from the sender. Nobody in the bus claimed to be the owner, and the bus driver was not obligated to tell who it belonged to. The next day the gentleman returned to ride the bus. At a road crossing an estate hostess got off the bus, and the driver said: “There is the lady that is missing 20 kilos of butter!”

Informers were common. When Eva Horelli went to the Population Supply office in Kuusankoski to honestly report that she had half a pig, in other words, she raised a pig together with another family, the superintendent said: “Good, then this case can be scratched.”

Eva had looked surprised, so the man had to explain to her that there indeed were people who were informants and that they had reported her pig.

During the fall slaughters people were allowed to buy their meat rations, here and in Helsinki. We had it good. Pulle’s moose was a tremendous help for us. At the end of November, the pig arrived from Mälikkälä, which also supplied us with fat and soap. It was getting more and more difficult to get soap, one was able to buy only 125 g (4.5 oz) every third month.

I had to give up the rations for a long time because of the pig, but that was okay, we had our meat. I got additional soap from two of the moose as well.

Where fat was concerned, an adult was only allowed 150 g (5.3 oz) during the month of December. There were places that had it much worse than Helsinki and Kymmene. In Varkaus the adults did not get a drop of milk. The milk rations were of no use; you couldn’t buy it anyway.

Varkaus was located on the railroad between Pieksamäki and Joensuu. All the military trains headed east to Äänislinna had to pass through it. Especially on this route there was a shortage of wagons. Many of the trains between Helsinki and Kouvola had to be cancelled, only a few overcrowded trains ran each day. The same was true for the freight trains.

The industries had a very hard time. In Kymmene the biggest problem was getting enough workers, waterpower, coals, and railroad wagons. Exports to England, Egypt, North and South America, were impossible due to the situation in the world. Germany bought more than usual, but not in such quantities that it would have made up for the losses. Most of the paper produced in Finland was newspaper grade, however the Finnish newspapers only used up one fifth of the total amount. Because of the surplus, new avenues had to be considered. The production was shifted to spirits, cellulose fodder, wall paper, bags for coals, paper towels and table cloths, paper underwear and waistcoats, etc.

There was an unnatural rise in the stock market, both industrial and bank stock rose many times above their face value.

HELSINKI AT WAR

This fall Helsinki was not the light, white city it usually was in peace time, it was gray and gloomy. The poorly kept, rough sidewalks were lined with meter-high piles of dirty snow. The food lines curled far out onto the streets from the market places and halls. The stores were emptied of their products and the salespeople were rude and nervous. Even the housewives were nervous. If one did get friendly service in a store, contrary to expectations, one was extremely grateful. It was not the fault of the salesperson that everything had run out. One has to appreciate an employee who, hundreds of times a day, had to answer a customer's question that this or that had run out.

But the "behind the counter" system was the fault of the store owners. It was embarrassing to want to buy candy and to be told there was none when you knew that certain customers were able to buy them. A lady from the country went to a colonial store where she was a regular customer and was told that what she asked for was sold out. Not until she explained that she was an old customer was the product shuffled into her bag.

I spent some time in Helsinki in November. Even though we now also had our own home in the capital, our girls were not there. Maj-Lis had organized the home very nicely, but it was much too big under these conditions.

The social life in Helsinki was modest. The theaters were running as usual, but contrary to the Winter War times, the concerts were few. A new sight in town was the German military in the streets, in the movie theaters, and in the restaurants. They were always well disciplined and well behaved.

The little joy to be able to buy French bread or buns with your wheat coupons was taken away from us. Even the pastries were made out of rye flour and looked strange, though they tasted alright. Other than by name, they did not have much in common with the bakery goods before the wartime. There were no cakes or biscuits. If one had visitors, one had to do the baking oneself, but since ingredients were so scarce, it was common for the visitors to bring bread and milk. Since the fall of 1939 it was also considered good form to bring sugar.

To serve dinner was not easy. The fish, including cod, was completely gone, and if one wanted to buy herring, one had to stand in line for hours. Vegetable steaks and meatless cabbage rolls were available, but it was not exactly something one wanted to serve dinner guests.

There was an article in the December edition of the Swedish weekly magazine, Weekly-Journal, about the life in Helsinki by a journalist by the name of Josephsson:

"When I left Stockholm, there were candles burning in the early morning, and fresh wheat buns were served for breakfast. It was warm and cozy inside, outside the temperature was mild; around freezing. A few hours later the plane landed at the Helsinki airport in harsh winter weather. The temperature had quickly dropped to -20 C (-4 F). The much earlier winter than usual has now been added to the many conflicts the Finnish people have to endure. Heavy snowfall and violent blizzards have torn through large portions of Finland. In the streets of Helsinki, the snow drifts are piling up a meter high (3 ft). One feels as if one has been moved to a Christmas fairy town for the short period of time of the day that daylight rules.

The mood changes with twilight around three in the afternoon. The white city becomes dark, quiet, and gloomy. The blackout is however not complete; here and there dimmed streetlights give a discreet shine; and through little openings in the shrapnel shelters, in the front of houses, lights are blinking during store hours. At around 6 to 7 pm, even these discreet shop windows are turned off. The entire great city becomes a large, dark, oppressive phantom town, the dimmed lights from the streetcars, as well as a few cars, are gliding by and reflected against the snowdrifts like ghost puffs. To a stranger the mood is heavy and filled with evil misgivings. The Helsinki residents, however, appear to be doing well in this, to strangers, gloomy darkness. The faint streetlights are somewhat of a relief to the blackouts. It means that the war no longer lies obsessively over the capital. The front is far away, Hangö, the coastal vacation spot in the Southwest, which had been lost to the Russians, is again in Finnish hands and the overhanging threat of losing the summer town does not exist anymore. The airports to the south of the Gulf of Finland are in the hands of the German allies. A few rare air raid alarms have sounded, but the Moscow visits from the sky have hardly been noticed anymore, and bombs, when this was written, have not been dropped for almost two months. Helsinki feels safe. The nightmares, of a time when one just about lived in shelters, are over. The residents of the capital are sleeping soundly in their beds while the winter is raging outside and the walls crackle in the freezing cold. The enemy no longer incites any fear. The Moscowites are driven out by brave soldiers through the dark and massive snow piles in the cold of the far east of Karelia, toward central Russia and the Northern Ice Sea. Other conflicts are more current."

I cannot write down the entire article, it would be too long. But I want to add that the last of the heavy bombardments of the fall happened soon after the elementary and middle schools had started their work in October. This is probably what Josephsson intended to say with the comment "at the time this was written, no bombs had been dropped for almost two months." Sadly, one bomb did drop outside a school, the shrapnel blew into a classroom and killed one student and injured several others. Because of this the schools were closed again, but the work was resumed in the middle of November.

Pi had completed middle school, so she was at home in Kymmene. During my visit to Helsinki I went to check on when the seventh grade was to start. The headmaster said that the class had already started, but it was voluntary for the students to participate. "Britta is such a strong student, I don't think it is necessary for her to come. I wonder if she would not rather stay in the country, but I will let you decide."

Pi started and soon it became mandatory for the seventh graders to go to school again. However, the schools did not work as usual. The classes were not allowed to be there all at once due to the bomb danger. This meant irregular lectures for Pi, only a few hours a day.

Josephsson continues: "Everything to the front and all for the front is the only thought I encounter in Finland. About 16% of the population is standing under the flying colors. This means that no other country at war has ever taken its mobilization to such an extreme."

It's exactly as Josephsson said: Just about every Finnish family has a close family member out at war. And I would like to add: Most families have accompanied a close relative, or a good friend, to the peaceful place from where they will never return.

Our faithful Mr. Saari, who built Mustaniemi, was killed in October. He left behind a wife with five small children, the youngest two months old. We all miss him, but especially Pulle. The two always got along so well. They worked on this and that, sometimes they went fishing or duck hunting. The gymnastics teacher Olavi Waalamo, whose wife and little boys lived in Mustaniemi in March 1940, has also been killed. Never, has such a large portion of the Finnish women been dressed in mourning, as during this year.

Josephsson continues: "The Finns are tough people, ready to face reality; otherwise, the fronts would not push as far into enemy territory during a war that had lasted half a year against such an overwhelming enemy; and otherwise, the home front could not be kept unified in such an unswerving manner and function with such remarkable inventiveness when it comes to collaboration and helpfulness. 'Wife, mix twice the amount of tree bark into the bread,' said the farmer Paavo."

Josephsson accounts for the food situation, but what he does not mention is how cold it is inside and the difficulties with gas and electricity, as well as the misery with the street cars in Helsinki. It happened that one had to wait forever for a street car, and when it came it was overcrowded. The lack of electricity lead to the cancellation of several street car lines. Bus lines had also been cancelled due to the lack of gasoline. The gas supply was weak and often turned off several hours a day. The inside of the houses was cold, which was caused by the shortage of wood and coal. There certainly was wood in the country, but there were problems with transportation. Warm water was not allowed to be used more than once every other week, that is when the whole of Helsinki took a bath.

"Why not 100,000 Finnish Children?" is the headline of another article in the magazine Weekly-Journal. Sweden received massive amounts of Finnish children in this war as well. The Social Department had a special section just for this purpose, the Children's Evacuation Committee was headed by school master Elsa Bruun.

It was the children of those who had been killed, handicapped, evacuated, or the poor who had the right to go to Sweden to eat and gain weight. On top of that private citizens and clubs gave other children the possibility to spend time in Sweden. This is how, for instance, engineers in the Technical Association took care of children. A member of the Mannerheim League of Child Welfare and one of the leading ladies of the Martha movement told a Swedish reporter about the children of Finland during times of famine:

"Births have increased by 21 per 1000, which better than anything else speaks for the Finnish people's belief in the future. At the same time the childhood illnesses are flourishing due to vitamin and fat shortage and mortality among children has risen fivefold. The children's hospitals are overcrowded, some rather serious cases have to be turned back due to the lack of space.

Baby outfits now consist of paper, even the ones handed out by the state with the maternity support."

During my Helsinki stay I also visited Irmelin von Troil at the Troiliana sewing club. The ladies of the family are still meeting every ten days. When I visited they were sewing a baby outfit for a mother in need. The material came from all kinds of old pieces, as new ones were not available.

At the needle workshop I met the nurse, Kekku Ehrström, who managed the child transports. She accompanied the children to Sweden and Denmark, even Denmark under German occupation accepted Finnish children. Kekku suggested that Mi should travel to Stockholm where a job was available at an orphanage. I got very excited and called Pulle. He thought it was a job for the motherland and also very suitable for Mi. Unfortunately, she was not interested. Later she did promise to travel there. It was difficult to get her released from her Lotta duties, but we did manage it in the end. But when everything was settled, she said that everyone at the hospital thought she looked ill and should be examined. Why she could not tell us earlier Pulle and I could not understand. The doctors could not find anything physically wrong with her, but they told her she needed to go home and rest and should not travel anywhere. She was exhausted. Not until Christmas Eve did Mi come home.

When I returned to Kymmene from the capital, I went to the needle workshop every day at twilight, where we made clothing, a very typical thing to do during the fall of 1941. We got one hundred checkered and striped wool scarfs from somewhere, in all kinds of colors, which we then made into shirts. The fringes were left dangling and I imagined that the soldiers in these creations looked much like the Indians in the books I read as a child, only the tomahawk and the feather cap was missing. The leftover pieces became warm and comfortable mittens with a lining made from fringes, and these were sent off as Christmas presents to our warriors.

Since the old deaconess, who during previous Christmases had delivered the presents, had moved, we were forced to take care of the delivery ourselves. Eva Horelli had received loads of presents from Sweden that needed to be delivered. The packages contained the most wonderful treasures like cookies, candy, chocolates, sugar, and wheat flour.

We delivered packages to the Lottas at their command posts. Mi got a white wool scarf, which went well with her Lotta uniform, a small bag with coffee, a sewing kit, candy, and stationary with envelopes.

When one encounters times of need and sorrow one becomes so overwhelmed by the paralyzing feeling of powerlessness. What is the point of the little help our needle workshop can supply; maybe just a helping hand for an exhausted mother? There are families who don't even have potatoes, not a single jar of vegetables, or a single salted herring in their pantry. Starvation is not far away. Wood is expensive, and those houses that are not owned by the company are both ramshackle and drafty.

Eva and I went to a family where the father of the household had just died. He left behind a wife and six children under the age of seven. There were families where I had the feeling that no matter how much we helped they were never going to make it on their own.

The executive families tried to give up some of their clothes to the countless collections. We did what we could, in many cases it was a drop in the sea, in other cases it was notable help. We were delighted that everyone was grateful, wherever I went I was met with kindness.

A lightning bolt lit up the political sky. England declared war with Finland, as did its colonies and dominions. Out of all these countries we could only really worry about England, from a military standpoint, South Africa could hardly come up here and bomb our cities. From a commerce standpoint it was, of course, very regrettable. But the Finnish people took it all in stride. The war in the East continued as before. And only the good news reached us.

I visited our war godchild and took some small Christmas presents to him, his mother, and brothers. We had taken over the god-parenthood for little Unto Kääpä, who previously had been Brita's and Willy's godchild. And then we sent a Christmas package to Mr. Saari's wife and children. I put a few candles in the package we had left over, they could use them more than we could as they did not have electric lights. And since there was a lack of petroleum, it could become a gloomy Christmas in the darkness with the loss of the husband and father.

For us here at home, and for Brita, I arranged for a few presents. And to raise the mood a little, I wrote my silly Christmas poems again. As usual, they gave rise to joyous laughter.

Brita had promised to come to us on Christmas Eve with all her children. They came around 6:30 when we had dinner. Mi was on her way but did not make it until we had already started eating. She did not look as bad as we had expected, she looked really chipper. But it still became a long, unpleasant illness with a stubborn slight temperature. I had tried to make the best food possible, although, apart from the ham, it wasn't the usual Christmas food at all. After dinner the packages were handed out and the Christmas tree was admired. We did not have any candles. Earlier Pulle had told Trolle not to feel disappointed that the Koskull children were going to get a lot more presents than he was. Pulle explained that it was because Uncle Willy had been killed and his family and friends had wanted to do something for his children. Trolle understood it completely and was adorably interested in all the things the others got. Ulla, especially, had been showered with presents. Christmas was a joyous occasion after all. The little ones had great fun and I don't think they thought too much about their father.

It was Brita's first Christmas without Willy. And it was very fortunate for her that her children were so unaware of the great emptiness that surrounded their mother. The adults drank a quiet toast to Willy. The void he left was painfully present the entire evening.

The second day after Christmas we went to Brita's place. She had arranged everything very nicely, her cooking was tasty, there was candy, and a few candles she had saved from the previous Christmases. New Year's Eve we were supposed to celebrate together, this was, after all, an old tradition. It was our turn to invite them for dinner. The Children were looking forward to the upcoming celebration together.

The National Help organization held a meeting in our community, but not until after Christmas. The institution, protected by President Ryti, heads the organizations that collect money. The intention is to support the families of the fallen, the handicapped, and those in need. Every community may keep half of the collected funds, the other half is spent in communities too poor to collect any money. The donations are given in percentages, those who want to participate give a certain percentage of their income or property.

Between Christmas and the New Year, we Lottas were mending pants, which were delivered to us from the Club House where some soldiers were staying on the bottom floor. The men were sitting in their beds while we were mending. It was a pretty nasty job since the pants were extremely dirty and torn up. It was also not very pleasant that many of us got fleas from these pants. But no one complained.

At 5 am the night before New Year's Eve my sister Caja called and told me her husband Rainer had died. His heart had long been in poor shape, he had had several heart attacks, but always recovered. Despite the heart problems he had been drafted and he took care of his job as the East Savolax Regional Chief, stationed in Nyslott. This is where he died.

Caja asked me to come to Varkaus. She was going to return home from Nyslott, where she had gone when called by Rainer's physician. I promised I would be on the first train, which was supposed to leave the next day, and would arrive in Varkaus late in the evening.

I called Brita and we decided that we were going to celebrate New Year's at her place instead, as it would be difficult at our place without a hostess.

It became a long trip with many delays. Finally, I arrived in Pieksamäki where I was supposed to change trains. There, I should have waited two hours, but it was three. Waiting at this station became a "war experience." The station house was full of military personnel, in the restaurant there were loads of soldiers and officers waiting for the train to arrive at the platform. There was talk and smoking, some were not that sober, they had taken a last encouraging drink before the long trip to the front.

I finally went outside. It was incredibly beautiful. It was wonderful to be able to stand in a fully lit place, compared to Kymmene which still remained in Cimmerian darkness. The trees looked as if they had been cladded in transparent drapes, as they were covered in frost. But it was cold, I could not stand still for long.

There was commotion when the train rolled in, but most did get a seat. I sat down in an ice-cold wagon in complete darkness, it did not have any lighting at all. The only light we saw was if someone lit a cigarette or turned on a flashlight– a will-o'-the-wisp that quickly went out.

Midnight was approaching. I was wondering what was going to happen at this hour. I sat in a train on the way to Äänislinna with military personnel and a few Lottas on the way to the front, and I was thinking maybe some passenger would get up and make a patriotic speech to greet the New Year.

The train rolled on kilometer after kilometer. I was wondering about those at home, wondered if they would cast lucky charms out of tin at Brita's place. I was thinking about Caja who had lost her husband, and all those out there at war. I looked at my watch, it was almost midnight. No one was moving, some were sleeping, some talking, then even they fell silent.

Was nothing going to happen? Were no clocks going to sound twelve deep chimes? It was midnight. Inconspicuously, we slid into the New Year. Nothing happened, there was only the sound of the wheels pounding the rails.

1942

Twenty-six countries signed the declaration of the United Nations in Washington.

The West for the first time hears about the Germans using gas to exterminate Jews.

U.S. forces enter Britain under the command of General Eisenhower and the first air missions are conducted over Europe. General McArthur leads the U.S. troops in the Pacific against Japan. The Manhattan Project is started to develop nuclear weapons.

Operation Barbarossa is a failure and the Germans also face stiff resistance in Africa by the Allied forces, including U.S. troops led by General Patton.

THE BIG PARTY

We stopped at a lit station - Varkaus. Bubi, Caja's son, came to meet me. He was stationed close enough to home that he was able to go to his mother immediately after his father's death.

Caja was in bed. She was unbelievably composed - not a tear. She was not alone, apart from her son, Murre, Greta Grotenfelt, Bubi's mother-in-law, was there. Tytti, her daughter, had not been able to come to Varkaus. She had been in Stockholm, for some time now, where her husband was studying.

Greta had made tea and sandwiches with ingredients from Järvikylä, they were very tasty after the long trip. While we ate, Caja fell asleep and we all quietly went to bed.

The next few days I was not able to help Caja much, she took care of everything herself. The phone was ringing constantly. A Captain from Nyslott, a lady from the Infantry Association in Helsinki, and a few others arranged the funeral, which was to be held in Helsinki on January the 8th. I felt useless, but maybe I was still able to do some good by just being there for her. Greta left on New Year's Day, as did Bubi.

We decided to travel to the funeral via Kymmene. Caja had caught a bad cold and did not want to travel to Nyslott, where Rainer's remains were to be sent to the station by military escort. Bubi went there by himself.

On January 4th, we all came together in Kymmene. Murre said he had gotten over his influenza. Unfortunately, he was placed in the same room as Trolle, and the poor boy got a terrible head cold, which lasted for weeks and infected me as well. Caja had white spots in her throat and a fever. But she categorically refused to stay in bed and thereby spread the germs all over the house.

Pi's birthday was celebrated in a somber mood. Poor little girl, it wasn't the first dreary birthday she had.

Rainer's funeral was beautiful, with military officiating. Afterwards Greta had organized coffee for the family. Caja told me that he had, up until the very end, worried that she would exert herself too much by having to travel to his sickbed. He had taken care of his duties, even in the last hours of his life. He held the telephone receiver in his hand shortly before falling asleep for eternity.

Out in the world the war was raging. We thought the Japanese with their fanaticism and their lack of respect for human life were capable of doing just about anything. When the Germans had gone into winter hibernation, things were reasonably quiet on the European Eastern Front. This was the case at our eastern border as well. There would be the occasional noteworthy event but then things got quiet again. "Nothing new in the West," one could say. It was as if everyone was catching their breath for a while in order to gather strength for the spring. What was going to happen then?

We were hoping the Germans would invade Leningrad, as the Russian planes were still a worry for our home front. Helsinki was "visited" every once in a while, but it was mainly Kotka that got hit including the coast east and west of the city. Strange enough Viborg was left alone most of the time, at least that was our impression. But, of course, there may have been things happening that we were not aware of, not all bombings of the city were reported on the radio, as it was not considered home front, but rather part of the war zone.

The transportation of children to Sweden and Denmark continued, thousands of kids were sent over so they could eat until they were full. I was wondering why nothing was happening in Kymmene and around Kuusankoski in this regard. I felt like I could not get mixed up in this matter that was handled by the head of the social department, Mr. Wallenius, and the community.

Pulle went to his staff location in Kouvola by bus every morning and returned around 5:30 pm. He had been eating dinner at home since December. The staff food was good, but contained only simple soldier aliment. I was not able to offer the same heavy food at home, but with the addition of vegetables from the jars, and the juice bottles, it became rich in vitamins and healthy. Unfortunately, there was still not enough food for everyone in the family, especially Pulle, who apart from his busy job in Kouvola also worked at home every evening. He was losing a catastrophic amount of weight. All we could do was to try to hang in there, as there was no light at the end of the tunnel. One did not know when the war was going to end or if Pulle was going to be released from his military duties. But because of his dedication, every task, including the most minute details, had to be performed with absolute perfection.

Mi was still at home. She had a persistent, slight temperature elevation that the doctors could not figure out. It was presumed she was exhausted. She had had long days at the hospital office and had not had any days off, not even Sundays. Her life at home in Kymmene was certainly very monotonous. She was allowed to go outside despite the fever, but due to her fatigue she did not want to go for longer walks or ski trips, which the doctors had forbidden anyway.

Pi went to Helsinki to her school. Nothing seemed to cause her any trouble. Among her friends she was like a fish in the sea and always had a lot of fun. Both in school and during her time off she was surrounded by her male companions. But she took all the wooing from a humorous side and preferred to just be good friends with them. “After all I am nothing special,” she once told me. But I thought there may be something special about her since she did not have to put on a show and was able to talk about things other than just chatter. She was having fun despite the hard times, she always made the best out of the situation.

Trolle got rid of his troublesome runny nose. The young man still had great ambition, mom was absolutely not allowed to check on his homework, he wanted to manage on his own. In his free time, he played with the “boys”; Willy and Peter von Koskull, and “Kurtta”, Kurt-Erik Rhen, and the “Sillers”, the Zilliaccus boys.

I went to the “Rag Studio” almost every day. We, the Lottas, were happy to be doing some good and to be able to talk about everything between heaven and earth. The world affairs and our children were discussed, of course. Some of our young husbands were out on the front, the younger ones had been called up for active duty or had joined up as volunteers. Out of the daughters, one had just completed her Lotta assignment in order to start nursing school, one had recently finished her Lotta job as a field cook and started her studies, and so on. It was only the very youngest that we were able to keep in the protection of our homes.

There was so much tragedy in some families. One of the Lottas in the needle workshop was Mrs. Gertrud Biese. She had, as previously mentioned, lost her second son Ernst Adolf during the Winter War. He was killed at the Isthmus of Karelia on Christmas Eve. Now she was sitting quietly, in full harmony, sewing, even though the oldest and the youngest son were out on the front. The youngest one had just been drafted at the age of eighteen. She often talked about her boys, one could understand that she held them in her thoughts all the time, but she never complained.

Where our husbands were concerned, most of them had also been called up. But they were well "placed". Lieutenants of the reserve and reservists at their age were rarely sent to the front.

We typically brought coffee with us if there was even the slightest reason to. The "coffee" was a concoction of dandelion roots or beets or something else like that. The main thing was having something black in the cup. And then we had a cake or a loaf of bread with us that we took turns serving. Every time, these food creations, or "master pieces", as we jokingly called them, were admired, and the baker had to explain how she had created this wonderful "cake" or "bread". The simpler the ingredients the more praise the baker got.

At the end of January, I was in bed with influenza when the Lottas had their annual meeting and elected me into the management. I almost got a shock when Eine called me and asked me if I was willing to accept the job. I really wanted to decline as my own health was not good and I had enough work outside the home. But as a Lotta I did not have the right to say no. On the other hand, I was happy I had been given this recognition.

By the middle of February, I felt like I was pretty much recovered and went to the needle workshop, but there I started coughing continuously.

"Haven't you come back too early?" One of the ladies asked, and some of the others agreed.

"I don't think it's that bad," I answered. "I can't be away forever."

"You know, tomorrow you are not allowed to come," Aina Henrickson decided.

I had to laugh.

"Am I not allowed?"

"No, absolutely not. You can go outside into the fresh air, but here inside the air is so terrible because of all the dirty clothes, so you had better stay away."

Aina was very determined, but then even she had to laugh. I did stay away and went to visit our godchild, Unto, instead, which I should not have done. It was a long way to his home and I was surprised by a blizzard and ended up getting worse. The next day I was in bed again, which gave me time to write about the Kymmene-Troil's war experiences. Had I been well, I would never have had enough time. Now, I was able to write up to seven hours a day in hopes of finishing it by Pulle's 50th birthday, March 16th, 1942.

Many evenings I would sit in the hall and write while Pulle was occupied with his writings at the dining room table or reading the newspaper. He could not understand what I was doing, but he figured out it had something to do with a birthday present.

"What in the world are you sewing up there?" he asked.

I smiled and let him think it was needlework.

Sometimes I read aloud to Mi what I had written, just as I had with Pi during the fall when she was still at home. The girls were helpful, told stories, and they were critical. But that was good, I was not used to writing and made some mistakes that I had not noticed myself.

It was not only about the book, I had also decided to compose a piece of music, a polonaise, in Pulle's honor. But the inspiration did not want to present itself. I was worried the whole composition was going down the drain, my nose was all blocked up and my brain did not want to work. But suddenly one day it was done, in f-minor.

The children were organizing their presents. Mi wanted to buy a briefcase with money she had earned herself at her Lotta job. When she could not find one in Kouvola, I got one for her during a visit to Helsinki. Pi embroidered a bookmark in the shape of the Troil family crest on a yellow silk ribbon, and Trolle was working on a garden cart for Mustaniemi made out of wood he had bought himself.

Pulle had long said he was going to escape to Helsinki for his 50th birthday. He was going to request leave from his staff headquarters, and then we would travel to Captain Street 11, where he could celebrate in peace with his closest friends and family. I had a tough job trying to explain to him that once in their life every person should allow themselves to be celebrated. The way he had struggled for Kymmene over the years, he could at least once reap the fruit of his labor in a few words of recognition. It would be good for him and make his family happy. Whatever difficulties there had been between various executives, Pulle had to intervene in order to make peace, and many private conflicts Pulle had sorted out by talking sense into the two parties. Now everyone would have a chance to recognize him.

"But how in the world could you manage the catering in these times?" Pulle asked.

Well, yes, this was a difficult problem, but if there is a will there is a way, I thought, and suggested that we should ask for help from Pulle's siblings, who wanted to oblige.

Pulle looked more and more worried.

"Just leave the food problem to me, I'll manage," I said, although I realized it would be difficult in a household where hoarding was strictly forbidden.

We wrote and called the siblings. Märtha promised to come, but Harry was not able to. Marga was in Stockholm with the Countess Bonde, who wanted to invite a person injured in a bombardment to stay in her home. Marga had received this strange offer, but promised to come anyway, as did Ebba. His brother-in-law, Tor, could not leave his job at the

Tilkka War Hospital in Helsinki. Holger said yes, and Lasse, who was now taking care of the community physician job in Mänttä, promised to take along his wife, Lisa. Maj-Lis said she was happy to visit us and Nisse asked his wife, Margit, to represent the family, as he was not able to get leave from his post far up in the north of Finland.

Where my sisters were concerned, Caja came to visit us in the beginning of March and I was able to talk her into staying until Pulle's birthday. But Greta was not able to leave Helsinki and Verner had to work.

We cleaned and scrubbed, all the silver was taken out and polished, the rugs were beaten on the snow, and the floors were polished as well as possible with the surrogate wax that was available. The guest room was put in order. Two were able to stay there and one more with Pi. The rest would be lodged in the management villa. I arranged for extra help and talked to Taina about the food, ordered black cock birds from Rovaniemi, went to Helsinki with Pulle and brought back loads of Vermouth for the reception before noon. Pulle talked to the director at the Fazer confection firm and was able to order three kilos of marzipan sweets, as we had not seen chocolates in this country for years.

But it wasn't just Pulle's birthday that occupied our thoughts. Pulle was to take part in a radio address and he was also going to be promoted. The Defense Department organized entertainment on the radio for the soldiers in the field, and on the 22nd of February, it was the turn of the Northern Kymmene River Valley District to make the address. We were able to send greetings to our boys at the front. The broadcast was especially meaningful, as our previous President Svinhuvud, also participated as a member of the district staff and old Kymmene valley resident. This is President Svinhuvud's greeting to the soldiers:

"The Winter War two years ago was very hard on us. Our sacrifices in blood were great and the peace in Moscow robed us of the greater portion of the beautiful Karelia. However, we did not let this battle stun us. We began rebuilding systematically after the damage from the war, improving our equipment, for we knew, with certainty, that the Russians were going to continue their destruction as soon as they had the opportunity. But we had also not said our last word to this treacherous neighbor. The game was not over on our part. Our turn to hit hard was still to come, to avenge the terror and unfairness we had been submitted to. The opportunity to do this came sooner than we had expected, Germany attacked Russia, and when Russia attacked us at the same time, we were eager to join the game. Now, a major offense is taking place from the Ice Sea to the Black Sea.

Under the leadership of the proud German army, many nations are taking part in this battle, we are also among them in an honorable position, which our boys in turn have handled with honor. The Russian has been driven out of Finnish territory and our boys have pushed far into the Isthmus of Aunus and into Russian Karelia to liberate our tribal brothers.

On the home front, we have continuously followed the bravery of our boys. Our thoughts are often with you, our boys. We ask ourselves how you manage in the cold and snow, and do you have enough clothes and food? How do you manage in burrows and tents and how are you even able to fight in the chill of the polar region? But the signals are telling us that you do manage well. Despite the hard winter the Russian continues to weaken. This has had a calming effect on our minds. We think the Finn will manage just as anyone else would.

But at the same time, we feel obligated to take care of the home front as well as possible, so that our soldiers can receive the support they need to complete their heavy task. We have to remember that in this ongoing trial of strength the Russians are to be crushed and Bolshevism is to be eradicated, otherwise there will be no peace for mankind, especially not for us! Therefore, the war has to be victorious, and we trust that our soldier boys, unceasingly, will continue their brave task. May God protect you, our boys."

The parliament representative Mr. Suurhonka addressed the farmers in his speech, a worker at the paper mill addressed his fellow workers, and Pulle, representing the Kymmene management, also addressed the industrial workers. A farmer from the Mustaniemi area, who had lost three of his four children (two sons and one daughter, who was a Lotta) at the front, gave a touching speech. The program had been recorded, so Pulle was able to listen to himself on the radio, which was a bit strange to him.

That same day he was promoted to captain. He did not really care much about it. Whether he had two or three stars on his collar was all the same to him. But I was happy about it.

Mi was starting to miss Viborg. Since the fever had finally gone down and she categorically refused to go to Stockholm, we did not have any objections to her return to Viborg. It however took three weeks before all the paper work was sent back and forth between all the authorities involved. She was not able to leave until March the 10th, which meant that she could not get any leave for Pulle's birthday a week later.

During the first few months of 1942 we did not really have any war action to speak of in Kymmene. Only the radio and the newspaper reminded us of what was going on out there in the world. Brita came over for tea just about every evening. She came alone– missing Willy immensely.

There was little joy in life anymore. The young had lost their illusions and the morale of the people was sinking. One tried to catch whatever little joy there was as it flew by. Therefore, we were looking forward to the upcoming fiftieth birthday celebration.

The Saturday before the party, Pi came home from Helsinki with Maj-Lis and on Sunday night Märtha, Holger, Hugo, Lasse, and Lisa arrived. Marga had caught influenza and was not able to come. Ebba and Margit were to arrive with the last train and go directly to the management villa where they were staying. We welcomed each arrival, and in a great atmosphere we sat down to enjoy the simple supper I was able to serve. All the fine food was to be saved for the actual celebration.

They were all so adorable. They came with loafs of bread, cakes, cheese, and preserved foods. Ebba brought a cod, packed in such a way that I thought it was a flower. We had been saving up on flour for a long time, but it would not have been nearly enough had Maj-Lis and Brita not been so good to give up two kilos each. Mrs. Tigerstedt had sent a little present from Mustila in the form of flour, eggs, and cream. No one, who had not experienced the bitter times of food shortages, could understand how grateful I felt.

After the supper, we sat in Pulle's room and listened to the radio. Trolle had been up and eaten with us, but was now sent to bed. Suddenly he came rushing in and said someone was singing in the yard. Pulle went out on the porch and found the choir, Kaiku (The Echo), there with its conductor, Headmaster Niinivaara. Pulle asked them to step inside and the headmaster made a speech which was appreciated, and two more songs followed.

On March the 16th, all the flags were at full mast for Pulle all over the mill, at the office, in the factories, and at the schools, and of course at home.

At 6:30 in the morning, I was awakened by some noise in the room next to me. Even Pulle turned around. I could not lie still anymore and got up as quietly as possible. Pulle looked up, surprised.

"You are not allowed to wake up yet," I said.

He put his head back on the pillow, just like a child pretending to sleep, but he couldn't possibly do so because of the excitement and anticipation.

Pi, Trolle, and Maj-Lis were already up and around 7:30 even Märtha came down from the guest room. The first thing I wanted to check on was the coffee table Rauha was setting and what Taina had been baking during the night to assure it was fresh. Cardamom rolls, ginger bread, and sandwiches... Everything was ready.

The birthday gifts were set up on Trolle's garden cart. Mi's briefcase, Pi's bookmark, a watch- which was my present- flowers and the beginning of the manuscript for my book, "The Kymmene Troil Family War Experience" were atop it.

The door to the bedroom was opened, Pi and Trolle carried in the cart with the presents while I played my polonaise composition on the piano. When I was done I went to congratulate Pulle. He was very moved and said he liked all the gifts and the composition very much. I pointed to the notebooks and told him that here lies the needlework. Pulle acted very surprised, he didn't have any idea about my writing. I read the prologue out loud, after which we hugged and cried a little, of course.

Pulle was still not dressed when Brita came over with the kids, Ulla with her almond cookies, Peter with a small flag pole he had made himself with Willy Jr., including a small blue and white flag. Willy's and Brita's present was a saucer in silver.

Pulle got dressed in his captain's uniform, he wanted to be polite to the expected military celebration and, therefore, did not dress in civilian clothes. The ones at home, Märtha, Maj-Lis, Caja, Brita, and I, were ready to have our coffee, but the others were late. Soon Holger turned up, and though the others were still sleeping in the management villa, we could not wait anymore. I had saved some real coffee. Taina mixed real coffee with some surrogate, a mixture we had not had in a long time. And wheat buns, when was the last time we'd seen them? One had not been able to get white flour for months, except on little children's ration cards. The war widows' children had been given Swedish wheat flour, that is how Brita had gotten some, but how Maj-Lis had gotten her hands on it I don't really know, I suspect she had hoarded some in Vasa, which, like Åbo, was a phenomenal "hoarding town". Yes, everyone was hoarding, except us, and we were therefore considered idiots.

We were sitting there waiting for the siblings to arrive. Finally, Märtha got so upset she lost her patience. Together with Holger and Maj-Lis they handed over the sibling's present, a rocking chair, which had been in Pulle's childhood home in Koskis Street in Åbo. Märtha thanked the jubilee for not only being the legal counsel for the siblings, but also their moral support. It was a recognition that surely made Pulle feel good.

At ten o'clock the official ceremonies started. The Kuusankoski community was represented by two gentlemen who congratulated Pulle with a speech and flowers. With the chief executive from the mill at the helm, Karl-Erik Ekholm handed Pulle a shotgun, a silver platter, and a birthday greeting bonded in leather with Pulle's initials, as well as a flower arrangement. The gentlemen were served coffee or tea.

Ebba and Margit had arrived, and finally even Lasse and Lisa. Hugo was not to arrive until later in the day. Märtha, Ebba, and Holger helped to keep the guests entertained. Maj-Lis went upstairs, she felt lonely, probably thinking about Dulle. Lasse and Lisa sat on the sofa like two doves and Margit faithfully kept them company.

At 11 o'clock the first guests departed and only the family was left. Lunch consisted of rye porridge and cold cuts of the salted pig from Mälikkälä. And the lean birds from Rovaniemi, which were served cold, were actually intended for dinner, but it would not have been enough for that meal. On top of that there were red beets and herring that Märtha had brought with her, as well as potatoes and preserved cauliflower casserole, which we were able to prepare thanks to the milk and butter from Mustila.

We had barely gotten up from the table when Headmaster Niinivaara from the Vocational School, together with four students, came to congratulate Pulle with Darwin tulips, daffodils, and two cast iron candlesticks. It would have been impossible to bake enough and invite everyone for coffee. Therefore, Pi brought in Vermouth for the adults and juice for the kids.

It was time to take out the best table cloth and old linen napkins in the house. In the middle of the table we put a glass platter and on top of it a Venetian bowl with the Darwin tulips and the Venetian fish. The sweets were placed in antique silver bowls, the wine decanters in silver containers were filled, and the glasses were picked out.

At 11:30 the area shelter organizations, the Lottas, the tennis club, military Captains, as well as writers of poems came to honor Pulle.

Former President Svinhuvud had intended to be present, but he had a last-minute hindrance and sent his personal greetings instead. All in all, two hundred telegrams streamed in, including one from Field Marshal Mannerheim and President Ryti. Of all the telegrams, Pulle was maybe most moved by the congratulations from the Salvation Army.

There was a strange atmosphere at the dinner table while we ate. Pulle and Hugo were very secretive. When Holger wanted to make a speech, Pulle asked him to wait a while– unbelievable I thought.

We had gotten to the pork chops when the phone rang. It was Kerstin Ståhlberg who had lived in the Koskull villa before Brita and Willy. We had kept in touch with the Ståhlbergs ever since 1928 when they moved to Kemi. After congratulating Pulle she wanted to speak to me. I went to the bedroom and stood there with the receiver in my hand when the door to the bathroom slowly opened and out came a pale, white haired creature in a black velvet dress– Marga. Have I gone crazy was my first thought? The second was to not scream, for I would have frightened Kerstin on the phone.

All was swirling around in my brain. Had something happened to Marga? It took a few seconds for me to realize, it really was Marga who was alive and standing in front of me.

"Don't say anything, I want to surprise everyone," was the only thing she said.

It was a difficult situation for me. Kerstin was asking what happened, as I suddenly became quiet.

"It's just something very strange," I answered, puzzled, ... "a person came so quickly." Kerstin could of course not understand what had happened.

Marga was in a brilliant mood. She could not imagine, that I, who had had too much to do for a long time and had been on my feet since 6:30 a.m. with hostess duties, could be frightened by suddenly seeing my influenza stricken sister-in-law appear like a ghost.

From a practical standpoint, it had been better if the hostess had been informed of Marga's arrival. But the siblings were delighted to see her. But there was one more who got almost as scared as I did– Pi.

The rest of the evening I was too tired to be able to share in the joyfulness. Holger made the first speech, followed by Pulle. I sat still, seemingly unaffected - as if I was paralyzed. But then the dam broke and I started crying uncontrollably. Pulle spoke about his life and said some all too sweet words about me. He said he had always put his work first and made my life without joy. Poor Pulle, he was always such a dutiful person, torn between the duties to the company and his family.

But as always, when the Troils were together, there were constant mood swings back and forth, or as one family member expressed it: "We had such a great time, and we cried terribly."

The next event for our family was Pi's confirmation. She had gone to confirmation school (Lutheran Church) during the spring in Helsinki and was to be confirmed at the end of March. Pulle and I traveled to this festive occasion.

I had gotten a hold of a white satin cloth and took it to a good seamstress. She made a dress that in its simplicity suited Pi well. After the confirmation, aunts and uncles were invited for coffee and champagne. Ebba and Tor congratulated her with a collection of the author Runeberg's writings, Marga and Hugo with an old family ring that had belonged to Pi's great grandmother, Caja with a book about the chemist Madame Curie, and Greta with a brooch. Märtha was not there, but from her and her husband Pi got a poem collection from five centuries, whereas Maj-Lis congratulated her with some sweets. From us, her parents, she got a decorative needle in gold and a bible.

I had not written anything on the first page of the bible, but when Pi asked me to do so, I wrote what my mother wrote into my commemorative album when I was about seven years old: “Treat others the way you wish to be treated.” I told my girl that I did not understand the citation at the time, and I was surprised that my mother had not written a common book verse. Much later I understood her and was grateful for the direction she wanted to give me. I was hoping that the bible citation, that had been my mother's loadstar, would in turn help Pi.

It was difficult to write down all the thoughts that followed my child in these days. But when I saw her, dressed in white, walking into the church, I prayed in silence that her life would become as bright as possible. Her youth had so far gone by in war and evil times, but at some point, we will have peace and see a brighter existence emerge.

BRITA IS MOVING TO THE CAPITAL CITY HELSINKI

Brita's life continued its melancholy path, but she did not let the grief get her down. She continued her agricultural studies, which were interrupted when she got married. She had gotten a job as a gardening consultant at the Helsinki farming clubs, a job which in every aspect suited her. The job was to guide youngsters who wanted to lease pieces of land for gardening. The arrangement was excellent from a national economic and educational standpoint.

She had recently been able to buy a five-room apartment at the corner of Eric- and Albert Street. It was a nice apartment, which suited Brita and her children well. She was going to keep four rooms for herself and rent out one room. But for the current school year she arranged it so her children stayed in Kymmene under the supervision of Siiri while she temporarily moved into her mother's apartment in Helsinki. Her mother, on the other hand, moved to Kymmene to help Siiri take care of the children.

It felt empty after Brita left. I was happy to have lots of work during that time, which helped to fill the void.

At the end of May, Ulla, Willy, and Peter left for Sweden. They had been invited by friends and were to spend the summer there.

When my family sometimes growled about my extensive social work, I answered jokingly, as long as I did not belong to the Salvation Army as well, they should be happy. The fact was, there was a little bit too much of the good. It was almost as if I had a job, as often as I was away from home this spring.

The area social department director, Wallenius, was about to go on vacation and asked me to select a committee to take care of sending as many children to Sweden and Denmark as possible in order to eat and gain weight. We were to work under the Department of Social Welfare and the Children's Transfer Office, and the Mannerheim League for Child Welfare in Helsinki. I was not completely happy about the assignment. I was busy with Lotta work and the needlework club, along with arranging a children's party on April 11th. The club had selected an organizing committee, but I was afraid that I, as the chairwomen, was still going to get my share of things to do. And that is exactly what happened.

The work with the children's transfer was a delicate one since there were already two ladies, Eva Horelli and Marianne Cedercreutz, who were arranging transfers privately. I pointed this out for Wallenius, but he thought the ladies couldn't possibly take care of everything just the two of them. This wasn't just for one child at a time, but rather larger contingents. I would be able to select the members to the committee myself, with the exception of two elementary school teachers who were obvious choices, according to Wallenius, one of them because she was the chairwomen for a care organization.

I chose representatives from the community. Eine Rhen from the Lotta Handicap Organization and some teachers who knew the children and their parents and were aware of the situation in their homes. Eva Horelli and Marianne Cedercreutz were also chosen. Marianne never participated in any of the meetings, but she did an excellent job out in the field. I also got a representative from Voikka.

I was very nervous before the initial meeting when I, for the first time, was to address a meeting in the Finnish language. I was also surrounded by total strangers. I wish I had a penny for all the different types that gathered there that afternoon. Without being rude, I can say that the gathering was eccentric.

Some expressed their concerns about sending the children to Sweden and Denmark at the meeting. A Dr. Virkkunen had been critical of our children's transports. He was among the language fanatics who were afraid the children would not stay Finnish enough. He completely underestimated the need for the children to receive the nutritious food that Sweden and Denmark were able to offer. Virkkunen's statements led to long debates in the newspapers. The Finnish people were split into two camps. There were those who understood that the children's health was at risk under the current condition of food shortage in Finland, and, that, therefore, the children should be sent to countries in better shape, and there were those who worried they would not be able to speak their mother tongue while abroad.

From a language standpoint, I thought it only beneficial that they would be able to learn Swedish while in Sweden. It could also be good for the kids, who were gathered from the poorer segments of society, to be able to experience the ancient Swedish culture. The only drawback was the Swedish and Danish families, in all their good will, would spoil the children. When they returned to their home country, they would have a hard time getting used to not even having their own bed to sleep in, which was their natural right in Sweden and Denmark.

It was also a shock for many of the youngsters to return to a Finland in blackout. In many poor homes the fire in the kitchen stove was the only light source. I heard of two youngsters who returned home and crawled up in a corner and yelled: "Mamma light! Mamma light!" And when poorly dressed siblings looked at an elegantly dressed brother or sister returning home from abroad, it caused slight envy, even though the one returning brought some goodies: cookies, apples, and candy.

But war is war. Better to have these inconveniences than have the children starve. I suppose, nothing in this world has only advantages.

We sent 181 children from Kuusankoski to Sweden, but unfortunately, we were not able to arrange any trips to Denmark as promised.

Before everything was arranged, we held many meetings which lasted for hours as we went through the applications. We would have been happy to send all the children, but transportation was limited. The times were challenging for the public health system. Therefore, we should be grateful to Sweden and Denmark that they took care of so many of our children and saved them from malnourishment. Additionally, these countries were sending food to our larger population centers, where massive amounts of children are fed. I wanted our community to receive some of the food donations and did not think it was impossible to do, but Wallenius was not interested. He promised to talk to the Kuusankoski County about it, but the community had already been feeding children for a long time and now wanted to expand their summer camp activities.

The summer camp turned out to be a blessing. It was placed at the Perheniemi farm in Itis. It was one of the farms that was part of the rapid colonization project, but it was still owned by the company. A children's camp was also maintained at the Itis parish, where children from Kotka had found refuge from the constant bombardments.

It may seem strange that we wanted to organize a children's party in the middle of raging war. The needlework club needed money in order to continue its activities and hand out the usual aid for Christmas 1942. We had held a party in the fall of 1939, and it had brought in a pretty penny. The suggestion of a new party was received with enthusiasm. Everyone was eager to arrange a nice evening with their own children and those of others.

There was to be “fishing” (a game trying to hook a prize blindfolded), a ring throwing game, and guessing games with prizes including a doll, a car, and a cake. One was also supposed to guess how many cigarettes there were in a box. It was not so easy to create all this, as sweets were almost impossible to get. The ingredients for the cake was, as usual, collected among our ladies: one gave the eggs, another a little margarine, and a third a little sugar.

Trolle played an old elf in a play and also the front legs of a giraffe in a tableau, Karl-Erik Rhen played the hind legs. In a dreadful shabby cloth, which was supposed to represent a giraffe, Trolle and Karl-Erik were striding around. The little children had unbelievable fun, which was also true for the adults. The needlework club received a net income of about 10,000 marks, a giant sum for our circumstance. The occasion had saved the 1942 Christmas distributions for the poor.

The children’s party also fulfilled another function. It provided a little happiness for parents and children, a natural happiness, which we all could use during such dismal times.

DISBANDMENTS AND MANDATORY WORK ASSIGNMENTS

When spring finally arrived the Germans had improved their positions on the Eastern Front. Where our front was concerned nothing much worth mentioning had happened. Those that were called up, especially the older age groups, were longing to go home and many were disbanded. A new age group was called in under the colors. Now it was the eighteen-year-olds' turn.

A teaching center was set up in the Community Club House bottom floor for the newly called up eighteen-year-olds. We saw the boys every day and mended, among other things, their pants. There was definitely nothing pretty about their lodging, but at least they had a roof over their heads. Many of the boys were still kids in our eyes and we were sad the day they were sent to the front. Pulle was able to report they were doing a good job out there. The older soldiers were not as bent on attacking as in the past, they had become more careful and were thinking more about their wives and children. For the youngsters it was an adventure to be able to go out to war "for real". They were not just little boys playing in their back yard, they had become men. Then one day they found themselves in the middle of the action, and like a bunch of whirling maniacs they caught the enemy off guard. They managed to get away from the adventure with surprisingly small losses, but in another battle, many of them were left on the battlefield.

On the home front, those who had reached a "mature" age were allowed to withdraw. For captains the age was fifty. Pulle was released based on this regulation at the end of May. He was able to return to his civilian life and started to go back to the office again. To carry the uniform and or to be in the military was not something that ever appealed to him. This even though he had always looked upon the army favorably. But because of a series of inconsiderate actions by the military in Kymmene, he had become bitter with time and could not comprehend the military's refusal to understand that it was in the country's, as well as the military's, best interest to behave with respect toward a company like Kymmene that had donated over seven million marks to the defense. But war is war, and there will always be poor judgement in the military as well as among civilians. It is often the result of a misguided executive decision or stupidity.

The forth of June Field Marshal Mannerheim turned seventy-five years old. This day he was honored with yet another title, "The Marshal of Finland". The day could not be celebrated with the same grandiosity as his seventieth birthday due to the current state of war. But something very unexpected happened: Hitler, in his exalted personage, flew in to congratulate him. The illustrious gentlemen met somewhere in the country, but where, no common mortal was allowed to know. That Hitler had been here the general population wasn't told either until his plane had left and was on its way back to Germany.

The German Chancellor's visit was an acknowledgement to our Marshal and also to our military. A few days later the Marshal flew to Germany for a return visit.

There was a great shortage of workers on the home front. In order to relieve the shortage all youngsters above fifteen were given mandatory work assignments. The boys' assignments were mainly farm work and log-floating. The latter was an important supply link for us, especially for the industry which needed the raw materials. The girls were mainly supposed to farm, garden, and do household work, as well as child care.

The distribution of these youngsters was different in different schools. The boys were not allowed to pick their assignments. Many boys in Kymmene, who went to school in Kotka, would have preferred to work in a workshop in our own area, as during previous summers, but they were placed in log-floating jobs. The girls, from the same school, were not allowed to stay in their homes, where they would have been fully occupied, but rather were placed among strangers. But on the other hand, the girls from Pi's school were allowed to stay at home if it could be guaranteed that they had work to do. In Pi's case we were able to make good on it. The garden in Mustaniemi was large enough that it gave her plenty of work. In terms of her health this arrangement was necessary, as she in no way would have had the strength to toil out in the fields and meadows for hours under the burning sun. The summer turned out to be cold and sun-deprived, though we could not have predicted it at the time.

The food question was a burning issue the whole spring. In our house we were especially short on bread and butter. Trolle did not gain any weight, which he should have done at his age, instead he lost weight. This made us decide to send him to Sweden. First, he protested vehemently, but later he calmed down and said he would be glad to go.

It was easier said than done to get him on his way, as we did not have any influential friends in Sweden. To send him for board and lodging at some place was not possible due to the rigorous Finnish currency regulations. No one was allowed to take more than 100 Finnish Marks in hard currency abroad. On top of that, all Finnish citizens had to declare all their Swedish money, if they had any.

Pulle, who was honest and could not be bribed, would have declared every penny.

The only other option was to hope there was a decent family that would be able to take Trolle. To send him by the usual children's transport was not possible, as these were chosen among the children of the fallen, the handicapped, the reservists, the big families, or those who had economic difficulties. Also, most of these children were younger, mainly below school age.

The matter resolved itself when our old friends from Kymmene, Glory and Olle Zilliacus, also wanted to send their oldest son, who was scrawny and thin. Glory was one of those who was responsible for the children's transports. It certainly was a post of great responsibility to, with a few other ladies, take care of groups of 30 - 40 children during the voyage across the Baltic Sea, most of them under school age. During one of those trips she talked to someone who took the initiative in the children's transports and was able to get our boys placed that way.

When the issue was settled I started to get Trolle ready to travel. Pulle's old gray summer suit had to be sacrificed and converted to fit the boy, as well as Pi's old rain coat, in order for him to have something decent to wear. To get something new for him was out of the question, one could not buy any boy's clothing. I was only able to find a cap in a store, but not a single pair of socks.

On May the 31st the boys were supposed to leave from Åbo. Glory and I traveled together with them to the capital to make the last arrangements involving money and passports. The tickets were bought with Finnish money and were valid all the way to Halmstad in Sweden. Because Glory was to accompany a children's contingent from Helsinki to Stockholm by boat, which was reserved for them only, she was not able to take our boys to Åbo as they were traveling privately. Therefore, I took them by myself. We spent a few hours with Märtha and Harry, who lived in Åbo, and then Märtha and I took the boys to the harbor. We were granted the honor to step on board and set them up in their cabin.

I stood down on the dock and waved goodbye to my boy, he put on a bold face when we'd left home, but when the boat left the dock he pulled his cap lower onto his forehead. What was on the mind of the little ten-year-old when he was going out into the big world with a friend of the same age? They were met in Stockholm by one of Glory's friends. She took them home to her place. The boys reveled in pastries and chocolates before they met Glory the next day, who then put them on a train to Halmstad, where the family they were staying with waited for them at the station.

Then Trolle's stay at the Wapnö Castle started. He got acquainted with the family's children: Sperling, ten, Elisabeth, seven, Brita, five-years-old, and little Boris who was still in his cradle. It was interesting for him to come to the 18th century castle with countless rooms and attractions. But he was not able to appreciate that at the time.

I had an empty feeling traveling home without Trolle. I had to console myself with the fact that the separation was not going to be long and that he would be well taken care of in every way.

STARVATION SUMMER

We had planned to move to Mustaniemi for the summer at the beginning of June, but that did not happen as it seemed that there wasn't going to be any summer. It was wet and chilly, and no one was longing for the country. Every Sunday, starting in the middle of May, we went out there to turn the soil, seed, and set potatoes. Taina and Pi had also cleaned the house. In the beginning of June, the house was ready to receive us, but the wet and chilly weather continued.

It actually suited me well to not have to go to the country. Because of my work outside the home, I had neglected some things. The garden needed to be put in order. Since I had my daughter with her mandatory assignment at home, she helped me do it, plus a bunch of other things, like cleaning up around the old books in the attic. The domestic help, Rauha, was on vacation, so we were pretty busy with spring cleaning.

On June the 20th we decided to move, even though it was raining cats and dogs. We had to do it because of the garden in Mustaniemi. Only part of the family moved, Pulle, Pi, and I. The Kymmene home couldn't possibly be left unattended, especially because of the big risk of burglary, so Taina stayed to watch the house, and Rauha came along to Mustaniemi.

Thanks to the fact that the bus traffic was working, Pulle was able to stay in Mustaniemi overnight, going back and forth between the country and the office every day. Even though it made the evenings shorter, he still thought he got a little rest and recreation. After eating dinner, he started the assiduous, heavy work. He laid new roads, tore up tree stumps and rocks, and chopped wood. Late in the evening he would go swimming and then to bed to get up again the next morning at half past six.

Pi's and my life became pretty monotonous. We cooked, baked, and cleaned, and if the weather wasn't too bad we worked three hours in the garden every day. The 15th of July Rauha returned from a trip, but the first thing she did was quit. She could not deal with Taina anymore, she said. Taina's mood swings had returned with increasing frequency. I realized that if the gentle Rauha couldn't deal with her colleague, no one else could. When I traveled to Kymmene I asked Taina if she could take care of the servant's job by herself, provided she would get help in every feasible way.

She agreed to the offer, but my family was not completely happy. They thought it would be too much for me, since I surely would start all the social activities in the fall again. Myself, I was sure it would all work out.

During our daily work, Pi and I had endless conversations about everything between heaven and earth, and I came to the conclusion that a mother never would completely get to know her children, that there would always be something new and interesting in a conversation with them. Pi's healthy, natural, thoroughly sound and honest way of viewing everything here in the world, made me happy. Her mathematical objectivity could be seen in everything she did and said, and it often made me break out in a good laugh.

Once, in the garden, we started talking about what Pi had experienced during our wars. When she talked to her friends at school it became apparent that none of them had experienced even half of what she had been through. Most of them had evacuated to the northwest or some other area far from the racket of the war.

One thing was for sure, Pi was never going to forget all the terrible things she had experienced, like the young mother and her two children who had to flee in the middle of the night when the Russians were coming in over the ice. Pi had been very upset on the bus when the woman told her little daughter didn't have anything else but her pink flannel morning dressing gown because she forgot her winter coat. Pi was only thirteen when she gained the woman's confidence.

We talked about Pi's heart problems, which she thought was caused by anguish when the front was getting so close and she was maybe going to be forced to flee without us.

"But dear child," I said, "did you really believe we mothers would abandon you! Did you really think that Stina would have left Gunnar? Maybe you could have fled with Trolle, but I would have tried to come after you as soon as possible!"

"Of course, but anyway, I was so worried," she insisted.

Poor child, at the age of fourteen she had worried about carrying the responsibility, by herself, of possibly having to flee with four little children from Mustaniemi, with the Russians at her heels.

Our brave girl never said a word about it during the summer of 1941. Not until now, a year later, did I find out. She had not wanted to worry her parents.

After Rauha left, Pi and I had to manage without help. The labor shortage was great in the entire country, and it would have been wrong for me to try to get a new domestic help during these times.

Since we did not have any help with the rough work, we had to do it all ourselves: sweeping outside, scrubbing, and taking care of the chickens. We were not able to lie around and be lazy with all this to do. To help the food situation we had bought five chickens from the northwest. It was not easy to get them. We were happy when they arrived, but unfortunately, the happiness did not last long. The fodder we had for them was not nearly good enough, just oats- and snail shells, and nettle stew (without milk of course). The poor birds flew at us when we stepped into the cage with the food cup. Sadly, they were not able to roam free due to the fox danger.

I did not give them our meager flour, as we were only allowed to buy 6 kg (13 lb) per person per month. The flour was our main food as we did not have much else but a little smoked moose and a few poor little jars of preservatives in the cellar. We still had a few strips of bacon, but no fish, a little milk and tiny little rations of butter. We were out of the roots from the previous fall and the vegetables were not ready yet due to the awful summer.

We ate potatoes in all forms. It goes without saying that there were no leftovers for the chickens. After laying a total of five eggs, two of the hens collapsed and died. On top of that we had pouring rain and strong winds the whole month of July, so the chickens got soaking wet in their drafty coop.

I am writing about the chickens because they did play an important role in our lives in Mustaniemi. We had hoped they would help our difficult food situation. We often went hungry, especially for breakfast and dinner, which often consisted of four little slices of bread and an insignificant amount of butter. I drank cup after cup of tea to try to trick myself with all that fluid, which at least gave the feeling of an ounce of satiation. Pi looked dejected, and I got so nervous I started crying my eyes out. Pulle also started to get thinner and his eyes more and more hollow with each day.

"It is so depressing to be hungry," Pi said, and she was right about that.

The day I cried, Pulle said we would start to buy on the black market, everyone else was doing it, we couldn't go on like this! It still took a while before we started to buy things under the counter, we were not used to it, and we did not have any connections.

We also had another problem that was like a recurrent nightmare for Pulle. The building of the sauna! In May he had agreed with Eino Saari's brother, Lauri, to complete the contract on the half-finished sauna after Eino had been killed.

But where can you get the labor or the materials for it? The two additional workers we hired turned out to be useless. The intention was for the sauna to be finished by midsummer. Midsummer and July went by and the sauna still remained half done. The chimney was made out of brick. It looked very strange, so Pulle brought an expert from Kymmene with him to inspect the mess. The chimney had to be torn down and a different bricklayer had to be hired. One of the useless workers was called up for mandatory labor, and a new one was hired so we could finish the carpentry work as well.

The new worker was seventy, a meticulous old man. And Lauri, the rascal, showed up now and then, expatiated and bragged, and thought he could fool us. In the end he was revolting in my eyes.

When we returned to Kymmene, September 14th, the sauna was still not finished. But we were still able to use it, when needed, during the last month. The worse thing about the sauna was that it darkened the summer for Pulle.

In June and July, I often wrote to Trolle in Sweden. The house was so strangely empty without him. He wrote two letters, childishly short and meager. Therefore, I did not know much about his thinking, if he was having a good time, or if he was missing home. Mrs. Stael von Holstein, who owned the Wapnö Castle with her husband, also wrote a couple of kind letters and had more to tell about Trolle. Eva Horelli had met him and thought he was doing well.

We had promised the boy that, if he went to Sweden, he would be allowed to come home in August to spend some time with us in Mustaniemi.

What promises you make to a child you also have to keep. We, therefore, expected Trolle to come home in early August.

He came, with a good tan and he had gained 5 kg (11 lb). He, and his travel companion, had brought with them all kinds of goodies in their luggage: bread, cookies, candy, etc. The boys had also gotten some new pieces of clothing. It was very kind of Mrs. Stael von Holstein to think about the difficulties we had finding clothing for children due to our textile shortages. It is going to be interesting for Trolle, when he grows up, to remember how he, during war and hard times in Finland, was welcomed and taken care of at a major Swedish estate.

I am hoping the friendships he established in Sweden, during the Winter War and during this summer, would last a lifetime. And as an adult he will understand how grateful he needs to be toward the people who helped us in our time of need.

One of the first day in August a little Lotta also came to Mustaniemi riding a bicycle. Mi had been granted leave. After five months of assiduous work, she was home. Now all our children were together again.

The weather was miserable, as mentioned. On the 27th of July, we had a hail storm, and two days later we had a major storm. Lake Urajärvi was covered with white caps. The temperature was 12 C (54 F) and the rain poured down. We had a fire going in our open fireplace, sometimes we even started the boiler for the central heating.

At the beginning of August things got better, but it was not a comfortable vacation for Mi. She bravely tried to go for a swim in the lake every morning until it started pouring and storming. She finally gave up.

The 16th of August she left, four days before my 40th birthday. It wasn't until after my birthday that we suddenly had summer; a nice heat wave swept over the country. But by the 1st of September, the frost came and caused severe damage to the garden. Considering the poor conditions during the summer, the crops were still pretty good.

Brita came to visit on my birthday. She had finally moved to Helsinki in June. Her children were in Sweden with friends since the end of May. Brita congratulated me with a handbag in gray snakeskin, which she had gotten from Stockholm through her sister. In Finland you could only get paper bags.

The weather was lovely. Lake Urajärvi was blank like a mirror, the bumblebees were buzzing and the crickets were singing. Pulle was home from the office and brought coffee to bed. Taina had baked cardamom rolls out of real flour, which we had saved for just this day, part of which was a gift from the Tigerstedts. Taina had come out to the country so that Pi and I could be a little lazy.

Before Pi's confirmation we had taken old "silver trash" to the goldsmith, and some of the trash was made into a dozen small coffee spoons, which Pulle now gave me. I also got two candle sticks in silver. Pi had knitted a kitchen cloth for me. Mi gave me a novel, and Trolle a cookbook with recipes to use in times of crisis.

Pulle knew I would have been glad for someone to come out to visit us, but because of our wartime commuting difficulties it would have been impossible. He, therefore, arranged a car from Kymmene that came out with Glory, Eine, Stina, among others, and they brought flowers and sweets. I was truly celebrated in many ways. We sat on the veranda and drank coffee with good bread, we really "splurged" on this birthday. It felt strange to turn forty.

Kpk. 2/1636

The field mail service in Viborg was split into five post offices. Kpk.2/1636 was Mi's address after she moved from the job as a Lotta telephone operator to the post office. We only heard about her work conditions when she came home on leave in August. She gave us a preview in a letter in July:

"The whole post office job here is pretty laughable because I am the post office manager and Ms. Siikanen is my assistant (a fifty-year-old teacher from Kuusankoski, who has been sent out here on a mandatory assignment during her summer vacation). Strangely, she is not at all the teacher type but rather lets me give the orders and decide everything. As I may already have written, I have four assistants. Am I a powerful woman, or what? It is up to me to make sure everyone gets a day off every once in a while"

Perhaps not powerful but certainly capable and well liked. Ms. Siikanen later praised Mi in every conceivable way: "What a mature woman Mi is for her age, quick and good at her job," she said.

I would have loved to be a fly on the wall to see her in action. Her post office had set opening hours, which meant the military personnel was not able to come and go as they pleased and disturb the sorting and registration of the mail. Mi had, therefore, received the reputation of being a somewhat proud noble lady.

Vegetables were expensive in Viborg, but nothing compared to the prices charged for blueberries. The reason was that picking the berries was life threatening. The terrain surrounding the city had been heavily mined by the Russians. Many civilians, who had been evacuated during the Winter War and now moved back home, were killed picking berries. Most sad was the situation with two little boys who were treated at the war hospital ward for civilians. The boys had innocently been playing outside when they stepped on a Russian mine and were badly hurt.

Mi had gotten accustomed to the war conditions. She wrote to me:

"Almost every night there is rumble from the air defense, but nowadays I don't here it at all, instead I just sleep like a dog. The others then tell me the next morning how they were not able to sleep, so I seem to have inherited your good sleep."

Mi could probably have been released from the Lotta job and started studying like other young girls, but for her that was out of the question. She wanted to continue to carry the heavy burden of duty and give her best years to a life in a gray Lotta uniform, far away from glory and luster. Who was going to remember a little Lotta, one in a thousand?

She always maintained that she had it good. Compared with her Lotta friends out on the front that was certainly true. She did have a bed with sheets, was able to work in decent conditions, and got good food, whereas the front Lotta sisters had to lay down wherever, get up in complete darkness, melt snow for the soldiers' coffee, and expose themselves to thousands of hardships.

Ever since the summer of 1941, when Mi started her job at the hospital in Viborg, she had "stood on her own legs". She is still saving some of the salary, and for that money I have bought her household goods.

In August we were informed that the body of Dulle had been found. The Russians had reported that he, as well as his fellow soldiers, were buried with military honors, something not one of us had believed. That it was a lie was confirmed when several bodies were found in a large bomb crater, half full of water, outside Viborg. Holger's son, Werner, was given the task of identifying his uncle's body. It would have been difficult had he not still had his dog tags.

The body was burned and the urn was buried on September 3rd in the family grave in Åbo. Along with his widow, Maj-Lis, Pulle and I were present, as well as all the other siblings, sister-in-laws, brother-in-laws, and even Mi, who happened to be home on leave. It was a solemn burial. Afterwards Märtha and Harry served dinner. As usual, when the siblings were together, beautiful speeches were held with the result that everyone shed a tear, only to be cheerful again the next minute. But, I believe one of us mentioned, it was entirely in Dulle's spirit: "Not with tears shall your memory be celebrated."

The 5th of September Marga's husband, General Hugo Österman, turned fifty. The party was held at the villa they had rented for several summers in Kyrkslätt. For Pulle and I, who lived in the country, those occasions, when we were able to be with the family, were an experience. The day was supposed to be celebrated quietly, but loads of officers and generals came out to congratulate him.

When Märtha saw Pulle she started crying, she thought he looked so miserably thin. She had lost 15 kg (33 lb) herself. The whole family was horrified by both of us, but mainly by Pulle.

Thanks to Pulle's vacation in the beginning of September, we were able to travel to Helsinki and Åbo. As I was worried thieves would raid the garden while we were gone, we decided that Pi and Trolle should stay in the country. This year no Russian intruders had invaded our community, but it was still scary to leave the children by themselves in the fall darkness. Ebba Rhen, who was familiar with the conditions in Mustaniemi, promised to help.

Pi had learned a lot in terms of the household during the summer and was now going to be responsible for the house. She cooked and, among other things, had to take care of Trolle who had been febrile with a cold. When we got back, Trolle was healthy and the house in perfect condition, a job well done for a fifteen-year-old.

Ebba also helped with the fall tasks. The most strenuous job was getting the red beets out of the ground. The tops were used for coffee surrogate. Also dandelion roots, parsnip, and chicory was used for this purpose. But we did not have time to prepare it all. The remainder was dried for Trolle's rabbits in Kymmene, where they were taken care of by Taina.

The crops were, in part, very good when it came to carrots and potatoes, but the peas and beans were a total failure. The summer had been too cold and sun-deprived, and the location of the garden in Mustaniemi was not very favorable. Despite that, there were countless bags that were loaded onto the truck bed when we left the place in the middle of September.

When we moved back to Kymmene, on this wet and chilly fall day, Trolle and I were squeezed into the front cabin of the truck. Pulle sat on the truck bed among laundry- and food baskets, potato bags, rabbit food, mushroom containers, and other junk together with his loyal hunting buddy, Reku. He got a lot of looks when we drove through the factory.

Kymmene felt deserted and empty. The neighbor's villa was undergoing repairs. We were missing Brita. She had become a part of our home, where she would come and go like a family member. The thoughts would return to the happy times when there was peace and Willy was alive, the evenings when he would say "let's walk", the endless conversations, the Sibelius symphonies, to all the joy we had experienced together, and finally, to Willy's coffin, covered by the Finnish flag, where it stood in the beautiful chapel, and the day, when his and Brita's home was taken apart and moved to Helsinki, where she was to live by herself with the children.

I told Brita it was good that we were able to stay in Mustaniemi this past summer, as it would have been difficult to have the repairs going on in the neighboring villa, right in front of us, reminding us that a happy chapter in our lives had come to an end, forever.

VOLUNTEER SPIRIT

People were preserving and salting, in short, collecting and collecting. Most house mothers had come to the realization that work had to be done here.

In Kymmene a spike-picking competition emerged. After the wheat and rye fields had been harvested, the fields were overrun by local people picking the left-over spikes to help with the flour shortage. What was remarkable was that they, with a few exceptions, were well educated people. Why did the working class not at least send out their children, they should have had the time? The unfortunate reply, "it isn't worth it!" kept ringing in my ears. This irresponsible lack of initiative and refusal to be useful, which a large portion of the people suffered from, was, to us, unbelievable. What valuable national economic resources could have been lost if the spikes had not been picked up!

Pulle talked to a few farmers about this. They could not understand the point, the picking only earned you two marks an hour.

"It is not a matter of money, but food," Pulle said. "And do you know what it feels like to live on 6 kg (13 lb) of grain products a month?"

No, that they did not know, for the farmers received more than twice the rations the rest of us did.

The food situation in our home improved when we started to get vegetables. Not to mention that we also, like surely 99% of the population, bought on the black market. We gained weight during the fall, which we no doubt needed to do. Despite that I developed a skin rash from lack of vitamins. Pulle's and Pi's eczemas were also flaring up. Pi's eczema in the elbow folds was, from time-to-time, a terrible annoyance.

The lack of fuel was threatening to become catastrophic in the whole country. Therefore, "wood volunteer days" were arranged everywhere. Participation was good and therefore mandatory assignments were not needed. The banks, stores, offices, and factories closed their doors for a couple of days and sent their entire personnel into the woods. Men from the Defense Corps, who were at home, Lottas, and single individuals followed in their footsteps. Everyone, who wasn't too old, too young, or unable due to illness, chopped at least one cubic meter of wood (35 cubic feet), or one "motti", as it was called. Many had never cut down a tree. In that case someone else would chop two cubic meters, and the one, who did not know how to, piled the wood instead.

Pulle actively participated in the work. Everyone who took part was eligible to receive a needle in the shape of an ax to wear on a coat or collar. A black ax was equal to one "motti", a silver ax four, and a golden ax sixteen "mottis". Before the volunteer work had started, a few individuals from the Kymmene office had, on their own initiative, chopped wood for some elderly and weak individuals, as well as for seven widows of soldiers who had been killed.

There were also other types of volunteer work. Pi picked potatoes for an elderly woman who had been evacuated. She also signed up for the office workers' volunteer work that took place further away from home by bus or truck, trips that even the managers' wives participated in. On one of these trips she ended up at the Knuuttila farm in Itis. There, the old owner of the farm had lost two sons and a daughter in the war. It turned out to be the same man who appeared on the radio with Pulle.

Reaping the harvest was life-sustaining for the entire country. The neighboring farm to Mustaniemi,

Arola Farm, which was owned by the Mynttinens, survived. The 52 hectares (128 acres) of cultivated land was supposed to be harvested by the farm's only farmhand and the farmer himself, who had been on active duty. In June he had had an accident after which he was released from military duty. Even before he'd had time to recover, he was working full time despite the fact that he also suffered from a stomach ulcer. But in July the farmhand was pulled into the mandatory workforce, and the farmer was left with only a few women by his side.

Pulle was very upset. He was not able to get the farmhand back, but through his officer acquaintances, he was able to arrange for five young soldiers to be ordered to spend one week at the Arola farm, which took care of the situation.

Unfortunately, one was still able to see some crops here and there on the fields, black and sour from all the rain in the fall. There were farms were neither the crops were harvested nor the potatoes picked before the winter.

Pulle hunted. Every Sunday, and sometimes even Saturdays and Mondays, the hunt was on for both hare and moose. Their hunting luck was not as good as usual, but he was not left empty handed either. We got a good boost in terms of food, although, Pulle gave away most of the moose meat.

THE HELP FROM SWEDEN HELD IN CONTEMPT

Even though our "civilian" life was considerably different, with all the food shortages and also having to save on wood, we were still able to forget the war for a few hours. More accurately, we had become numb and did not react as strongly anymore to the war news bulletins. A later generation may think we were too indifferent and cold. But the fact is that it was a natural reaction, otherwise our nerves would have shattered from the constant tension.

On the Eastern Front the Germans were still doing well, which gave us a sense of security. Kotka, however, was bombarded beyond description, whereas other areas were pretty much left alone. Helsinki had only been exposed to a few bombardments. In September, Kotka had already counted up to eight hundred alarms and was thereby second in the bomb statistics after Malta, which held the questionable world record.

Kotka had become very desolate. House after house in ruins and the inhabitants often had to sleep with their cloths on– if they were able to sleep at all between the bombardments.

Those children from Kymmene who went to school in Kotka, had been moved from the student home to an elementary school, where they slept with their clothes on in order to dash out to the shelter during an alarm. There was no shelter close to the student home.

On November 8th Helsinki was bombarded with a devastating result. One single plane, flying very high, dropped two bombs. One of them hit the Five Corners were five major streets merge. The alarm came late, and according to regulations, the audience at a movie theater was ordered to leave and go to the nearest shelter. Just at that time the bomb exploded. The following days, many deaths were reported in the obituaries.

Pi had returned to her school in the capital and was staying with Brita, but she happened to be at home in Kymmene on that unfortunate day. Mi was on leave and the sisters were able to meet.

There was a constant lack of textiles and leather products. Adults were not allowed to buy a new pair of leather shoes if they owned more than two pairs. Even if one managed to get a permit for a pair of shoes, there were usually only paper shoes available.

Children under sixteen were entitled to one pair of leather shoes per year. I was lucky to find a brown pair for Pi. But not for Trolle. Elementary school children were supposed to get their shoes through their respective schools. Some got them–others did not. Many would have managed without new shoes if they'd been able to get their shoes repaired. It was a true miracle if one could get half the soles replaced. Galoshes were not repaired due to the lack of glue. One was able to buy new ones on the black market for a hair-raising price.

There was also a lack of undergarments. Even if one had coupons, one could not buy anything with them. I wanted to buy a nightgown for Mi for Christmas. After days of running around town looking, I managed to buy one, but a daytime chemise or pants were nowhere to be found. Nor could I find any fabric to sew them myself. The situation was the same with children's clothes. If a mother was able to get any piece of clothing for her children she told her friends about it, who the next day ran to the same store. The supply was already gone by the time they got there.

Sometimes one was able to get a hold of silk stockings. Gentlemen's suits made out of surrogate cloth and ready-made women's coats and dresses, at sky high prices, were still available. But even the shoe laces ran out, as did beeswax, glue, and hair-lotion. Candy was rationed, as well as tobacco.

Those who had aluminum trash were able to buy a pot in exchange. Only young couples, who had announced their wedding day, were able to buy sheets, pillow cases, and towels, and then only four sheets per couple. But what did all this matter as long as the country was ours, as long as we were able to keep the Bolsheviks at bay! One day the war would end, everything was going to be alright– God willing.

The anguish, however, did sneak back at times to disrupt the peace. We tried to console each other with the fact that Germany was doing well. Crushing Bolshevism would become our rescue.

An insidious danger for our solidarity and loyalty were the so-called whispering campaigns, which were initiated by less desirable elements. On top of that, people created loads of rumors with their thoughtless babbling.

That fall a slander campaign flared up against those who had sent their children to Sweden. Instead of all the classes in society being grateful for what the Swedes did for our children, there were accusations that the children were not treated well by our neighbor.

Mothers in Kuusankoski demanded to have their offspring sent back. The women were hysterical and thought they had committed a crime by sending their children away. But the women were not able to explain what the actual crime was.

The Social Department arranged for free travel for the children to return home. We advertised in the newspaper that those parents who wished to have their children returned should report. About forty parents did, including some families that were economically so badly off that they were supported by the community. We asked these families if it wasn't better for Jack or Jill to stay where they were well taken care of, but it was like talking on deaf ears.

One fall morning I went to the Kouvola station to meet an extra train operated by the Red Cross. The lady in charge of this children's transport was irritated, and I had to endure numerous sneers from her due to the foolish behavior of the mothers. That these poor women had come to the station was by no means my fault. We had specifically asked them to come to two different places in Kymmene where we were taking the children by bus.

When I finally sat down in the bus, surrounded by a bunch of kids, I felt a deep sense of relief. The children were happy and fearless. A little girl asked me:

"Does the lady speak Swedish?"

The little girl was completely lost.

The strange thing was that many children had forgotten some of their mother tongue after being away for just four months. They were all well-dressed; fine sports shoes, good pants, hats, dresses, and coats. Everyone had with them at least one large package with wheat flour, sweets, sugar, cookies, and other goodies. Many also had clothing for their siblings in their suitcases.

But it was no joy to again be forced to realize that the factory workers never will learn, or don't want to learn, a little decency. One would have thought that those, who had their children lovingly cared for, would have written a thank you letter to the foster parents. Few did so, which led to worried Swedes contacting us to find out if the children had gotten back alright. It is embarrassing.

It is hurtful to be treated with such obvious nonchalance and unfriendliness. Afterwards, when I met some of the mothers in the streets, they would not greet me. Pulle said that I was too demanding of people who had not had the opportunity to learn anything.

At the post office and in the stores, one could hear women complain that their sons did not get enough to eat in the army and that they had to share their own meager rations so the boys wouldn't go hungry. One time I boiled over and said that they were talking nonsense. At that point they did stop talking. The whispering campaign was like a boil. In poor neighborhoods and factory centers it easily burst. The worst to talk rubbish in Kymmene, those who talked about how badly the children were treated in Sweden, were truly silenced when the children came back healthy and well-dressed with lots of goodies in their luggage.

One day a couple came to see Eva Horelli and apologized for listening to the rumors. Now they had seen, with their own eyes, how good the children had it. But the worst thing was that these children were not happy at home and wanted to go back to Sweden. Which of course was out of the question.

Unfortunately, our little Swedish travelers brought with them diphtheria. The illness had been running rampant in Sweden and it resulted in an epidemic in Kymmene and many other places in the country. One of the children had died while in Sweden. Her body was sent back to her native land and was buried at the Kuusankoski cemetery.

Work cannot always be joyful, and one cannot help that there will be misunderstandings sometimes. Luckily, most of the time, I've been met with kindness in my social work. Some other ladies and I, representatives for the needlework club, were shown touching gratitude when we, just before Christmas, handed out monetary assistance and gifts to those in the community who needed help. Mothers and many children, invalids, drunken men, the sick, and weak elderly ladies were helped. It was a dismal group accepting the gifts. In order to keep track of these people in need, we kept a list. It was called the "gray list".

Honesty was not always upheld in this country during times of war. There were thefts left and right. When Pulle and I traveled to Åbo, I had packed a thin summer coat into an unlocked suitcase, which for a moment was unattended in the train compartment. When I opened the suitcase, the coat was gone. Handbags and bicycles were in constant danger. The dark streets gave criminals excellent opportunities for assaults and robberies. Furs, shoes, and handbags were frequently stolen.

Even little children were victims. In Helsinki and in Åbo, unattended children suddenly disappeared, and when they were found again they had no clothes on.

One child was found in the bitter cold in a gateway in the capital city. Nothing that happened on the home front compared to these kinds of crimes.

I have so far only mentioned the downside of war on the home front. There were also things that gave us encouragement. I am mainly thinking about our ally's military success and the fact that we've been noticed for our optimism, especially by journalists from Sweden.

However, we just can't understand why these newspaper people let themselves be invited to one lavish dinner after the other in our starving country. But then again, we have been raised in such a manner that we pull out the last of our storage when we have guests.

Kymmene was visited by the Swedish Working Women's Association. Pulle and Mr. Wallenius, head of the social department, welcomed them. The ladies, all of them journalists, were very interested in what they saw. This included the Voikka Paper Mill, the Vocational School, and the Central Elementary

School, undoubtedly some of the finest schools in the country, and a few other points of interest. The chief editor for the Women's Magazine asked how our nerves were holding up with all our burdens. I thought it was a strange question, we didn't really have a choice, they had to hold up.

The Swedes have not always understood us politically, even when they have helped us tremendously with food and child transportation support. But they have not related to our political views. We had to regret this, and we hope that one day our neighboring country would realize that our battle against our mighty neighbor in the East was a fight for our lives, our freedom.

Here in Kymmene we can continue to live in our altered homes while those on the front have to lie in their burrows or tents month after month. The Finnish soldier is tough, although often a coarse fellow, whose emotional life does not hold much softheartedness. But it may be our luck that our warriors are not overly cultivated or overly sensitive by nature.

We had heard about atrocities in the Russian prison camps during the Winter War 1939-1940, about horrifying evil deeds against the poor warriors who had ended up in Russian hands.

Caja's oldest son Bubi, who had served for a long time on the front-most lines, made several patrols into enemy territory. During one of those trips, two of his men suffered leg injuries. Their comrades were not able to take them to a first aid unit but were forced to leave them on the battlefield in order to later fetch them with stretchers. Bubi had doubted this decision, but the wounded themselves wanted it that way.

Bubi made sure they both had their Brownings at hand and told them not to give themselves up alive to the Russians if help did not reach them in time.

When Bubi returned the men apparently did not have the courage to give themselves the mercy shot. They were found dead with their hands nailed to tree stumps.

Pi met a soldier on a train who talked to her about the fact that it was forbidden to dance. During the entire war, dancing in public was prohibited. It may be abominable to be dancing here at home while soldiers are dying at the front, but on the other hand one can understand that our soldiers would like to amuse themselves while on leave. They want to forget the seriousness. At all too young an age the fun has been taken away from them. The way it is now, they are not able to properly entertain themselves. Some will reach for the bottle. The drinking has increased at an alarming rate.

The soldier on the train told Pi his whole leave had been one hectic runaround from one bar to the other. "One chases a happiness that does not exist." After that they have to return to the burrows and trenches, and then again back to the hometown and the bottle and wandering from one cafe to the other for the next ten days. Where is the enthusiasm that was there during the Winter War?

There still was an order for complete blackout in Kymmene, which was dangerous for pedestrians, cyclists, and automobile drivers. One dark evening I twisted my ankle on the slippery ground and had to sit with my ankle wrapped and elevated for several days. I could not move without crutches for more than a week.

I sent Mi small packages with Christmas tree decorations and books. She was not granted leave and was for the first time going to spend Christmas with strangers. She did not feel sorry for herself for not being able to come home. One thing is for sure,

Christmas at a war hospital was going to be very festive.

My Christmas started with Eine Rhen and myself distributing gifts on Christmas Eve morning by horse and sleigh to our war invalids who were part of the Lottas' responsibilities in the caretaker program. It was a giving and educational trip. We experienced quiet peacefulness and contentedness, little, well-tended homes, and happy children. But we also saw illness, bleak poverty, and the inability to maintain a decent home.

I was deeply moved by all this. Most of all by the men who had done so much for their native land.

We quietly celebrated the holidays– just the four of us. Then Brita arrived with her children, and once again we were able to keep up the old tradition of celebrating the New Year together.

1943

Dear Reader,

In the original Swedish version and the Finnish translation of this book, my father, Sten von Troil (Trolle), wrote about the year 1943 for continuity. At the time, Brita's 1943 notebooks were missing. Later, two small notebooks were discovered. Brita probably was not able to write as much this year as she herself fell ill.

My father had captured the year remarkably well. Brita had written about many of the same events my father had described. However, two excerpts have been added from Brita's notebooks; the first about work duty for women, the second about Brita's own thoughts about her illness.

Stella von Troil

EVENING PRAYERS FOR MAMMA

Written by Sten von Troil (Trolle)

The most important event for our family in 1943 was mother's illness. Her appendix had been removed in the 1930s without any complications, but in the winter of 1943 she suddenly came down with severe stomach pains. The company physician, Dr. Forss, diagnosed adhesions that were strangling the gut. These were thought to be scars from the appendix surgery. The adhesions were removed and the pain resolved. But after a few days the pain returned, worse than before. Dr. Forss immediately wanted to operate again, but my father first wanted to consult his brother-in-law Dr. Harry Elving, who was one of the best surgeons in the country. Harry realized the seriousness of the situation and would have come from Åbo to Kymmene to perform the surgery himself, but he was unable to do so due to another acute surgery he had to perform.

He recommended a few colleagues, and in the end Dr. Biaudet from Lovisa jumped on a bus and came to Kymmene. The operation was started without delay and further adhesions were removed. The situation was critical and we did not know if mother would survive.

Late one night, when my father came back from the hospital, he entered my room. I had already gone to bed.

"Have you prayed for mamma in your evening prayers?" he asked.

"Yes," I answered.

"Do it again, she is very sick."

Pi was called back home from Helsinki, but Mi was at her Lotta job at the front. What were we going to do? In cases like this the radio was used as a way to communicate. One could often hear after the news, for example: "Soldier NN Kpk.xxx, immediately contact your home, your mother is seriously ill."

One wanted to give a son or daughter the chance to see a dying parent one last time. Leave was granted "automatically". My father contemplated this option but decided against it. If Mi had suddenly turned up at mother's bedside, she may have interpreted this as her doomsday with serious psychological consequences. Mi was instead informed by letter.

Mother slowly got better but continued to suffer intermittently from stomach pain. She was only able to eat easily digested food and was even more tired and weak than before. Despite this she continued, the best she could, to participate in the Lotta work and the needle workshop activities.

The year 1943 had been a definite turning point in the war. The Germans had suffered a bitter defeat in Stalingrad. A whole army had been taken prisoner and was pushed into Siberia in icy cold and dreadful conditions. After the defeat, the German-Russian frontline moved continuously toward the west.

The war in Africa had ended. Rommel's troops gave up and hundreds of thousands of Germans were taken prisoner. Now the allied troops were able to invade Italy. This German ally, which had caused more trouble than good, actually capitulated. Mussolini was overthrown and replaced by Badoglio, but the German troops continued to fight.

Churchill and Roosevelt met in Casablanca. They decided to continue the war until Germany and Japan had surrendered unconditionally. Finland was not mentioned in the official documents. The next major meeting was held in Teheran, where the three big ones met: Roosevelt, Stalin, and Churchill. This time Finland was addressed as a separate matter. It became clear Stalin was mainly interested in the nations between the Soviet Union and Germany, he gave in on the matter of Finland, which Roosevelt and Churchill were determined to keep as a democratic nation. Stalin agreed not to go any farther than the 1940 border between Finland and Russia, but demanded additional war restitutions. One contributing reason for the decision was the fact that the Soviet Union and England were going to be in great need of our wood manufacturing products after the war.

To what degree details of these meetings actually reached the political leadership I cannot remember with certainty, but some information did leak out via Vilhelm Assarsson, the Swedish messenger stationed in the Soviet Union.

The day in 1941, when Germany declared war against the US out of solidarity to Japan, my father realized that the Germans were going to lose the war. He only mentioned it to those he could trust and to good friends. After all, one was not allowed to stir up unrest. This realistic view soon took over the entire country.

Opinions changed radically. The first steps were taken through Stockholm to try to reach a separate peace agreement with the Soviets. This did not, however, lead to any results. The Germans, of course, became aware of the contact that had been made between Finland and the Soviet Union. The Germans protested and threatened to stop the grain transports to Finland that had been of vital importance and life sustaining.

A group opposing a peace agreement, including well known politicians and cultural personalities, became so vocal that some persons in leadership positions were imprisoned. The future president, Urho Kekkonen, held a speech in Stockholm that attracted attention. One now realized that the idea of a Greater-Finland expanding its territory into Eastern Karelia, based on the great success of 1941, was less intelligent wishful thinking. Now, Mannerheim's unfortunate speech and Svinhuvud's address to the soldiers was seen as a burden in respect to the peace negotiations, which would begin sooner or later.

One of the consequences of the change in opinions was the construction of a water power plant on the River Kymmene at the Kuusankoski rapids for electricity production. The government was afraid we were going to lose the power supply from Imatra in the East, which could lead to severe power shortages. The "boys" and I watched the progress of this enterprise which demanded an enormous amount of labor. Three turbines/generators were delivered from Germany and were installed, but the forth was destroyed in a bombardment by the Royal Air Force in the Hamburg harbor. The new power plant was connected to the grid in Keltti. The cables between Kuusankoski and Keltti were placed on concrete pillars. Steel, which was the most common material, could not be used, it was needed at the front.

There was an increasing knowledge about the atrocities of the Nazis toward the Jews. Everyone was understandably upset about it. The only large newspaper that dared to oppose it was the Swedish language paper Huvudstadsbladet (The Capital Paper), otherwise these atrocities were kept silent.

The murder of the Danish author Kaj Munk was especially upsetting.

I often spent time at the Mustila Estate that spring. I traveled there from Kouvola on a bus which had a wood burning carburetor. I thought it was wonderful to be able to eat as much as you wanted. We often had a delicious veal steak for Sunday lunch.

I also remember hunting sparrows with an air gun with Axel Tigerstedt, who was the same age.

There was a map on the wall in Mustila which showed the frontline between Germany/Finland and the Soviet Union by using pins and thread as markers. It was very depressing to see how the line, which had gone all the way to the River Volga, now was moving west.

At Mustila I met many German officers who were on leave. The road home from Lappland to Germany was long, and hospitable homes had opened their doors to the warriors so they could rest. Mrs. Tigerstedt came from the Baltic States and German was her mother tongue. Her husband, the estate owner, was also fluent in German. I was learning German in school for the second year, so I was able to pick up a little bit here and there at the dinner table, but I was not able to take part in any actual conversations.

Like many estates, Mustila had received fourteen Russian prisoners as laborers. These men were poorly dressed but still had warm clothing. But since in these times nobody looked elegant, it was hardly noticeable. The prisoners were completely unguarded and lived in an old building. A cook saw to it that they were fed. They worked with the estate staff, especially in the garden. Timonen, the master gardener, was a refugee from St. Petersburg and of course spoke fluent Russian, but really terrible Finnish. As both the estate owner and his wife got by in Russian, the prisoners were able to express their wishes and these were carried out if feasible. Some of the prisoners spoke German, Axel and I tried to speak with them, mainly to be able to brag about it to friends of our age.

One time a few of the estate farmhands and a prisoner were traveling by horse and sleigh across Elimäki Pond when the ice broke and the horse fell into the water. The estate farmhands just stood there petrified, but the Russian jumped into the water with cold-blooded courage, he freed the horse from its harness so it was able to get out and was saved. The estate owner was informed about what had happened. The Russian, who had rushed back to his quarters soaking wet to get some dry clothes, was given a number of glasses of liquor to prevent a cold. But that was not all, he also got a pair of pants!

One of the German-speaking Russian prisoners talked about his son at every opportunity. The son fought for the German Wehrmacht and we were shown a picture of him. How he had ended up with the Germans and the father with the Red Army I do not recall. The prisoner had tried to contact the German embassy in vain. Now he made another desperate effort. Dressed in the pants that were mentioned above, he traveled to Helsinki by bus. If he ever made it to the embassy we never found out, but he was quickly recognized due to his Russian steel teeth. Later, a very polite Swedish speaking sergeant from the military police questioned both Mrs. Tigerstedt and us boys about the circumstances surrounding the escape. I can remember Mrs. Tigerstedt's final words well:

"I hope he gets in touch with the German embassy and is treated fairly."

In 1944 when these prisoners had to leave Mustila and, according to the peace treaty, were to return to the Soviet Union, one could witness a tearful good bye. The estate owner thanked them for the work the Russians had done and they in turn were grateful for the extraordinary treatment they had received. Obviously, I did not understand what was said but I could see that each party, mutually, wished the other all the best and God's blessing. The Russians cried the most, they were, after all, aware that in the Red Army there were no prisoners, only deserters, who all were mercilessly executed. We could only have a presentiment of what was going to happen to these unfortunate men.

On the front there was a position war going on. Inside the country it was relatively quiet. The Kotka harbor was important as the connecting link to Germany. A lot of the war materials traveled this route. The Russians were, of course, aware of this and bombed the town frequently. Even though the town's schools were functioning reasonably normally, it was considered too precarious for the final year high school students to have their final national examinations, "Student Exam", there. Therefore, all the students from the Kotka Swedish High School were placed with company employees' families in Kuusankoski, where the exams were held, one of the many special arrangements during the wartime.

Mi was moved to the Lotta Regional Office #6 in Aunus. Every army corps had such an office. Aunus was situated in East Karelia, between the 1939 border and the River Svir northeast of Lake Ladoga. Mi became an office worker there. Luckily our cousin Margaretha Österman was the office manager and the two were able to share a bedroom.

Aunus was a village with four roads that crossed each other. There, the Finns had built a hotel named Lottahovi (The Lotta Court). There were also some shops. The supply of commodities was scant, but there were books. A theater had performances, occasionally with actors from the National Theater. A great portion of the working population was still left, but there was no bustling social life. Mother often read Mi's letters from Aunus aloud and the family would laugh out loud at her hilarious descriptions.

With all possible means, one tried to stretch the scanty rations. Rabbits were popular. Our new neighbors, the Cedercreutzs, had several cages with a grid bottom. These were moved around on the fairly large lawns in front of the houses. The rabbits reproduced very rapidly, no assistance needed.

We had sheep, two of them most of the time. During the day they were tied to a tree with a long rope and were able to graze. They often got tangled up in the rope after which terrible bleating could be heard, so one had to dash outside to untangle them. During the night the sheep were put into the playhouse, causing severe damage to its floor.

Picking mushrooms was a major activity in the fall. I enjoyed roaming the woods and got to know my home district better and better. On the other hand, I really despised picking berries and gardening but was forced to participate anyway. One of my specialties was to dig up dandelion roots, which later were roasted to be used for coffee surrogate.

We put out fishing traps in Mustaniemi. The catch was not particularly good, but it was enough for fish soup a couple of times a week. Some of the perch was used for crawfish bait. The shellfish were not only a delicacy but also a joyful subject in an otherwise rather gloomy existence.

In October there were volunteer days to pick up beets and potatoes at the nearby farms. The plentiful provisions made these occasions especially attractive. Therefore, I tried to go to as many of them as possible, but getting time off from school was a limiting factor.

It felt empty not having Willy and Peter living next door anymore. But I did not have to be without friends. Axel Tigerstedt came to stay with us in the fall. He had had a private tutor in the past in Mustila, but now his parents thought it would be better with a real school. We consequently became classmates.

In the fall I went to visit Axel almost every weekend in Mustila, and on Monday morning we returned with highly appreciated food items. Mustila had a truck which we got to ride on. The wood carburetor had developed in a positive direction, starting– or other problems– were rare. A typical war phenomenon was that people who had a car would let others use the vehicle for transportation. Mustila's truck transported mainly farm and nursery products to Koria station and to Kouvola. On the way back, all kinds of items were loaded for stores in Elimäki near Mustila.

Axel and I participated in the on and off loading. One time the estate dog Lux returned with the truck. If I am not mistaken he had been called to duty as a guard dog in Sandhamn. Now Lux became a civilian again and returned home with one of his puppies, Nix. The joy when he recognized the people at the estate cannot be described in words.

Another time we were reminded of the realities of war when we loaded and unloaded a coffin that contained a war hero's remains.

I am convinced the transports were done for others without economic compensation. It was part of the Winter War spirit, which really did not end with the Winter War, something my mother sometimes feared.

During the fall my father made a visit to the front, to the Isthmus of Maaselkä to be exact, where a large portion of the company's workers were stationed. The idea was for him to deliver a greeting from their employer and to tell them about a social benefit they were to receive, unfortunately I do not recall what that was. Once he had returned home he reported that the mood among the workers/soldiers was good. He had seen quite a few East Karelia communities and pointed out:

"They are at least fifty years behind us in their development."

One tried to keep one's spirit up in all possible ways. Finnish Film did their part with their screwball comedies. The humor was partly supposed to show how stupid and uncivilized the Russians were.

Suomen Kuvalehti (Finnish Picture Magazine) had a comic figure which also acted with similar intentions.

The longer the year went on, the more pessimistic people became in terms of the final outcome of the war. Secret peace negotiations were carried out in Stockholm with the help of Swedish middlemen. The Soviets were represented by Mrs. Kollontai. She had also been in the picture during the Winter War. Her family ties to Finland were undoubtedly to our advantage, she wanted to keep Finland independent, but as a Bolshevik state.

What was going to happen to our country? This serious question was keeping us all occupied. When my mother, Brita von Troil, discussed a possible Soviet occupation with Brita von Koskull, the latter Brita, said:

“If I end up in a situation where I cannot tell you the truth in a letter, then I will sign with “Brita”. Otherwise with “Muku” (her nickname).

“Good, then I will sign with “Brita” or “Musti” (my mother’s nickname).

WORK DUTY FOR WOMEN

The labor shortage was severe. In order to help the situation before the upcoming summer farming campaign, not only was volunteer female help organized through various women's organizations, but there was also a summons to which all women, from cities and other densely populated areas, between the ages of 18 and 45 were summoned. Exceptions were made for those who were pregnant, as well as for mothers with children under six years old.

In Kuusankoski we had the summons at the end of May. I also went there. It was a pretty odd experience, and because it was so characteristic, so labeled by war, I will describe it in detail.

The summons took place in the new fine Community House. I went there on a cold and rainy day in May, when persons whose names started with the letter T were supposed to report. The summons was to start at ten o'clock, but I went there early to avoid being the last in line. When I arrived, I found a quacking gathering of women who had mainly been recruited from the working class.

At ten o'clock the chairman of the summons and the head of the social department, Mr. Wallenius, came out to explain the principles of the summons.

Class I: Women completely healthy, able to perform heavy duty.

Class II: Women not completely healthy, but who could do light duty.

Class III: Women with a dubious past, imprisonment, etc.

Class IV: Women who were sick, not capable of doing any kind of work.

Additionally, the classes were divided into A, B, or C, depending on the importance of the work the person in question was currently performing. In other words, class IA was certainly going to be placed on farming duty as her health was good, and the letter A indicated that the woman in question was not important in her current position. The letter B indicated that the woman's abilities could be utilized but preferably only for a short time. The letter C indicated that even if the woman's health would allow a work order, she would be out of the question as she was needed in her own position. This could, for example, happen to a mother with several children, even above six years old, or a maid in a family with children under the age of two, or someone employed in an office, or similar situation.

After this explanation, I had to stand in a crowded line for an hour and listen to all kinds of rubbish.

Thereafter, I came into a room where I got a card with my name and my address.

"Please, this way," and I was placed in another room with another line. The room was divided by a curtain behind which two physicians were sitting.

"Are you healthy?"

"Yes."

One could hear the noise from stamping.

"Move forward, next."

"Are you healthy?"

"No."

"What is wrong with you? Take your clothes off."

And so forth with lightning speed. For once, I got to experience that the Finnish people were in a hurry.

Then it was my turn. I went in to see the sweet female physician Dr. Tarkiainen.

Short and straight to the point: "Are you healthy?"

"No."

Only then did she look at me.

"What is wrong with you?"

"Heart problems, I have spent eleven weeks in the hospital a long time ago, but after that I have had to be careful."

"Take your clothes off."

I was probably not the first one to complain about heart problems. It was obvious to see that Dr. T. thought I was trying to get out of the work duty by simulating. She did not hide her surprise when she observed abnormal heart function.

"Pretty sensitive heart, really, sensitive heart," and she looked truly concerned. She started to interview me about my home situation. I told her that I had a maid, but that I was going to stay in Mustaniemi over the summer and that I was hoping to get Pi to come and help with the kitchen and garden duties, as I couldn't possibly get, or even claim to get, a maid to come out to the country as well.

Dr. T. said that she was compelled to stamp my card with class II, but she sincerely hoped that the next authority would completely exempt me from all work related to farming.

The following authority looked grand and impressive. Wallenius was sitting in the place of honor with a secretary and another person next to him. A doorman made sure only one person was let in at a time.

Wallenius was smiling a bit. It must have amused him to see the company women, one after the other, come in and receive their verdict during the days he was chairman of the committee. He probably was grateful for not having such a serious labor problem in Kuusankoski and that the need for our predominantly factory workforce was not really that great in the surrounding communities either, so he was able to act in a less stringent manner. For rigorous regulations in a mill town would not have been nice, especially for those who would have been in charge of monitoring that these regulations were carried out. In any case, the company official's wives were surely going to be more loyal and likely to follow the regulations than the female laborers, something that later turned out to be the case.

Wallenius took my card.

"Class II - is that so. How old is your boy?"

"Eleven-years-old."

"The letter C," was stamped on the card.

I must have looked a little astonished because Wallenius said: "We have tried, whenever possible, to let mothers with small growing children stay at home and take care of them and the home."

I felt extremely grateful. In my mind I had already seen myself thinning turnips or picking weeds on a farm in Itis or Jaala for eight to nine hours a day, and I was wondering how the family would be able to take care of Mustaniemi and themselves, and what I would look like after only a few days under such conditions.

But there were many that had to go through with the work duties that summer. Among them Clara Ekholm who was the wife of the company CEO, Karl-Erik Ekholm. She had to pick potatoes in September. This also happened to Mrs. Sevon, who had to get by without her maid and also had sheep to take care of. She had to leave everything for a couple of weeks. Her husband had to manage the best he could while she picked potatoes.

There were also farmers of various kinds. On one farm owner's porch sat the daughter of the house and watched how those on work duty were working, Mrs. Sevon told us, the girl herself did not do anything at all, but she did seem to revel in the situation.

The work orders lasted between two weeks and four months and included farming and garden work, as well as peat harvesting. In 1944, log floating for women was added to the program.

But as I already mentioned, not everyone turned out to be loyal. There were women who never showed up for their work duty, and to keep the whole thing from coming to a head the police did not chase after them, at least not in Kuusankoski. It often happens that the lazy and the insubordinate get away with the most.

BETWEEN LIFE AND DEATH

It is a strange feeling to find oneself somewhere between life and death, to lie there and wonder if one was still going to be alive the next day, or in two days, it sort of becomes a curtain for the future. At times I was hit by a great anguish. I did not want to die but hung onto life with all the willpower I could produce in my weakened state.

Doctors and nurses were so sweet to me, I got the best imaginable care.

On the 26th of October, I went home. I was very weak, but I was alive. A merciful God had let me stay with my husband and children.

1944

Heavy bombardments continue in the capital city of Helsinki and the bloodshed continues on the Eastern Front in the fight for Karelia. Can Finland hang on while the rest of Eastern Europe is slowly annexed to the Russian sphere of interest as the German army continues to retreat west?

June 6th, D-Day, Allied troops land in Normandy and Hitler's days are numbered as the German empire is now attacked from the east to west, and from the south. As the Allied forces move towards Berlin the concentration camps are liberated one by one.

THE CAPITAL IS BURNING

Trolle was standing in front of the mirror in the bathroom brushing his unruly hair. I stood next to him, smiling, checking his suit and tie. Were the hands clean? Yes, most definitely, it showed that the young man was on his way to the dance school's season-ending ball.

Dancing was prohibited, but this did not affect children.

"Remember not to whip your arm about, Trolle," Pulle shouted.

"He is just setting the rhythm, don't you understand," Pi was trying to defend him.

"Yes, of course, but it just looks so funny."

Trolle put a hurt look on his face, stubbornly put his chin in the air and thought: I will dance exactly as I please, mom and dad don't know anything about swing, they are so old fashioned.

Pi and I sat on a bench and admired the little brother who flitted about the dance floor, but kept whipping the left arm about carelessly. The slick hair just got more and more obstinate as the evening wore along, and after about the twentieth dance and the seventh bottle of lemonade he was so hot his hair went into wild disarray.

"Can't you take your jacket off," I whispered to him when he got at arm's length.

"Impossible," he answered and gave me a humiliated look.

"Dear Mom, don't you understand, Trolle has to look good," Pi cut in.

Yes, of course. And then things cooled down a bit. Whatever the ice cream machine had produced was rolled in and all the kids stood in line to get some of the desired product.

This is how idyllic January was at home in Kymmene.

I traveled to Helsinki to meet Brita and Pi, who had returned to school. For me it was a break from all the duties. At about the same time Mi made a trip to Kutujärvi with her Lotta group to entertain the troops with theater. Out to the front they traveled by car and out to the lines by horse. Sometimes they were so close to the lines that they were able to hear the rattling from the machine guns.

The girls were performing at three canteens. At one of them they actually had a real stage and a hall with room for three hundred and fifty people. The halls were filled to the breaking point by an enthusiastic audience. Some of the soldiers came in by cross country skis from the outermost lines just to be at these events. Concertina players filled the air with their music during the breaks. During the program a soldier stood guard outside with a machine gun.

Mi Acting as a Male Character

There was going to be a lot of work for me this spring. Among other things we were preparing for a Lotta course. The needlework shop needed money. And we also had to think about our customary children's party.

But Pi had not been feeling very well, so I traveled to the capital again to be at hand, she was, after all, going to take her National High School Final Exams this spring. On February he 4th, the last day of actual classes for the seniors, the traditional "penkkis" party was to be held. It was undoubtedly going to tear at her strength too much, but neither Pulle nor I could tell her not to go. She got home the next morning, all bushy-tailed, after being up all night dancing and having fun, and then slept to the next day.

Many of the school's boys had been called up for duty, but they had been granted leave in order to take part in their "penkkis" celebration. Their school work had taken place in schools near the frontline and their exams were also to take place somewhere at the front. If the times were not very favorable to final exams, it was even more unfavorable to those who had to stay out in the fields. Luckily one had cut down on the demands for those on duty.

I visited friends, went to the movies, and mended clothes. I also washed for Pi, as she had a hard time doing it herself with her hands constantly covered in eczema.

The 6th of February I was out in town when the first alarm signals sounded. A new system had been introduced in Helsinki. Two signals were given for air danger, the first was only a warning, the second meant there was imminent danger and one had to go to a shelter. I was happy I had the time to get home to Brita before the second warning signal.

Brita was visited by her mother, and Pi had a friend over, who had lost her home in bombardments during the first day of the Winter War. When the second warning went off, Brita wanted to go into the windowless hallway for shelter. We did not hurry at first, but when the air defense started shooting we moved briskly.

We had just taken our seats when we could hear the first detonations.

"Bombs!" Brita said. "Shall we go down into the cellar?"

"The hostess should decide," I answered.

Brita had her old mother and her boys at home. I could understand her talk about the shelter, although I thought it was not necessary. I was simply too lazy to get out of my comfortable chair. But on the other hand, I had some degree of responsibility for Pi's guest.

So we did go down, and Pi and I chose the shelter at 44 Albert Street. It was a nasty establishment, a low cellar supported here and there by thick beams. Brita had gone to another shelter that was a lot more comfortable and, therefore, quickly overcrowded. Outside, it was cracking and blasting.

It is a strange feeling to be in a city that is under bombardment. One is completely helpless, one can only wait, waiting like a rat who wants to get out of its trap. I hated to sit behind the boiler. We were going to be cooked alive or be scalded if there was a direct hit.

Time was crawling forward. The girls where chatting just like they were walking in the school yard. When the noise became deafening they looked up astonished. "It really is cracking," they said and went right on with their chatter.

I was watching the people around me. There were ladies knitting, quiet and reticent, children sleeping, and a baby sucking on her milk bottle. She was looking at us with her big clear eyes untouched by everything that was going on around her.

There was a violent bang followed by a strange jingling sound. People were screaming, but the next moment everything was quiet again in our cellar, but outside one explosion followed the other.

We sat there for three long hours that evening, from seven to ten o'clock. Once we got out we could see that the Russian embassy was burning. Huge plumes of fire were slung out of each window. The whole house looked like a giant torch. It was also burning across Erik Street towards Sandvik, the sky was red and huge smoke clouds were rising.

When we got back to the apartment Brita was worried about her daughter, Ulla, who was on her way from Kymmene to Helsinki. Her train was supposed to arrive at the station at 7 pm according to the timetable, just around the time the first bombs were dropping. Now she had no idea where her girl was.

In Brita's home the windows had been blown out and the flowers were on the floor surrounded by the crushed pots. In the dining room the curtains were fluttering. The table had been set with tea, bread, and butter, but now it was covered in shards of glass. Together we cleaned up. Brita wanted everyone to get something hot to drink and something to eat, plus a schnapps.

Pi and I continued to clean and put the food back while Brita hurried to her sister who lived in her mother's apartment. She assumed the house had been damaged as she lived right across the street from the burning Russian embassy. She soon came back with the sister, her little foster son, and the maid. Their faces were sooty, all three of them, and their hair was hanging in strands.

When the alarm had sounded they had rushed to the shelter, but when they ran across the yard a bomb hit a house nearby, which led to the plaster dropping off the sides of their own house in big flakes and rained over them. The home was now uninhabitable, the windows were blown out, the furniture and the kitchen gadgets had been thrown all over the place by the air pressure wave. Now they needed a place to stay overnight.

We sat down at the table. The conversation was about the evening's happenings and the thoughts constantly went to Ulla, who was on the train on the way to Helsinki. When she finally arrived she burst into tears, almost hysterical.

"Are you alive?" were her first words as soon as she got through the door.

She had sat on the train with some of Pulle's good friends from Kymmene. They had made it to Malm outside Helsinki when the alarm signals went off and the train stopped. Ulla had run out into the woods, frightened and panicking, and only returned after the all-clear signal had been given. She had walked through the city, which was in flames, all by herself.

Countless people were looking for their loved ones. Pi and I had to go to sleep despite the blown-out windows. I wanted to reserve rooms at Hotel Socis but the phone did not work. Pi thought we should lie down in the little hallway next to her room. There we organized beds for ourselves. She fell asleep quickly, but I laid awake for a long time.

Soon after midnight the sirens went off again. I laid there wondering what I should do, I did not really want to wake up Pi. She moved about restlessly and muttered something about not being left alone.

I stayed there for a while and listened to the bombs blasting, it was not a pleasant situation. Suddenly the room became lit up like a flame.

I told Pi that we had the Russians over us and I could not be responsible for what was going to happen if we did not rush to the shelter. But Pi muttered that she had lain in her bed before while the bombs were falling over the city. Despite her sarcastic attitude I felt weak in my knees and anguished. If something happened to her it would be my fault. She got up, tired and a bit angry that she had such a squeamish mother. "If a bomb hits us in the head, it hits us in the head, so what?" she proclaimed.

"But there could also be a bomb that just took an arm or a leg, that would be worse," I tried.

Finally, she gave in, but she was not going to go all the way to the shelter, just to the staircase.

Said and done, we got set in the staircase on the bottom floor. There were already a bunch of people there. I looked into the shelter that was nearby. It was filled to the brim. Brita also sat down in the staircase with Ulla who was shaking and crying.

I was leaning against the wall and Pi, who was sitting one step below me, rested her head on my knees. We sat like this for hours while it roared around us without interruption. It was as if it was thundering continuously, and intermittently there were sounds of horrible explosions that caused our ears to lock up, as well as clinking, crashing, and whistling noises.

"That was close," someone would say and, "now there will be a big bang." Someone else would comment on the strange whistling of a falling bomb that would forebode an explosion. But here, on the stairs in the cellar, there was the most exceptional orderliness. Not one tear, not one nervous movement, only calmness, control, almost apathy.

"It's about time it stopped, it's getting tiresome," someone said and everyone agreed.

At about half past four the bombardments started to die down and Pi and I went upstairs to lie down. My train was supposed to leave at nine in the morning and I had to pack before that, so I did not have much time to sleep. We were already between the sheets on our mattresses on the floor when the all-clear signal sounded.

The next morning I met Brita. She threw some clothes in a suitcase and asked me to take it with me. This was about evacuating things, to save what could be saved, especially clothes that were impossible to buy. We were both convinced that this bombardment wasn't going to be the last. I had the feeling I was abandoning Brita, but thinking sensibly I realized I could not be of much use here. To sweep up the glass pieces was something the maid Siiri could do, and only Brita herself could decide on what clothes to pick out for an evacuation. I was also convinced that if I missed the nine o'clock train it would take a long time for me to leave, as there was going to be a mad rush to get out of town.

Helsinki was a strangely empty town, with shards of glass everywhere. The streetcars did not run, there were no cars and only a few people. But on the way to the station I did not see any of the real devastation.

Outside the station there was a long line out into the street. I was wondering how I was going to get to the platform and went up to a policeman and showed him my ticket. I was allowed to pass the line which consisted of those trying to buy a ticket.

A part of the station house had burned, the windows were gaping with emptiness and blackened. The tin roof was torn up and large pieces were fluttering dangerously in the strong wind. There wasn't a foot's width of ground that wasn't covered in glass pieces. On one of the tracks was a fire damaged train.

I had to wait a long time for my train to roll in. More and more people were gathering, mainly adults, but also mothers with children. The pavement was still not filled to the point of crowding, but for the later trains the lines would grow horribly.

I had to wait one and a half hours. It was cold in the piercing wind. When the train arrived, I got a seat in a freezing wagon with one of the windows smashed. It was boarded up with a piece of plywood and the temperature did go up significantly during the trip.

Pulle had gone hunting to Pargas, west of Helsinki, and heard about the bombardment of Helsinki on the radio. He had decided to return home on Monday, but he took the train via Riihimäki in order to avoid the crowds and all the difficulties at the station in Helsinki.

Up until Riihimäki the trip was moving along as usual, but then he had to change trains. He boarded a different train, which had left Helsinki a few hours earlier. The wagons were full, every single seat was taken. Pulle realized it would be impossible to try to squeeze into a regular passenger compartment and instead jumped up into the conductor's cabin with the dog, shotgun, and backpack. It was full there as well, but not from passengers, but from strollers, laundry baskets, suitcases, bundles, and packages of all kinds. Apart from Pulle there was a poor man in the cabin; whose job it was to throw out the right stuff at each station, a complicated job, when the things were piled up in complete disarray all the way up to the ceiling.

This was not an express train but stopped at every station. At the first stop after Riihimäki the train had to stand much too long. The poor man could not find all the luggage that needed to be off-loaded. Pulle helped him, organized and took over, and with the help of the man the entire wagon was reorganized from top to bottom when the train was rolling again, and at the stations the things were quickly off-loaded.

Just as the train was leaving Herrala Station, a woman came running with a baby under her arm and holding another child by the hand. The train was already rolling, with the big door to the conductor's wagon still open, when the half hysterical mother put the baby down on the floor, even though she was still half hanging outside. Pulle rushed to get a hold of the baby.

I would have wanted to see his face when he stood there with a crying and struggling baby in his arms realizing the mother was not going to make it onto the train. What was he going to do? Was he going to take the child home to Kymmene?

It soon turned out that the woman was from Kuusankoski and was soon united with her baby, everything turned out well.

Helsinki had been targeted with bombardments before, but the city had not seen anything like this air raid, ever. As I had predicted, there was a rush to get out into the country. Everyone, who was somehow able to, got out. This was much easier to arrange when the schools shut their doors for everyone under fifteen, which included those who went to middle school. Only the high school students continued their classes. The authorities encouraged mothers with children to evacuate voluntarily. Later, a mandatory evacuation was probably needed.

Every home was organizing and preparing. Children were placed with family and friends, valuables were packed, rugs were rolled up and sent to the country or put in the cellar. Silver items were put into bank vaults or at least taken out of the city. All of the clothes were sent off, if possible. Furniture was the most difficult to move, as trucks were only available for those whose homes had been bombed and now stood in the streets with what they were able to save out of their belongings. There were many pitiful loads on the way to Åbo going west and to Tavastehus going north.

Brita had arranged everything exceptionally well. Her sister's husband, Åke Wahlroos, was the manager at the Lahtis glass factory. He sent a car full of window glass to cover the most urgent need for windows. Instead of the car returning empty, Brita was able to send her mother and children, and a bunch of things, out of the danger zone. The mother was evacuated to the Wahlroos family in Lahtis and the children to Mustila. Brita stayed in Helsinki with Pi who had turned seventeen. The maid, Siiri, left the city a few days later to help out in Mustila.

The relative calm that had engulfed the city now turned into a restless pressure. There was desperate activity all over the place, not only homes were evacuated, also hospitals, offices, stores, in short, everything that could be moved was moved. A business moved its office to Nystad, another to Jacobstad. The banks sent a large portion of their personnel to work at another location.

When was Helsinki going to be bombarded again? Strange enough, one day after the other passed without anything happening. Pi moved in with Brita, who did not want the girl to sleep alone and maybe not wake up if there was an alarm. Also, the provisional cardboard piece that had been put over the window in her room could not quite keep out the cold.

One day Pi got a sore throat and a high fever and had to stay in bed. She had once before lain in bed with influenza during a bombardment. Brita sent a telegram to my brother-in-law, Tor Aschan, an ear, nose, and throat doctor, who diagnosed her with diphtheria and she immediately had to be taken to the epidemiology hospital by ambulance. She was placed in a room for two on an observation ward, but in the beginning, she stayed in the room by herself.

In the evening the 16th of February, the sirens went off at full blast, and a moment later there were thundering explosions after the bombs hit. A nurse rushed into Pi's room. She had to put a coat over her shoulders and go down into the cellar, which was only halfway below ground level and as such was not a real shelter, but at least it kept possible shrapnel and splitters out.

There were several patients with diphtheria who were sitting or lying down on stretchers or some sort of beds. The room was overcrowded, and Pi only got an uncomfortable place to sit. The patients were seriously ill, screaming piercing shrills while the bombs were raining over the city for almost ten hours.

Pi was not afraid, she had become a fatalist. But she was cold, she only had a nightgown under her coat and a pair of knee high socks. She did not have the time to get any more clothes on. Strange enough, she did not get a cold, and a few days later she was able to be discharged from the hospital. It turned out she did not even have diphtheria!

She returned to Albert Street 44, but she was tired and spent, her heart was bothering her, and her knees gave out. She, again, had to stay in bed.

The second bigger bombardment caused more casualties and greater material damage than the previous one. In one shelter the air ran out and in another there was a sewer breakage and people were standing up to their knees in unsanitary water. A third shelter suffered a direct hit.

That same evening, I was at the Lotta management meeting in Kymmene. When I walked home I could see the flame-lit sky as Helsinki was bombarded. I knew that my girl was there.

There were new regulations for the evacuation of Helsinki. All schools were shut down, including Pi's school. The children were allowed to continue their studies in any other school in the entire country. In the spring, they were to be advanced a grade as long as the teachers at their remote school thought they had met the requirements. The children were also able to study privately or send tests directly to their teachers.

Brita's children were in the same situation as many others from the capital who had to relocate to a place with a school. Brita did not, by any means, want to add to the "invasion" of Mustila by sending her boys there with a home teacher. Pulle and I, therefore, offered a home for Willy and Peter, and Tigerstedt's son, Axel, with us in Kymmene. Ulla was to stay with our neighbors the Cedercreutzs.

Standing Left to Right:
Trolle, Axel, Willy
Sitting: Peter

We rearranged the furniture a little for the children, and the boys became a source of joy for us although they sometimes also caused some trouble. There were times when Siiri cried and poor Ulla's nerves were totally spent.

On the 20th of February, Pi came home still sick and pale. She stayed in the guest room, which now served as her and Mi's room. That is, if Mi ever was able to come home on leave.

On the 26th of February, Helsinki was bombarded for the third time in the same month. This time the enemy held the inhabitants of the city under unbearable suspense for twelve hours straight. On the 6th of February, about two hundred planes had dropped their load over the city, on the 16th, there were about four hundred planes and now, the 26th, from six to seven hundred planes. They flew over their target in one wave after the other.

The city's fire brigades were overwhelmed. The brigades from nearby towns were immediately sent into action, but not even that was enough. Firemen from towns over 150 km (93 miles) away were called in, but in spite of this, it was impossible to put out all the fires quickly. Pulle's cousin, Walter Ehrström, had a direct hit on his home. Just about everything was destroyed.

After the night of bombings my sister, Greta, called. Her home had not suffered any hits, but the windows and doors had been blown inside and their frames had been torn out. The house was uninhabitable. She had temporarily stayed with an acquaintance and asked if I could let her stay with us. Of course, I could, even though our house was already overcrowded.

We had two rooms for the maids. Our maid, Veera, stayed in one of the rooms, Siiri in the other. I asked the girls to move together, after which Axel and Trolle moved to Siiri's room. That way Pi moved back into her own room and the guest room was reserved for Greta.

Now I was only waiting for Caja to announce her arrival. She was still staying in Kotka, which was like living in an inferno. Helsinki had had three air raids in February of 1944 that defied all descriptions. The inhabitants had been forced to sit in shelters for hours. The Helsinki residents had seen a lot during the war, but those in Kotka had seen more. There were often German war and transport vessels in the harbor, which led to the severe attacks.

The 29th of February president Svinhuvud died. The country's great son did not have to see the end of 1944.

THE INGERMANLANDERS ARE ARRIVING

Greta's daughter, Margaretha (Tippan), had finished her nursing course and got one week of leave before starting her commission at a Mänttä war hospital. She had no home to travel to for her leave, and since Greta was staying with us, it was only natural that Tippan come to Kymmene. A few days after her arrival her brother, Paul, arrived with their father Verner Gustafsson. Paul only stayed that afternoon, but later he came to stay a few days. He had become a tall, dark boy, happy and open minded. He was joking with Trolle, who with childish admiration followed him like a puppy. Paul had, for some time, been a junior officer in the air defense artillery and had spent time at the front.

On March the 12th Pi had to be back in Helsinki, she was to have her first oral test as part of her National Final Exams. She did not exactly have a calm work environment. She had announced a long time ago that as soon as she turned seventeen she was going to become a Lotta. This was the age limit between a girl-Lotta and an adult Lotta.

In the middle of February's unrest, she called one day to ask for permission to do some on-call work at a telephone center, night work, which her Lotta manager had offered her. I knew how eager she was, so I gave her my permission, something Pulle could not grasp. He thought she was putting all of her finals at risk. Pi subsequently realized herself that she couldn't possibly handle the job. Shortly after that she became ill.

All her oral exams went well, and when she came home she had with her a friend, Brita Stark, the same girl who sat with us in the shelter on Albert Street on February the 6th.

Caja came to us off and on when Pi's bed was available, and her son Bubi came to visit his family. Pulle and I were happy we could be of use, even if it sometimes was quite tiresome.

For many years I had hoped to one day be able to take part in a Lotta course, so I signed up for one. Pulle, of course, was right when he thought it would all be too much for me. My strength, after all, was not what it had been before my operation. I often felt silly sitting on a school bench with Lottas in their twenties. It was torturous for me to have to be there at a certain time, to stand up when I answered a question, to listen to snubbing from those ranked above you, in short, to feel like I was a little school girl.

But I had enough ambition and discipline to realize the rules had to be the same for everyone. A Lotta course was a good upbringing but was more suitable for a young girl than for a forty-one-year-old board member of the Lotta corps. After six weeks I did my written exam and received the white course star.

The Finnish state had received the people from Ingermanland when the Germans had evacuated and placed them in camps. Now, the camps could no longer be maintained, and the immigrants were placed in various places across the country. The local community authorities were to arrange lodging and provisions for them, which, in part, became a job for the Lotta organization.

But where were all the Ingermanlanders going to be placed? It was thought that mainly the big estates and farms would receive them and give them food and a roof over their heads. Those capable of working were allowed to work for a fair salary.

My contribution started with visiting the labor authorities in Helsinki to get information on how many and what kind of persons could be placed in the already densely populated Kuusankoski. I got a list of some suitable families. Among those able to work was an old lady who knew how to spin.

At home, I contacted the community, the chief of the workforce, the mill's social director, a few farms and estates, as well as my Lotta helpers. I got three families placed and was very happy, although none of the families were exactly what the farms or estates wanted. Everyone was hoping for young and agile men while I, for the most part, could only offer women, older men, and children. There was only one man at a suitable age on the list.

After a job well done I contacted Helsinki by phone, but got the surprising report that all "my" families, except for the spinning lady, had been promised to another community! I was supposed to get a new list. I got all wound up and explained that the families already had lodging and work. I could not guarantee that new families would be just as well received.

I was informed that the department had given the orders to dissolve the camps and twenty-seven people were going to be sent to me on March the 27th. I went into panic and wondered what would happen if we did not get them placed.

"They are coming March 27th," was the answer. "It is your job to see that they are taken care of!"

What should I do? I had to start the whole job over again. But I managed, much because of an excellent Lotta helper, who knew the people on the farms. She was able to coax and talk them into it.

On the 27th of March, I stood on the platform at the Kouvola station and received "my" Ingermanlanders. We nearly had to turn over heaven and earth for them. There was a mother of around thirty-five (she looked like at least fifty) with three boys, the oldest being thirteen. Then there was an old woman and her fifteen-year-old granddaughter, and a twenty-nine-year-old woman with a five-year-old daughter.

No identification markers were needed, I could have picked them out among hundreds of people and could have said that they all are from Ingermanland. They were dressed the way I remembered Russian women when I was there as a child. They had a shawl wrapped around their heads and a short, patched coat over a long, wide skirt and felt boots on their feet.

They had loads of bundles, and they explained that their bedding was coming later as luggage. I was able to understand the old woman the best. She spoke Finnish that was pretty similar to the language I had heard in Karelia, but the mother of the three boys had a typical East Karelia accent. The younger woman spoke Russian and also some German.

We took the train to Kuusankoski, where two farmers were waiting. I first took the mother with her three boys to the company mess hall for the workers and then to a traveler's lodge.

The old woman was happy the entire time, friendly and composed. Her granddaughter looked like a scared duckling. The twenty-nine-year-old woman was quiet and closed. The poor mother with the boys was overly talkative up until I placed her in the simple traveler's lodge, then she burst out crying. She was upset about all the trouble she was causing me and refused to live in such a "fine" room. But she did not want the boys to stay in a separate room by themselves, and she did not calm down until the hostess suggested a primitive small space for all four together.

I often had difficulty finding the right words and felt embarrassed. As a Lotta it had become much easier for me to find things to talk about, but this time there was nothing. The tears of the Ingermanland woman got to me, I understood that she was missing home.

The next day I was to accompany them to the train to send them on to Voikka, where they were to meet a transition Lotta at the station, as planned, who then was going to take them to a village near the factory there.

I went to the traveler's lodge in the morning and became desperate when I found that all of them had left. Where could they have gone? They did not have the right to move about wherever they wanted without police permission, for example, they were not allowed to travel to Kouvola. But it turned out they had just gone to the mess hall to have breakfast. The mother was very happy to hear that she was able to travel that same day with her boys. During our long walk from the traveler's lodge on the Kymmene side of the river, over the bridge, to the Kuusankoski side, she kept asking questions. The factory had left an impression on her. The oldest boy used a kick board, on which the largest of their bundles was placed. He had never experienced anything so much fun. All the boys were well behaved and perfectly brought up.

Before we went to the train, I took them to a police station to report them. I noticed that they were ill at ease, but I had to stick to the regulations.

I thought I was going to get some rest from "my" Ingermanlanders. But the owner of one of the farms called and was very upset. He said he had been deceived. The newly arrived woman in his house only spoke Russian, cried all the time and did nothing, would not even wash her plate after eating. I asked him, if despite this, he could keep her for at least a while. I explained to him that I did not have the authority to move her without first talking to the head of the labor department. The farmer got mad. What a mess, he thought, and the situation got unbearable. I managed to get her a job in a garden owned by the company. She was able to get lodging with an elderly, quiet lady, who owned a drug store. She gave up her summer cottage, which was not far from the mill. A few other persons were already staying there, all of them for free. The Ingermanland woman was to get firewood herself. I organized that for her. Despite all this, she was extremely rude to those staying in the same house because they would not engage themselves in her sad fate.

My first visit in her new environment still went fairly well. We spoke German as far as her vocabulary would take it. Then we used our hands for help. She kept her things nice and tidy and her dress was to the utmost Spartan, whole and clean.

One day I asked a company official's wife, who was born in Russia, to come with me. With her Russian charm, she managed to soften the woman somewhat, but she was still reserved. It turned out her husband, who was Estonian, was imprisoned. We could not figure out if he had been imprisoned by the Russians or the Germans.

I wanted to know to which denomination she belonged and started to apologize for not having an orthodox church in Kuusankoski. She answered that she did not believe herself to belong to any faith. Her little girl was happily skipping around in the cottage while we were talking, completely oblivious to her mother's and her own tragedy.

At seven o'clock the next morning the mother was supposed to be at work in the garden. When we asked what we should do with the girl while she was at work, she answered that she would lock her up. We couldn't possibly agree to that, but she resolutely turned down all our objections and said that the girl was used to being by herself as long as she had food.

A few days later, one of the other guests in the cottage had surprised the girl when she was playing with matches. This led to a change in the rules. The nice lady who owned the cottage took care of the girl while the mother was away and let her stay in the store, dressed her when she went out to play, and gave her one meal a day.

One could have thought that the mother would have felt grateful for all this kindness, but no, the opposite, she was hurt. I made a visit to the drug store and spoke to the owner. I expressed my dislike of the ungrateful and rude woman.

"She is a devoted communist, maybe that is the problem," the drug store owner said. "She is not happy here."

I was surprised, but the lady continued: "But that is human. After all she has never experienced anything else, how could she not be a communist? That she is rude to everyone could also be caused by her nerves shutting down. How would we feel in her position, being transported to a foreign land and having to live by yourself, without her family with the exception of her little girl, with whom she cannot reason?"

I stood still for a while and then said:

"Then I can understand that she dislikes me the most, as I always visit her in my uniform. I want them to know that I am coming to see them as a contact Lotta, not as a private person. I have, through a translator, explained to them that they can turn to me with their problems, it is part of my job and my responsibility to help them the best I can. Can you let me know if she needs any help? Everything should be arranged in terms of her job and livelihood, support, firewood, grocery ration cards, and lodging, which you have been so kind to provide her with."

She promised to keep me informed. I left completely convinced that I had succeeded in arranging everything materialistically, but had failed on the pure human and emotional level. I had surely sounded both cold and arrogant. But I could not have acted differently, even if I now felt numb inside. There were others who hereafter took care of this matter.

The Ingermanland woman never came to me, and I was never called for either.

April 25th the community held a party for the people from Ingermanland, to which I was forced to go. Mi had been at home on leave and was going back to Aunus that same evening, and I wanted to be with her. On top of that, the needle workshop had a meeting in the morning. I wanted to miss this meeting, but because my sister, Greta, (the opera singer) was going to sing for the ladies, I had to go to accompany her on the piano and to show her that we were grateful for her coming out to sing for us. Her song was appreciated by everyone, but I felt like screaming out that I wanted to be at home for my girl's last day of leave and say it the way another Lotta once said it:

"Now my boy is at home from the front, I refuse to come to the board meeting, and I have the right to do so. I don't know when, where, or if I will see him again, he comes first."

Mi had left everything and sacrificed the best years of her youth. She never complained, but I had a feeling that I was hurting her. Eine Rhen was also at the celebration and could see that I was suffering. When there was a brake in the program she said:

"Go now, go now, immediately!"

I was hesitant, but I left. Or better said, I half-ran the long way to the gates of the club. When I was only a few steps from the train, which had stopped at the end of the Kouvola-Kymmene factory track, it whistled and started. Someone saw me running and thought I wanted to get on the train and stopped the train headed east with Mi on board. Hence, I was able to hug Mi one more time.

LADIES STOCKINGS AND WHEAT FLOUR

Out in the world the war kept raging. The papers had showy headlines of the furious bombardments of Berlin, where entire blocks were annihilated. Here at home we lived in a constant state of uncertainty. What would the rejected peace agreements mean for us?

Despite the gloomy future outlook, people had the intractable desire to entertain themselves the best they could. Of course, it was different in Kymmene than, for example, Helsinki or Kotka. In our neck of the woods our social life prospered the way it hadn't for years. We were regularly invited to black tie dinners and even arranged a very successful one ourselves. It was exciting to take out the old evening dress from the closet, old-fashioned of course, but so what? During the parties there was only meaningless chatter. There was an unwritten rule not to talk politics, but to only have fun. Just a few years ago one had talked about the war forever, dabbled in politics, discussed and argued, back and forth.

The socializing had spread all the way to the youngest generation. Trolle and his friends went to the children's ball every Saturday. Once we organized one of these little events for thirty kids. I ordered seventy-five bottles of lemonade, a terrible concoction sweetened with saccharine, but it was appreciated. Last, we served ice cream and tea with simple bread. The boys thought it was a grand party. There was enthusiastic dancing up until midnight, when the final waltz was played on our rickety old gramophone and the young guests started to go home.

It upset the minds of the adults that, for them, it was still forbidden to dance. For me, personally, it was an annoyance. I did not belong to those who openly condemned dancing, but I was critical. I did not want to be demonstrative during our private dinner parties, so I went for a swing or two, even if it did not please me.

But when dancing was resumed at the Club my reaction was even stronger. One evening I did join them, but the whole time, my conscience was eating at me: the officials at the mill should set an example for the workers.

In April the needle workshop held its annual children's party. It was a success and the income was excellent. At one of the preceding meetings I had brought up the question of dancing. What did the ladies think, should we allow dancing later in the evening or not? Some thought it would be alright, I was hesitant myself and explained that we were sitting in a glasshouse. Evil tongues could say that the children's party was nothing but camouflage in order for the Kymmene residents to have some fun. No one opposed, so I called the Club's chairman, Baron Curt Cedercreutz, and suggested that there should be no dancing after the children's party. He agreed to the suggestion.

When the children had gone home and the adults were sitting around small tables, eating supper, someone suggested that we should do some dancing. I referred to the fact that it had been forbidden, but after I had left the place, some of the youngsters from the office started up the gramophone and there was dancing anyway. It hurt when I heard about it. I thought they behaved irresponsibly.

While I, in Kymmene, from time to time could dress up in an evening gown, put on some lipstick and go out to have some fun, Mi's life at the front in

Aunus was, for the most part, moving along in gloominess.

Her sleeping quarters had a bumpy straw mattress underneath a number of blankets. On top was her favorite Christmas present, a sheep's wool fur coat which Pulle had bought through an advertisement. It was cold in the room when she got out of bed, so she pulled on the fur coat before getting the fire going in the stove. The wood was wet, it sizzled and spat. Mi sighed, shivered and rubbed her hands. Finally, the fire would start to burn.

It was warmer in the sauna. There, the Lottas would bathe.

The officers were to be entertained and given food and surrogate coffee. But this activity was more for the higher-ranking bigger fish, to whom Marga's daughter, Margaretha, belonged. The only thing that bothered Mi was the pickiness of the manager. She realized it was jealousy that affected his behavior as her social status was above his. For the same reason the manager hated Margaretha and made life miserable for her as well. At the front, one would have hoped, there was a different attitude.

Rats, that had been rude enough to invade the house, were supposed to be eradicated. They had become so impudent that they would shamelessly snatch something eatable right in front of the inhabitants. During the night, it happened that they would get tangled up in the Lotta's hair curlers.

Poison was put out everywhere so efficiently that it resulted in a massive death toll, but it also caused an unbelievable stench. When brother-in-law Nisse went to visit Mi and Margaretha, he could not stand the smell in their lodging. In this stinking house the Lottas had to live and work, there was no other option, where were they supposed to go?

With her humor Mi could give her experiences a special touch in her letters. For example the following, about her first visit with her new friends from Karelia, Sandra and Masa:

"In both rooms there were enormous brick walls and in one of them a small whole had been cut out for a stove, but it was so low down that it couldn't possibly be comfortable cooking on it. It was very neat and clean, white bed covers with a broad lace edge, as well as two piles with several pillows stacked high on each bed. There were photographs on the walls in oval frames, the kind that were used around 1915 for engagement photos, and of course samovars, even two of them. When we left, the other Lotta showed us a hole in the entrance hall. That was the toilet. One cannot say that these people would be used to luxury."

In another letter she wrote:

"Last Thursday, Maundy Thursday, we were all invited to Masa's place, alias Maria Bogdanova, for morning coffee. It was truly an experience of its own. We sat on raggedy chairs and had to eat massive amounts of all kinds of bread and pies and drink one glass of surrogate after the other. Then she played the gramophone for us, or truthfully, the gramophone rattled and then the unavoidable photographs came out here as well. And what photographs!"

Mi customarily sent most of her sugar ration home, which was a lot more for someone in the military or a Lotta on duty than for the civilians. In return I tried to, as I had done before, arrange small packages with coffee cakes, which she could enjoy.

This sending of packages to loved ones at the front had become a duty for the Finnish people, a true ritual. The people living in the countryside could allow themselves more extravagance in this regard. The city residents could not give up much as the rations did not go very far, and the hoarding was both difficult and expensive. But no matter how simple these packages were, they were received with joy, and it was considered part of good comradeship to share some of their contents with the other soldiers in the dug-out. It also happened that people sent packages to the "Unknown Soldier" and then received touching thank you notes in return.

For us, the food situation had improved with Axel Tigerstedt moving in. His parents were always quick to help.

When it came to clothing, an odd exchange trade was taking place. For example, one could advertise in the paper for lady's stockings in exchange for wheat flour. What was remarkable was the candor of the people. One was not concerned with being accused of trading on the black market, it seemed. There were the most curious advertisements. A puppy could be offered in exchange for cigarettes.

While Mi was living her simple Lotta life, Pi was studying for her final exams. The poor seniors in Helsinki were not able to take their written tests in their own schools. Pi's class wrote them at the Esbo Defense Corps House outside Helsinki.

Strangely enough, Helsinki had not been under any further bombardments. Nothing of much importance was happening on the home front. Out on the frontlines the troops were lying in their positions, and the soldiers had plenty of time to engage in woodwork and crafting jewelry in their dug-outs. The whole country was waiting and holding its breath in suspense.

Life in the capital slowly started to go back to the old normal. People returned home, as long as they still had a home to return to. If not, they stayed with family or friends. The opera opened its doors again and Greta, who was employed there as a mezzo soprano, had to leave us. I was sorry to see her go, as I had enjoyed it tremendously to have her around. She did not want to go herself at all since she couldn't live in her home anymore, so she had to stay with one of her friends.

Our four wild boys in Kymmene were all little personalities. Adults don't always understand children, and I probably made many mistakes during the spring, but I hope that all four will one day know that I had their best interest in mind.

The Koskull boys had a passion for collecting junk; old rusty nails, pieces of rubber hoses, screw-nuts, bolts, glass pipes, mercury, anything was good enough. They got these precious items partly from the cellulose factory where their father had been the manager. Willy and Peter were met with kindness, especially by one of the older office workers who presented them with trash of various kinds.

Pulle was not pleased about this collecting mania. It was strictly forbidden to give away anything of the factory's property, no matter how worthless it may have seemed. It was wartime, after all, and there was a shortage of everything. He especially did not like the electric stuff, copper wiring, and the mercury, that the boys had gotten hold of. He tried to calmly and sensibly talk some sense into them, sometimes he scolded them, but nothing helped. He told them to take back everything they had snatched. They may have done so, but they probably got something else for it. One time they swiped calcium carbide and made a lamp out of an old tin can and lit it up, which caused it to explode. It all luckily took place outdoors and no one got hurt.

Axel had a keen interest in chemistry. He collected the most peculiar glass test tubes and had bottles with mysterious concoctions. But when he started his laboratory activities I did not want to take the risk to see him, or any of the other boys, get hurt.

To their disappointment, they had to leave the laboratory in Kymmene. In Mustila, on the other hand, where they sometimes went over the holidays with Axel, it was open season. Axel's parents had more understanding for their interest in chemistry. In Kymmene they at least had an outlet for their energy with electric experiments, which were probably not quite as great a fire hazard. I may not have been consistent, but I was less worried about all the lines, plugs, and wires, than about the chemical mixtures, despite the fact that the wall switches burned out and it occasionally caused a short circuit.

The fact remained that the Koskull boys carefully hid items, which we found in their room when they left for home the last day in May. There was a trash basket full of strange toys, plus a bottle that contained a small amount of wine. Not only Pulle and I, but everyone that heard about the bottle was thoroughly amused. Such rascals!

When it comes to the volunteer work the boys felt right at home. There was a book in which information was entered about how much each one had collected of various materials. They gathered rags of both cotton and wool, pine cones, paper waste, and bottles. They were rewarded with either a bronze, silver, or gold button. Trolle received the silver button.

Peter was fabulously diligent collecting bottles and rags. Shamelessly, he called up all the ladies at the factory.

"This is Peter Koskull from the Troils, does the lady have bottles or rags?"

He usually got a satisfactory answer, after which he resolutely took his big brother to help him haul the bottles and rags home. He systematically went from door to door and asked complete strangers if they had anything to give away. Peter and Willy gathered four hundred bottles as well as a whole lot of rags and old newspapers, which were bundled up. After a few days the Koskull's room was filled to the rim with junk. There was a huge box with bottles on the kitchen steps, and beside it a cardboard box with broken glass pieces and broken off bottle necks. When the bottles were washed the water went all over the kitchen sink, the table, and floor, over the entire kitchen.

Axel and Trolle took care of things in a different way. They were not as eager, but still very diligent, and they had the patience to complete their projects. Taking Willy's and Peter's bottles to the collection center became terribly hard work for me. At that point it wasn't fun anymore.

On June 1st Pi started a Lotta course. She was a member at the Lotta Svärd Drumsö 27 location and wanted to take the course so she could complete her mandatory work order as a full-fledged Lotta. The last two summers she had not enjoyed doing her work at home, and her friends even claimed that she had gotten off easier that way. Pi really did work her share, and at the same time we were able to account for her poor health, which was crucial.

Pi's manager surprisingly sent her to a course held in the Finnish language in Kouvola, even though she came from a completely Swedish-speaking department. It was also an odd coincidence that she was sent to a place so close to Kymmene. She had a good time with her teachers and friends, but had a hard time physically getting through the program. She especially had difficulty standing during the morning and evening prayers. In the end, the teachers and Pi herself realized that she could not go on like that without a few days of leave.

I took her to Dr. Tarkianen's office. She explained that her heart had been strained. She was not going to be allowed to do any Lotta work for two months and was released from her Lotta duties. She was extremely disappointed. But there was nothing one could do, the experiences during the spring had been too strenuous for her health.

THE BOLSHEVIKS ARE COMING

Out in the world there had been several important events. The Allied Forces had thrown themselves over Italy, and the Germans were forced to retreat. On the 4th of June, the British marched into Rome and the following day the Italian King Victor Emmanuel abdicated. The 6th of June the British and the Americans started the invasion of Normandy.

Early in the morning the 9th of June, Pulle and I woke up from the shaking of the windows. First, we did not know what it was, but we soon learned that there were hard battles on the Isthmus of Karelia and that it was the cannon fire that caused our windows to shake.

On Saturday the 10th of June, we drove to the country as usual and returned in the evening the next day. When we stepped out of our car Kurt Cedercreutz met us on the porch. He looked very worried.

"Have you heard anything new?" Pulle asked.

"There has been a break through on the Isthmus, we will see what the papers are saying."

I was overcome with an uncomfortable feeling, but I wanted to hold it off, hoping it was just something temporary.

"The Russians have started a General Offensive on the Isthmus of Karelia," it said in a bold, black print in the Swedish-language newspaper, Hufvudstadsbladet (The Capital Paper). The article continued:

"Twenty-Four Russian planes were gunned down and ten armored vehicles were destroyed. The official report June 6, 1944: On the Isthmus of Karelia the enemy started a general offensive early in the morning with powerful artillery fire and a strong air force. The offensive's various locations were stopped, with the exception of a few small limited breakthroughs. The enemy suffered significant losses in casualties and more than ten armored vehicles had been destroyed. Our fighter planes and air defense shot down a total of twenty-four enemy planes. The battle continues.

In other parts of the front there is patrolling activity."

This is how the sad tale started on the Isthmus of Karelia. The events followed one after the other. Our troops had to give up their positions head over heels, which they so heroically had tried to maintain. Retreat was the only option against an overwhelming force.

A large portion of the civilian population had gone back to their homes on the isthmus during the last two years and had started to rebuild what had been demolished. Now, they had to, for the second time, flee toward the north and west. They were people of all ages, women, children and elderly. There were farmers who had had time to put the horse in front of a cart and take with them the bare essentials like food and clothing, others drove their livestock in front of them through the woods and fields. There was a story about a mother who was in the sauna when she suddenly saw the enemy run into the yard. The woman fled into the woods, but her small children remained in the house by themselves, and she was beside herself with grief and frustration.

What the army had to endure during these weeks on the Isthmus of Karelia no one who has not actually been there can describe. It was hell on earth! Our troops did not have the manpower, and reinforcements were called in from other fronts. But it seemed nothing would help. The number of obituaries in the papers were increasing at an alarming rate. On the 16th of June, the news came that Holger's son, Werner, had been killed. Poor little Marianne and poor Holger!

Werner

Lasse was going to turn fifty-years-old and invited us to the party, which was to be held close to Helsinki. Were we, again, going to be in the same situation as three years earlier when Lasse and Lisa celebrated their wedding? We realized that we could not go, and soon after we got word that the party had been cancelled.

The canon fire could be heard day and night. We were afraid to turn on the radio or open the newspaper, afraid to constantly hear or read about new Russian advances. If the battle had come to a halt one day, one was relieved and hopeful, only to be met with bad news the next day.

Viborg had to be evacuated quickly. For most of the city's residents, the departure was so sudden that they were not able to take more than they were able to carry.

The War Hospital #13 in Viborg again was forced to pick up its property rapidly and return to

Kymmene, where it had previously functioned almost three years earlier. Mi had, as a young Lotta, worked at the hospital in Viborg in 1941.

It was best to just work and continue working, the fear did not let up. Most of all, a desperate thought was churning inside me: Where was Mi now? There was at least a dreadful relief in the fact that she did have her little revolver. She was not going to give herself up alive. It was all so atrocious.

When we came home on Sunday the 18th from Mustaniemi, we were again met by alarming news: the floodgates were about to burst open. Was nothing going to stop the approaching enemy?

Marianne and Curt Cedercreutz came to visit us. They had stayed up all night with the Horellis and decided that Marianne, Eva Horelli, and Pian Gripenberg would flee to Sweden with their children. We wished Marianne a good journey and wondered when we were going to see her again.

Brita called from Lahtis where she was visiting her daughter, Ulla. Willy and Peter had, after a few weeks in Mustila, traveled to Artsjö, where Åke Wahlroos had rented a villa for his family. Brita said she was also going to take Ulla and the boys up north and from there over to Sweden. Ulla was going to leave her mandatory work assignment in Lojo.

Brita wanted to take Trolle with her. Up until this day I had been able to keep my spirits up, but now I was broken. I did not think the situation was so serious that it would be necessary to send Trolle away. Lisbeth Tigerstedt had tried to talk me into letting the boys come to Mustila, but we did not want to put such a great burden on her shoulders. She had her own children and other's children, adult evacuees, and the estate staff to take care of.

We decided that Trolle should travel with Brita to Kemi. There, he would wait for his passport in order to be allowed into Sweden. Pulle sent a telegram to Wapnö Castle and asked for an invitation for the boy. This was necessary for the passport formalities. We did not have any Swedish currency and had to ask the Staels to also pay for his trip on the Swedish side from Haparanda to Halmstad.

The departure day was a nightmare. The same day Viborg was lost. The tidal wave passed over the Isthmus. If this flood could not be stopped, we did not have much time before we would have to leave our homes.

Brita was surprisingly calm when she arrived. On the phone she had sounded agitated. Now it was she who had to console me, I had completely broken apart. But I had to take care of the practical things. In the last minute I washed, patched and packed Trolle's things. He sat in his room, quiet and sad, with his beloved saloon rifle, which was a gift from Pulle. He slowly stroked the rifle, carefully packed it up and put it aside. I couldn't stand it, I had to leave the room. But then I went in again, took the boy into my arms even though he was twelve-years-old. We sat quietly for a while and then talked about things maybe getting back to normal one day. He had to be brave, then things would turn out well for him in Sweden.

In the evening Pulle came to the idea to let Trolle take the rifle with him to Sweden, at least try to get it through customs. The boy was happy with the suggestion. The next morning he left. He was calm, but I had to fight desperately to keep my composure. Pulle stood on the porch and imprinted the picture of his boy onto his retina. He thought that this may be that last time that he would see his son.

After Trolle left, I packed a few clothes and our most valuable small things. Everything was to be taken to Mustaniemi, which, just like during the Winter War, again became the storage place for our, and our closest friends', personal belongings. There hung tail coats, dinner jackets, coats and dresses of all sizes. There were shoes, rugs, paintings, an old cabinet from my family home, and loads of little things we had scratched together.

One morning we also received the announcement that Pulle's cousin Walter's son had been killed. It had taken a long time before his remains could be found.

It was the second tragedy for Walter and his wife Walborg. First, they'd lost their home and now their older son. Earlier, I had visited Walborg when I went to Pi's graduation. She and Walter were, at the time, staying with Walter's father, Otto, and the sister Kersti. Walborg was tremendous, calm and composed, even though she had just lost her entire home.

"The main thing is that the boys are alive," she said. "The home is, after all, just things."

Despite her grief Walborg soon continued her charity work. She had, for years, transported children back and forth between Finland and Sweden. This work is what she absolutely needed now. The worry about their younger son would otherwise have become a constant pain.

On June the 23rd, the Russian troops invaded Aunus. The next day the thermometer showed 8° C (46° F), there was a full storm and it was raining cats and dogs. Lately, we had had beautiful summer weather and we were happy the evacuated Karelians out on the roads did not have to freeze. But now they were going to be drenched in this horrible weather.

The German Secretary of State von Rippentropp visited Helsinki. German help was going to be sent to the Isthmus of Karelia. The help was mainly going to be in the form of air support. If it was going to have any significant effect on the outcome of the war was impossible to predict. Pulle and I were pessimists, but there were also those who thought now suddenly everything was going to turn around. It all depended on where one lived. During the entire war, we, who lived in the East, had seen everything from a more serious perspective.

Despite the fact that the papers had urged people not to travel more than absolutely necessary, in order to give room to the evacuated, the trains were filled with vacationers. The suggestion to cancel the midsummer holiday travel was ignored. Only from Helsinki about ten thousand people left.

Before the trip, Brita called and said her brother-in-law had changed his mind. Based on the situation at the front, he thought his boys did not have to travel. Pulle could not comprehend this. Our positions at the front did hold for a few days, and since Viborg had already been lost the situation had come to a standstill. But no one could know if this meant a definitive halt to the Russian advances. Had they stopped because the resistance had gotten tougher or were they just biding their time only to again throw in their giant forces? Then, all dams may brake and the flood could spread all over the country.

Pulle was of the opinion that Brita should continue toward the north, and then suddenly her brother-in-law, Wahlroos, changed his mind again and his boys were allowed to go along.

The mood between Wahlroos and Pulle was getting strained due to the change in the decisions. For us it was important that Trolle got to the Swedish border. If it really came down to it, one could even just ignore the passport issue. There was always a way to get out of the country. Massive amounts of deserters had reached Sweden in open boats over the Gulf of Bothnia. There were surely others who had done the same thing when it was difficult to get passports for anyone but mothers with children born after 1933. Trolle's passport had also once been denied on the same grounds, he was born in 1931.

After a long and tiresome trip, Brita and the children arrived in Kemi. But when they looked up the family they were to stay with, only Brita was asked to come in. The children had to wait outside and were taken to a children's crib, where they had to sleep on sawdust mattresses on the floor, even though the family had a large villa at their disposal without any other evacuees accommodated. Ulla was insulted deep into her soul.

The woman in the house claimed it was not necessary to send the children to Sweden.

"I was just at a coffee get-together," she said. "There was a lady there who said she could not comprehend this rushing over to Sweden. Of course, there is room for our children in Finland."

"Really," said the always quick to answer Brita. "How many children would the lady be willing to take in?"

The woman was at a loss for words and a little embarrassed. She did not have any evacuees and had no intention of housing any either. Luckily, Trolle was too childish to understand how unwelcome the poor children were. But he did suffer from the bad food and the children's crib's unfriendly supervisor who scolded the children.

The children, luckily, had an abundance of bread coupons. Trolle's June card had not been touched and I had, on top of that, given him my own card. We had done the same with the butter rations. Otherwise, things could have been really bad.

And so, the days crawled ahead in the wait for the passports.

On the 25th of June, I started packing the family's most necessary clothing, dearest memorabilia, and other little things into big boxes that were still left in Kymmene. I also packed some kitchen utensils, one of Mi's table sets, a few coffee cups, sheets and towels, etc. The things were sent to Pulle's cousin, inspector Erik Ehrström, in Kristinestad, which is located between Vasa and Åbo on the West Coast. So far, there was no mandatory evacuation, but the company and the community were working desperately to get everything organized for all eventualities. The office was to be evacuated to Högfors and giant boxes with office materials were sent there. The factories were to send away machine parts, straps, etc. The Kymmene residents were to be sent to Närpes in Ostrobothnia, not far from Kristinestad. It was a strange coincidence, we did not know this when we contacted Erik and Edith Ehrström.

Pi and I were preparing to go to the Ehrströms in Kristinestad as the first leg of our journey. Then we were going to get an apartment unless we had to go all the way across to Sweden. The last option was very unlikely and would only be considered in an emergency.

Pulle was going to join the office in Högfors. Trolle was hopefully going to be doing well in Wapnö Castle. But how was Mi going to get home? And, her winter and other clothes were packed up. We were hoping to get in contact with her from the other side of the Gulf of Bothnia in Sweden, if that was where we were going to end up. Even Pulle would be able to join us there. The possibility of having to become an evacuee was not appealing, and deep inside I had the feeling that I would never have to become one. I was hoping that at least Pi and Trolle were going to be saved. When it came to Pulle, myself, and Mi, I had very little hope.

This was all, of course, just speculation, but the people of Karelia, west of Viborg, already had to leave their properties and land. The trains were overcrowded. At the stations, Lottas were serving food to those fleeing. If the enemy was going to continue toward the west, we would also have to get going soon.

Pi was a fatalist and the calmest of us all. She almost seemed not to care. But she could be irritated about small things, which was a sign that her nerves were not alright. But she actually thought that she felt healthier now.

Pi and I had the most peculiar conversations with each other. We spoke about the future. Could it possibly happen that we would soon be without a home and never see Kymmene again? If there ever was peace, where would the border go?

Sometimes, I thought about composing a tango. Since some popular music composers had been able to get their creations published, why should I not try? But nothing came of that. Instead, I focused on sewing boys' shirts, which could make some money. It was a big relief that Pi had become a "student" (one who had passed the National High School Final Exams) and as such would get a job or get by with giving private lessons.

Pi in her Student Cap

In my mind, I could see myself in an apartment with one room and a kitchen in Kristinestad, on the West Coast of Finland. Well, why couldn't one become happy in Kristinestad as well, under simple conditions? Then, Trolle might be able to come home again. The main thing was to be able to live in peace. Again, I got the feeling that only Pi and Trolle were going to have a life after the war. But I realized that my speculations were caused by my nerves being on edge, too much anguish, too much restlessness.

Worst was my frustration over the fact that Mi had not contacted us. We had only heard about her through Margaretha, who called from Helsinki and let us know that the Lottas had left Aunus, but it did not answer the question about where the girl was now. Margaretha had been granted leave just before the Russian invasion of the Isthmus. Now she was under orders from the Lotta district not to return to Aunus.

Pulle's brother-in-law, Verner Gustafson, was able to tell us that Mi was in Pitkäranta on the northern coast of Lake Ladoga, about 20 kilometers (12 mi) from the 1939 border. On the 27th of June, we received the first sign of life from her.

"2579/5 Kpk.
20.6.44

Dear Ma!

The birds will know when you will get this letter, hopefully it will not be lost. So, one ended up in an entirely different place. I have a Lotta from the "Border Office" as company. The work is completely different than before, even though this is still office work. Yesterday we moved over to this troop installation. But I don't really have a clue about this job yet, as we have traveled almost the entire day. The world is so upside down, I did not believe a month ago that one wasn't going to be at the old location anymore.

I saw today in the newspaper that Werner has been killed. Where do you think the rest of the male members of the family are who are in the military? I am so tired and confused, so I will stop and go to bed. The bed is the floor with the blanket on top of it. We simply don't have the strength to fill our mattresses (with straw)."

Some of the postal services to the different troop installations were disconnected and at times very irregular. Due to the frequent moves, it was not always possible to reach the recipients. Everything was done to get the mail to all those out in the field, so they could stay in touch with the home front. This was considered extremely important.

That Mi's letter was a bit sphinx-like was caused by the fact that she was not allowed to reveal her location and also not say what her job really was.

"Dear Ma!
23.6.44

I wonder if you got my letter from the troop installation 2579? I feel like the real "flying strap", that is to say, I feel like a loose end flying about in the wind. We have been moved over and over and will surely continue to move in the future again. There is no point in you sending any mail, it would just be passed around.

As you can imagine, we are not at the old location anymore. Here, we have three rooms, a kitchen, and a hallway. The best furniture has come along, so the hoggish Karelians were left with long faces. They had, during the last days that we were there, flocked in and claimed that they were allowed to take everything if we left. In the end, a soldier had to stand guard at the house so the old women would not get a chance to hoard.

Of course, there were also other types of people there, but the majority of those who did not go to Finland were absolute pigs."

The strong comments about the "Karelia pigs" were directed toward the Russian civilian population that had remained in the area occupied by our troops.

Ten days after the Russians had stormed the Isthmus of Karelia, Mi got the order for decampment to Mäkriä, and as a Lotta office worker was assigned to a center for the fallen soldiers. But the next day she was told to join a troop installation close to the old border. She arrived in Pitkäranta by "coincidence ride", that is, by hitch hiking. This was the result of taking her entire heavy packing and going out to the side of the road. When a car came she stopped it and asked to come along. The world is small; on the back of the truck bed sat a young boy from Kymmene whose parents were among our acquaintances. The youngsters had a moment to chat before their paths were split again.

In Pitkäranta, Mi was caught up in an air raid from the feared low flying enemy planes that, with their machine guns, shot at the railway stations and the trains at the platforms. The attack came so quickly that there was no time to seek shelter. Mi ran a bit but realized it was useless and hit the ground and lay flat until the attack was over.

She often traveled back and forth between Pitkäranta and the border. She was the "flying strap", as she wrote in one of her letters.

On June the 26th, Werner von Troil was buried in Helsinki. Pulle was not able to participate in the funeral, he had to remain in Kymmene to prepare for the evacuation. There still had not been an official order to start, but one could not know if or when that was going to happen.

I continued the packing. There were huge boxes standing in the dining room and hallway. I was told to visit the war hospital with the Lotta management. The hospital was a sad place, I had a very hard time going on rounds with two other Lottas and the head nurse. It felt as if the wounded soldiers wanted to be left alone and wanted me to get the hell out of there.

The 29th of June I made the following note: "I have been missing Trolle horribly. I can barely think about the moment when he said goodbye to his rifle, which he then to his delight was allowed to take with him, or the farewell, without starting to cry. Mi's absence is also a rock in the road. But there are others who have it worse. It is like Pulle says, I was much calmer during the Winter War. I don't know why, but I assume I have experienced too much war so that my nerves have gotten worse, or it has been my illness that has made me nervous and weak. Somehow, I just don't have any energy, all work is repulsive, I am numb. Nothing wants to move along; the joy of working has been blown away. One should not loose one's spirits, but it is difficult to keep it up."

Most homes are gloomy, not just ours. Pulle is also feeling very down. But life has to be lived and the work has to be done, even though one would have preferred to just melt away from it all. But I am not alone and I cannot just think about myself, one has to try to keep one's head up as high as possible, and one wants to hope, despite it all, that we will one day have peace again.

WE BECOME TREASURE HIDERS

July started with bright sunshine and tremendous heat. Pulle, Pi, and I went out to Mustaniemi for the weekend. The water level in Lake Urajärvi and the whole Kymmene River system had risen almost catastrophically. Our half-finished sauna was floating out in the lake. The pier was under water. In order to get to the end of it one had to balance on the railing, which was still visible. The bench had completely disappeared under the massive amounts of water.

I don't have any notes from the day we became treasure hiders, but I believe it was this very day. We wanted to preserve our old von Troil family silver and the other house silver for the afterworld. We did not dare leave the valuables at home in Kymmene, or at the office, as fire and exploding bombs easily could destroy the houses. We also did not know how the border would be drawn in the event of a peace agreement. In Mustaniemi we at least were on the west side of the Kymmene River, which during the entire time of war was a great relief to us.

Pulle dug a hole in the ground out in the woods, and while we hid the silver I was thinking that the two of us probably would never see it again. But we hoped that our children, one day, could come back here and then Trolle would dig up the treasure of his father's great grandparents and my grandmother's bowl from 1806.

We did not bury any jewelry. We were going to take it with us, along with a silver platter, candle sticks, and a few other small items. A strange mood had come over us. We felt like treasure hiders from the middle ages.

The Russian invasion had been stopped after Viborg had been taken. Small invasion attempts did occur but they were only partially successful. These heated battles took many lives, among them many young men, really young men. Pi's fellow student, Gustaf Ahlfors, was among those who lost their lives for the fatherland. He had been a strong competitor to Pi in mathematics as they both aspired to be the best in their class. Another friend, Bjarne Melander, was wounded and taken prisoner by the Russians.

The 13th of July the enemy pushed forward to the northeast of Lake Ladoga and the 30th there was a breakthrough on the frontline Pitkäranta-Loimola and at Lake Tolva. The Germans had abandoned Narva. I wrote down a little reflection: "What is of great importance and what is of really great importance? I am about to lose all sense of proportion."

The entire population was upset about the assault and killing of civilians in northern desolate areas by Russian partisans. It was still many kilometers from Kymmene to the front, which now had been stabilized. We did not feel like we had to abandon everything tomorrow or even the day after tomorrow. Now, we were able to think, "maybe next week."

Pulle was inundated with work up to his eyeballs and Pi and I continued to pack our things. No matter how grateful I was for all we owned in these days of shortages, I could not help but think that we had too many of these worldly possessions.

I started working in the Lotta cafeteria. We had arranged for a so-called wandering cafeteria between the hours of six and eight in the evening at the war hospital. The work was both physically and psychologically strenuous. We carried heavy lemonade baskets and gigantic coffee pots up and down the staircases. We went from ward to ward and bed to bed. From a psychological stand point, it was difficult to see all the misery. In addition, there was the horrible stench that always comes with a war hospital. I was tired and Pulle demanded that I stop working for the cafeteria. Of course, this was the only reasonable thing to do.

Instead, I started to drive to the Lotta needle workshop in Voikka. But I was so tired I would have preferred to stay at home and take in every moment while I still owned a home. After all, one could not know when it was going to be taken away from you.

Mi's life in Läskelä went by in the company's old clubhouse, which had had all its furniture removed. The factory was owned by Kymmene. In the beginning, she had to stay in a work hall, but when she and Captain Renfors went to see one of the remaining company officers and introduced themselves, she was given lodging at the Club. Mi writes:

"Uncle Verner (General Gustafsson) had told a colonel he should take care of me and I have certainly been taken care of. The colonel, in turn, had told Captain Renfors that he should take care of me, with the consequence that when we moved, I was not allowed to go in a car by myself the way we had planned, but instead, I was escorted by the Captain himself. My bed, dresser, and a chair were brought along, as well as the floor rug, and a wall rug above the bed. I am now staying in a huge room by myself. There is military order everywhere. It has to be that way, as we never know who comes knocking on the door."

Mi took care of her office work, cooked, baked, washed the dishes and cleaned, patched and mended. She became the soldiers' big sister who listened to everything, looked at all the photographs, and took part in everyone's joy and sorrow. She was given the most peculiar presents as proof of the men's appreciation. Among other things, a big cat with five kittens, a rabbit, candy, a pocket-knife, and a pair of birch-bark shoes. Her life almost became a normal everyday existence, only the bombs over Läskelä reminded her of the war. On the 25th of July, she wrote that she was going to move again. It was toward the north to a small station community.

On July the 2nd Brita called from Helsinki where she was trying to resolve the children's passport formalities. The only one who had gotten his passport was Peter, but Brita did not want to send him alone to Sweden and said that she had to get Willy to go as well because of his poor health.

Trolle had a good time in Kemi. Together with the other children they did a kind of volunteer work. They debarked logs for four hours a day. The proceeds were given to the Brothers in Arms, and after completing the job they received the volunteer ax in silver.

At the end of July, it had become so peaceful in the land that we decided to bring the boy home.

As there were no lodgings available for the families of the wounded at the war hospital, the Brothers in Arms had arranged for a simple apartment where the mothers, sisters, and fiancées could stay. Some private families offered to take in temporary guests. Even we were able to do so as our guest room was empty.

One day, the young Mrs. Oker-Blom stayed with us. She was married to a Captain who had been good friends with Werner von Troil. He had also been at Kuuterselkä where Werner was killed. The Captain had been wounded in his lung during a reconnaissance trip to the enemy side. He had crawled back until he came upon two medics who carried him on their stretcher. But the two medics were both killed and Oker-Blom had to wander several kilometers, with a lung that had been pierced by a bullet, before he got a ride with a truck to the first aid station.

The 1st of August President Ryti resigned. The Marshal of Finland, Carl Gustaf Emil Mannerheim, took his place.

We were again three that traveled to Mustaniemi for the weekend, in other words, Pulle, Trolle, and I. Pi had left for a Lotta assignment. Despite the raging war we were able to do, what seemed to be, trivial things. We made jams and preservatives for the upcoming winter, even though no one could know if we were still going to be in Kymmene and need vegetables and preserved berries.

I also hired a home seamstress who made new things for us out of fabric pieces, discarded items, and old curtains as one was not able to buy any new fabric.

The company received guests from Sweden, who, under the direction of the Mannerheim

Association, visited their Finnish foster communities. We had two pleasant days at the management villa.

On August 9th Pulle had a day off and we went to Mustaniemi. I had been without a maid during the summer weekends, but this time I asked Veera to come along, as I needed some rest. The next day we got the message that her fiancée had been killed. She was, of course, allowed to go to the funeral, but she stayed away for three weeks, which was hard on me during this time of making jams and preservatives in glass jars. It was actually against the law; no one had the right to more than half of one's vacation time. She should have been allowed one week, not more. But I had a hard time denying a grieving fiancée's wishes to stay with the mother of her fallen fiancé for a while.

The Romanians turned their weapons toward the Germans. Turkey cut the diplomatic ties with Germany and the allies landed in the south of France. Paris was captured. Romania asked the Russians for peace and got it, but with very severe conditions.

Brita had finally managed to get her boys to Sweden by referring to Willy's weak lungs.

During the summer, I received several letters from the ladies Pian Gripenberg, Marianne Cedercreutz, and Glory Zilliaccus who now all were in Sweden with the children. They wrote about their difficulties, about missing home, and about the restlessness. Due to the regulations, the ladies were not able to take with them any money. Economically they were completely dependent on their hosts to give them some money or lend it to them for an undetermined time.

Pian had come to a property in the middle of Sweden through an acquaintance of her acquaintance. You could read between the lines of her letter that it wasn't all that much fun to be dependent on people you don't know. She did not stay there very long. Her hosts probably belonged to the magnificent part of the Swedish population that took in refugees even though they really did not have the economic means to do so. Pian did not want to look for a new place to stay but returned home with her children at the end of August, despite the uncertain situation here at home.

Marianne ended up with her father-in-law's good friend's widow, who did not want to know anything about her or the children. The lady gave Marianne some money and told her: "Take care of yourself!" I don't know how much money she received, or what the prices were in Sweden in 1944, but I understood that Marianne had a very difficult time. She wrote to her husband that she now knew what it means to be "the poor one in the family", which of course was descriptive of her situation.

She moved to a traveler's lodge in the south of Sweden to be closer to Glory at the Wapnö Estate and Eva Horelli in Stjärnarp. The hostess of the lodge could not understand Marianne's request for separate beds for her and her children in the little room that she had at her disposal. In the room she had to sleep in the same bed with one of the children. In the end, the practical Marianne resolved the issue with a little box for the smallest girl.

Marianne was, to the utmost, in control; she was able to meet all the challenges without falling apart. The oldest girl was taken care of by good folks and that helped a lot. If she had not had the two little children occupying her day and night, she would have looked for a job. But as it was, she was forced to live at the mercy of others.

Glory wrote the most temperamental letters. They were lively descriptions about life in estates with parties and people in elegant evening dresses. Everyday life consisted of good food and wonderful cakes with their afternoon tea and all other imaginable comforts. The Stael von Holstein family was just as loving toward Glory and her children as they had been toward Trolle and Claes Henrik two years earlier. This time, her oldest son was not able to come along, he did not get his passport. Glory was very worried about leaving him at home in Finland with her husband and her elderly father.

There was a shortage of maids in Sweden, so even though she wasn't exactly healthy as a horse, she had to clean and wash. She also had to take care of her youngest child. Her hosts wanted her to participate in their parties, but she did not always have the strength to go along.

In August, two nurses and one nurse's aide moved into our guest room and the room where Trolle and Axel had stayed during the winter and spring. All three worked at the war hospital.

Pi did not have a good time at home. The restlessness and feeling of uncertainty had been worse for her than for us, as she had not felt healthy and did not have any regular work. She was, therefore, immediately willing to accept an assignment her Lotta manager offered her. But she was forced to first see a doctor. He thought she would be able to travel.

She reported to the district in Helsinki but was told her papers had been sent to Kouvola. The trip to Helsinki, in other words, was completely unnecessary. When Pi asked where she was going to be sent, she was told "to the north". She had to accept this vague answer until she, in Kouvola, was told her destination was Kajana.

Pi became an office worker at the War Hospital 31. Her job was essentially to keep a register of the entire inventory: tables, chairs, surgery instruments, table dishes, etc. On top of that, she had to do some typing and other office work. She sometimes also took care of the tobacco sales, which meant she was allowed to spend time with the wounded in the sick wards. This wasn't always so easy. I had seen a war hospital up close myself and knew how gripping it was to be in contact with the warriors on their sick leave. It was surely a challenge for a seventeen-year-old to see the suffering every day, but she had a really good time at her job.

She was also given another task, which caused her family to put on a big smile when we read about it in one of her letters. She was supposed to represent the hospital, together with her closest manager, at celebrations and concerts that were arranged for the soldiers in Kajana. We thought it was very peculiar that our Pi, seventeen, would arrive at the festivities with her manager, and be taken to one of the best seats. Her manager's name was Henry Sysimiilu. He liked to sing and performed all kinds of popular songs, even arias.

Her first room in Kajana was tiny. She shared it with a nurse that she did not really get along with very well. The room was filled with distasteful things. Pi's bed was a couch pieced together from boxes of various sizes with a straw mattress on top. During the day this hideous piece was covered with an orange blanket with a brown edge. Above it hung a wall decoration with gray and purple as its dominating colors. There was also an old-fashioned wash basin in the room with a lid covered with a black cloth with green squares, white curtains printed with yellow butterflies, and a radio.

Her next lodging was in a gigantic room, big and desolate like a desert, with an alcove where two other Lottas slept. Pi slept in the other end of the room tormented by her roommates‘ dirt and mess. They left their dirty socks, torn undergarments, and shoes everywhere. The girls also had to stand in line with the host family's own three members and two other gentlemen that were lodged there to get to the bathroom, which had the only toilet in the house.

To make things a bit more bearable, Pi bought a cooking platform. I sent a pot and some bread, so she could boil tea and also heat up water for washing. A Lotta on assignment was never allowed to be fastidious.

The hostess, who initially had been very unfriendly, softened at the end and invited Pi to celebrate a name's day. She absolutely wanted Pi to accompany Henry Sysimiilu on the piano. Pi wrote:

"Can you imagine anything so crazy, that I, with my meager talent, would agree to accompany someone on the piano. But the lady is a bit nuts, she plays herself full scale with one or, at the most, two fingers, and of course she believes I am pretty much a genius."

Pi reported to her Lotta manager in Helsinki that she had started her job and received a nice letter in return, and in September, when her raincoat got too thin, she got a thicker coat. She was allowed to keep it for as long as the assignment lasted.

CEASEFIRE WITH HARD CONDITIONS

The 2nd of September the prime minister, Antti Hackzell, held a radio speech, in which he reported that the government had taken the first steps toward a resolution with Russia and that the action had been accepted by congress. The Russians had demanded, as a condition for the negotiations, that the German troops in Finland leave the country within two weeks. Our government had asked the Germans to do this.

The 4th of September it was announced that a ceasefire had been reached at 8 am between Finland and Russia. Despite this, the Russians were shooting full blast at several frontlines all day and the bombardments did not stop until the next morning. It was claimed that the reason for this was due to Prime Minister Hackzell's failure to mention in his speech that the Russians had demanded, and we had promised that unless the Germans left willingly by September 15th, they should be disarmed and be surrendered as prisoners of war to Russia. The last demand, according to the Russians, had to be published in our newspapers for it to become commonly known.

The German troops volunteered to leave from the south and the middle of Finland. The Reserve Officer Association declared, in a written statement to Marshal Mannerheim, that their members would not wage war on their former brothers in arms. The statement was read on the radio. But there was fighting and shooting. The reserve officers were not able to keep their promise.

The 6th of September our delegation left for Moscow to start the negotiations for peace, and the following day the commander-in-chief and Marshal of

Finland, Mannerheim, published an Order of the Day, in which the following was said:

"The country's independence and our people's future cannot be secured without a confiding relationship with our neighbors. With this in mind I have, in agreement with the government, communicated to the Russian government the desire of Finland to move toward peace negotiations. This action has been approved by congress.

In an agreement with the opposing party I have given the order to cease the fighting at the Finnish army's frontlines."

On the 8th of September, Prime Minister Hackzell had his first meeting with the Russian authorities. That evening, the Finnish delegation saw a play about Wilhelm Tell at the Moscow Theater.

Meanwhile, the entire world was up-side down. Romania and Hungary were at war. The Soviet troops marched into Bulgaria and demanded all German soldiers be handed over as prisoners of war, and all German ships were also supposed to be handed over. Only with these conditions could a ceasefire be negotiated.

The war also spread across the Baltic States and, in the end, reached Eastern Poland. At the Western Front, the Germans were pushed back.

Strange enough, we experienced two air alarms in Kymmene, despite the ceasefire, on September 6th and 7th.

In terms of our private affairs, Mi enjoyed a short week of leave at home. She celebrated her birthday with a crawfish party for three, including myself and another Lotta, Mrs. Tarviainen. She was her best friend from the time in Viborg, the same Lotta that had, one year earlier, celebrated Mi's coming of age (21 years) with us. Now she had been moved to Kymmene War Hospital 13. Despite the difficult times it was still possible to steal some fun for oneself. Not everyone had the strength to constantly immerse themselves in the misery.

At the end of her leave, Mi traveled to Joensuu where she became an office worker at a border office. Margaretha was working at a similar office in the same town. This is how Mi described her work conditions in one of her letters:

"In general, there are only old folks here of various ages who cannot get along without quarreling, so the air is charged off and on. Whose fault it actually is, I don't know. They are all equally stubborn and cannot give in at all. It is strange that female old folk never can get along well. The mood here is, as you can see, terrible.

I am staying with a few others in a hallway a few blocks from the actual office. This hallway is a walkthrough area for the local Lottas, which leads to a large room and a warehouse in this building. The house we had in Aunus was a paradise compared to this one. It is so ridiculously drafty that even the Lottas that stayed here in the summer were shivering from the cold. We are going to try to get another place to stay, a hallway cannot ever be really warm. I did not dare to take my clothes off when I slept on the floor but rather put more cloths on before wrapping myself in the blanket. I did not have a mattress either, just lay down straight on the floor. I can assure you it was warmer on the floor of the station than here.

We were all, by the way, invited to Margaretha's border office tonight. I could not go as I have big, almost skinless blisters on both heels. I got them yesterday when I had to walk several kilometers."

I was deeply upset about this information. Had all this happened during times of war I would not have said anything, but now we had ceasefire and Joensuu was on our own side of the border, in Finnish territory. It was nonchalance toward people. Mi's rheumatism, which had worsened during the war, now took a hard hit. She was in pain and it only got worse.

Pi sent funny letters from Kajana. She had answered her call for teaching by instructing a fifty-year-old field officer and a thirty-year-old Lotta in the art of keeping a register. Pulle and I had to smile as we imagined with what eagerness and precision this would have been carried out.

We thought she was a long way from the danger zone, so we did not have to worry about her. But it did not take long before I was gripped by an untamed concern for her. We had heard about the strangest rumors from the north. The Germans were retreating, but they used the scorched earth tactic as they left. We did not know what to believe.

Pi did not disclose where in Kajana she was working. We assumed that it was at the war hospital, but we did not know if it was Finnish or German. We waited day in and day out for any information from her. I got bent out of shape with restlessness; if it was the German's hospital, they would possibly take the whole personnel with them if they were forced to leave Kajana.

I did not want to worry Pulle with all my speculations. It wasn't until Pi called home, in reaction to one of my desperate letters, that I disclosed my fears to him. He laughed, but Pi did not. She had seen the hysterical mood that had gripped Kajana. The town was overrun by Germans preparing for the retreat. They had run around the streets with the town girls; shouting, making noise, and partying. The whole town was in uproar.

The Germans, at least, announced in advance that they were going to blow up a bridge. But this respectfulness quickly turned into the opposite when they had gotten further north. It was maybe human to react that way, we had betrayed them just as the Italians before us. But we thought they should have understood that we were forced to do so, as we had no choice. It was all so horrible. There was an outright war between them and us now. They burned and destroyed, and we were bitter over our former brothers in arms. There were whispers about atrocities in Norway, and we knew about the unrest in Denmark to some degree. But, for example, the concentration camp Bergen-Belsen, at least I had never heard of it. It was around this time that the dark veil was lifted and one became aware of the unspeakable disgrace in the Nazi system.

There was a similar situation in our country as there was in Norway with the "German girls", that is, girls that had become girlfriends of German officers and soldiers and now had chosen to go along with the retreating German troops. Many family tragedies unfolded. In the last minute, the parents would get word that their daughters were on the way up north with their fiancés, which caused the fathers to leave in panic to bring them back. As there still were Germans who were friendly in general, it happened that the matter was resolved and the young daughters returned despite their wild protests.

Many girls, even wives who had had a little affair with some German officer, went along with their boyfriends. Some of them surely listened to their love-struck hearts and conscience, some probably did it out of recklessness or for adventure. For some, the relationship had gone so far that they did not want to stay behind alone with the shame. After a while a large group of these women returned from Norway, where they had been abandoned by their fiancés. Not all returned alone, there were those who had delivered a baby during the escape.

One of the first noticeable acts of war on Finnish territory happened on the night of September 15th when the chief commander on the island of Hogland was given an ultimatum by the Germans to surrender the island. This ultimatum was not accepted which led to fighting. The Capital Newspaper (Hufvudstadsbladet) reported about the intermezzo:

"At around 1 am, the night of September 15th, German war ships arrived at the port of Hogland. A German officer came to see the commander of the Finnish forces and presented an ultimatum that the island was to be surrendered, a demand that was immediately denied. At the same time troops were surprisingly put on shore from the German ships at the port of Suurkylä and these even managed to form a bridge head. The German war ships fired in an attempt to support the landings on other parts of the island as well. Our artillery fire was able to ward off the landings and forced the German ships to leave and destroyed six landing rafts. The counter-attacks by our light vessels sank an additional four German ships and vessels. Through the counter-attacks of our troops, the part of the island that had been conquered by the Germans was shrunk throughout the day and at 18:55 the Germans gave up the fight. Over seven hundred prisoners were taken, out of which two hundred were wounded."

A Russian air squadron of about sixty planes made several attacks at the German fleet and during the day bombarded the German troops that had landed on the island. When the Germans finally left Kotka, they mined the passage.

In the newspaper on the 18th of September, one could read that German fighter planes had shot at a civilian passenger plane on route to Stockholm from Helsinki.

The time frame that had been given to the German troops in Finland to voluntarily leave our territory had passed on September 15th. The Germans, however, did not retreat from other parts, only from the south. Full-out war erupted. At first it was "quiet" and "friendly", but it soon turned into a bloody battle when the friendly German troops were exchanged for the tough SS-troops, which were not shy to burn entire villages, blow up railway bridges, in short, destroy everything that could be destroyed. Rovaniemi became a city of ruins, the magnificent hotel of Pallastunturi was also ruined. The railroad bridges between Oulu and Kemi were destroyed so that the track was out of commission for a long time and all the traffic had to be handled by sea.

The people of Lappland and the county of northern Oulu had to be evacuated in haste. We got a package from Kerstin Ståhlberg from Veitsiluoto with a few quickly scribbled lines: "Please keep the package for now. We are currently packing here as fast as we can."

On the 19th of September, the radio announced in a descriptive sentence about the evacuations in Lappland: "Our roads are crawling with creatures." The Capital Paper wrote:

"There have been negotiations with Sweden about the transfer of the inhabitants from the west of Lappland to Sweden. A positive result has been reached and the transfer of the people has already begun. Finland will provide for the transports as far as the border and Sweden from the border onward. Those that have been transferred to Sweden have been placed in camps, where they are staying in military barracks. In every camp there is a so-called social caretaker. The people have only been able to take a few personal items with them, but on the other hand, they have been able to take their cattle with them. The evacuations are taking place under difficult conditions due to the long distances in Lappland, as well as the lack of means of transportation."

During the whole month of September, we Finns were terrified of what conditions the Russians would demand in order to achieve a peace with us. We could, however, never imagine how tough they actually ended up being. The deathblow finally came the evening of September 19th when the secretary of internal affairs, Ernst von Born, read the ceasefire conditions on the radio, we thought that we had just gotten a noose put around our necks and wondered when it was going to be pulled tight.

"The signing of the agreement entails that we immediately start the withdrawal of our troops from beyond the border that was established in the peace agreement in Moscow in 1940. Karelia, in other words, was lost and our hopes of at least a correction of the economically unsuitable circumstances, in regard to the border, have not materialized. In addition, we have been forced to give up the Petsamo area, which the Russian government in the Peace of Dorpat had surrendered to us as part of fulfilling an old promise. As a third territorial point, the lease of the Porkkala Peninsula (west of Helsinki) should be mentioned, with all its vast water and land areas, as a military base to the Russian government for fifty years. We also have to, although just for some time, give up the airports to the allied forces in the South and Southwest of Finland, as well as our merchant fleet. In addition, we have to be prepared to support the allied forces with certain material deliveries.

Author: Central Intelligence Agency Employee
Modified by Stella von Troil
Map of Finland 1996
REPOSITORY Library of Congress
Geography and Maps
Washington, DC, Unite States
http://hdl.loc.gov/loc.gmd/6960.ct001018
CIA released the image into PUBLIC DOMAIN

Areas ceded to the Soviet Union in 1944:
Petsamo
Salla
Karelia
Islands in the Gulf of Finland
Porkkala Peninsula (lease agreement 50 years)

A serious situation is that we have to disarm the German forces in the country and surrender them to the allied forces, and we must urgently prepare to put our army on the peace path. These demands placed on our troops are by no means unimportant, even though the south of Finland up to Oulu already is completely free of German military.

In regard to the future peace time conditions, special attention has to be paid to the circumstance that Finland has to, during a six-year time period, pay a three hundred-million-dollar war compensation cost. This compensation is actually only half of the sum that was intended for us during the peace talks last spring, but even then, it is considerably more than any war compensation placed upon any nation after the First World War."

I will never forget the evening when I sat alone in the living room listening to the radio. I got a strange feeling. It was as if a wall was slowly rising between Finland and the West. The fear was beginning to be overwhelming for me. But I knew that we all had to fight to keep our heads up high, we were not allowed to fall apart into some state of apathetic frustration. "The Lord will only challenge, he will not cast away" - maybe that was it. But why would the Lord challenge us so hard? I felt empty and cold inside, I was bitter.

Brita came to visit us in Kymmene the 20th of September. She was going to stay for a while to rest, as she had had a lot of work the whole summer as an instructor at the Swedish Farming Association.

The mood was oppressive, and a gloomy seriousness lay over our home and the whole country. When Brita heard about the evacuation of Porkkala, she said she had to leave to help out. She traveled to Helsinki to get instructions and was ordered to oversee the transport of the farm animals.

The people in Porkkala had eight days to harvest crops, pick the potatoes, pack, and leave their homes behind. It was an old community of Swedish culture with many beautiful estates from ancient times that now were going to be handed over to the Russians for a period of 50 years. There was grief in the land, grief everywhere, especially for the fate of Porkkala. It affected the Swedish-speaking people. And we who were part of it, grieved.

While the people in Porkkala worked and toiled, the people of Lappland left for calmer areas toward the south and west over the border to Sweden. The people of Karelia, already spread all over the country, were allowed to stay where they were and saw their hopes of returning to their homes fade away.

People worked night and day in Porkkala. If there was time for a little sleep during the night, it was on a hard bench, on a floor, or just about anywhere. There was a shortage of vehicles, everything that rolled and could be given up was sent down there. There was not much time until the deadline, on September the 28th, the area was to be emptied. Sigyn Alenius analyzed the mood in a newspaper article:

"Close to twelve thousand people started their journey, in these days, toward an unknown destiny in a new home and place. The number is not exact, one cannot yet accurately estimate how many are affected by the transfers, but together with the local community leader in Kyrkslätt, Eric Westman, I calculated this number.

'We have lived here since 1684,' Mr. Westman states. 'It is not easy to leave, and there is probably no one that today actually knows where we will be going. But we know that we have to leave, and it doesn't get any better by complaining. There are also enough practical tasks that have to be resolved in these few short days, so one does not have the time to think that much."

Straight across the street, on the Stor-Hila Estate, the owner of the estate, Sigrid Söderström, is methodically and carefully packing the china, silver, and furniture.

'None of us have really thought about what this really means,' she says. 'In the end, we have to get out in time first, the actual moving process requires all our strength and demands all of our attention. I guess it is okay for the people, but the fate of the animals is so unspeakably sad. What is going to happen to them? To be forced to leave them after all these years. One should never get close to earthly things, I know that but...."

On the 22nd of September, the first group of Russian inspectors came to Helsinki, and the following day seventy military officials arrived.

This was the beginning. Slowly more of them arrived and entire hotels were occupied by them and many apartments. The tight living conditions got even worse. But the Russian military's discipline was irreproachable. No women were assaulted, and one never saw a drunken officer or soldier in the streets, and in the restaurants, they behaved correctly.

We did not dare think about the future. Were we going to survive the fall? And the winter? We were like sleep walkers roaming around in the dark. Mi wrote from Joensuu that the leadership had declared her living quarters uninhabitable. She had to move. That was good news. Mi wrote:

"You know, I have moved to another lodging again. I am staying with two others in a small drawing room in the house of an engineer, but the Misses of the house is downright insolent. In the entrance hall we were met with the words: "It is so unfortunate that you are coming to stay here since I am a dentist and I am gone all day, the same goes for my husband."

What a nice lady, don't you agree? We probably look so rough that they think we are thieves. It felt a bit dreary until we got into the room which blew away any anticipatory mood, at that point I most of all would have liked to jump up and down with laughter. This "drawing room" is about 6 x 8 m (20 x 26 ft) with three windows, a long sofa, eleven chairs, a bookcase, a round table with a knitted table cloth, which takes my thoughts to a sewing machine. On the walls eleven paintings, a picture in plaster, and wherever one turns, one can see loved ones, or Mannerheim, or raging rivers."

Veera turned in her resignation. I was very surprised, I had thought she liked it here. One reason for her resignation, she told Ulla, was that she did not have Sundays off. She, who had been off almost every weekend during the summer, except for one when we picked the potatoes in Mustaniemi!

I could not even think of getting a new maid, for our life was too uncertain. I therefore asked Ulla to stay and help me, which she did until the 1st of November when her school started.

On the 29th of September, Caja's and Rainer's son, Bubi, was killed at Olhava by the German forces. He was killed on a mined bridge over which he and two other men had volunteered to be the first troops to cross. His road as a warrior had been exciting and filled with danger. He had been wounded three times and was nominated for the Knights of the Mannerheim Cross for his personal bravery.

Pulle went to the office every morning as usual, tired and dejected. I had never seen him so pessimistic. In order to suppress the constantly nagging gloomy thoughts, he went hunting as much as possible. He shot two moose, and the meat was shared as usual among the hunting buddies, the families, friends, and acquaintances.

Mi's letters were calm and serious and never breathed of any hopelessness. She had gotten a terrible cold which led to puss in the sinuses and headaches. But now she was feeling better. Her leadership did not get along among themselves. She remembered with sadness her friendly troop quarters, where she even had her own room. In a letter from the 20th of October she wrote that she had moved again:

"Yesterday we moved quickly to a bigger, but oh-so-dirty apartment. The reason was that the family, whose apartment we had stayed in, had returned from their evacuation. We had just one day to get another apartment and this was the only one available. We scrubbed and washed all day yesterday, we even had time to get paper curtains, so today we are feeling very happy with the result. We are now all staying here, as we got as much as four rooms and a kitchen. But everything went down the drain today when we heard that the gentlemen, who arranged this, had messed up and given us this apartment by mistake, it had already been promised to someone else. And so we had to pack our bags again, but where we are going to move now no one knows. It really felt as if our feet were pulled from underneath us, it is truly a strike of luck if you can find a corner for your mortal clay in this place.

You do know that one can buy soap with clothing rations? I managed to find one today, will see what it's like."

Pi did not have much time left in her assignment in Kajana. She had, contrary to her sister, friendly people around her.

"You cannot imagine how well the Lotta mangers have taken care of me. I got a letter from one of them some time ago, and then the day before yesterday from the other one who asked what my shoe size was, she wanted to send me a pair of boots. She also sent a package of notepaper, paper napkins, and liquorish. Isn't it sweet? Even my closest Lotta manger here, the "Lotta Oldest", actually cried today when I left. She is going on vacation, so we may not meet again. It feels really sad to leave this place when one has learned to like all the people here."

Ulla and I took care of our household. At the beginning of the month, I did not even want to hear anything about getting a new maid after Veera had left. But now, when everything seems to stabilize, I have after intense urging from Pulle thought about trying to get some help for the kitchen and someone to help take care of the house.

In a letter to Mi I shed some light on our everyday life. We have recently had a visit from Walter and Walborg Ehrström's younger son, our little cousin Freddie, who currently is stationed in Kouvola. He was there fighting during the horrors at the Isthmus of Karelia.

"He is so sweet, a small boy, who looks like a Bernhardiner puppy and pretends to be an adult. I had today thought about making a very simple dinner, but it would not have been enough for Freddie, so we went to the Club. It was very nice since I that way had a bit less work today. Ulla has been to a birthday party and is now at the movies. The boys have traveled to Mustila. Their hands are just as dirty as usual, and it is the same battle as last spring to try to get them to keep their room halfway tidy. As you can see, nothing has changed. I have been running to meetings and here at home we have cleaned, so I have not been lying around. But hopefully we will get a kitchen aid and a domestic help soon. Then, I will suddenly feel like a guest in this house. I hope to have some time to play the piano and write some. I really want to do it, my playing has gone down the drain, it is about time for me to get some practice....

Pulle is feeling well, he does have a lot of work, of course. Tomorrow he will go hunting. He has a terrible problem with Topi and Reku, as they always want to fight and are about to kill each other. To be honest, I am not so thrilled to have two dogs in the house, and sometimes three. They have put a leg up in the dining room, for example, they lie on Trolle's bed, and so on. The worst thing they have done was when Topi sat on a chair and lapped up sheep's fat from a plate on the kitchen table. This, after we slaughtered the sheep mainly to get some fat."

Greta was very sick and had an operation on her intestines followed by complications. Caja had worked, for a long time, as a nurse's aide at a war hospital in Varkaus. But soon after hearing about her son's death, she got sick with pneumonia. When she was just about back to health, she tripped on some stairs and broke a bone in her lower leg and wanted me to come to Helsinki. It would, of course, have been difficult for me to do that. If either one of my girls had been at home, it would have been a different matter. I could not leave the responsibility of taking care of the house, Pulle and the boys, as well as getting the food and preparing it, to Ulla, who had just turned sixteen and was still a child.

Finally, Bubi's lacerated body arrived and was released to his wife. Due to Caja's health, the funeral was to be held the 29th of October near Lahtis. Pulle and I wanted to be present at that time. Bubi had lived in our home for three years as a child and we were very close.

We made the decision that I should travel to Helsinki on the 26th to visit Greta and from there go to Lahtis. There, I was to meet up with Verner and Pulle and continue to Järvikylä by car. Bubi's brother, Gunnar, was also supposed to come along with us.

Unfortunately, Pi came home the same day I left. It was sad to immediately have to part from her since she was going to stay at home for only a few days and then travel to Helsinki for the start of her first semester at the university on November the 1st. In other words, she was going to leave before Pulle and I would be back from the funeral.

She was in good spirits and happy but 6kg (13 lb) lighter than before she left to Kajana. She came like a ray of sunshine back into our lives. She was happy to be home for a while and be able to wash, patch, and mend her cloths before starting at the university.

The next morning I went to visit Greta. She was in bed at home, but she was in such bad shape that she had to be taken to the hospital by ambulance. Her daughter, Tippan, came back the same day on leave from Kemi, where she had worked as a nurse in a war hospital. Her description of the trip from Kemi to Oulu was typical for the times. It took place by boat as the Germans had blown up the railroad tracks. Even her brother, Paul, had been given extra leave to visit his sick mother.

On the 29th of October, Bubi was finally laid to rest. It was extremely sad.

Among my diary notes and newspaper clippings from the month of October I noted, among other things, that the Germans took one hundred and fifty northern Finns hostage. Among them, one town hall director, several priests, policemen, and county commissioners and threatened to shoot them if the war operations in Lappland did not stop. The hostages were, however, soon released without any bloodshed.

The chairman of the commission for the inspectors, General Colonel Shadov, arrived in Helsinki on October the 5th. "All Finnish citizens above fifteen years of age who have resided in

Germany have to report to the police," it said in a declaration.

The fighting around Torneå, close to the Swedish border in the North, was raging with great force. On the 8th of October, Kemi was conquered by our troops; the devastation of the city was vast. The Prime Minister, Castren, reported on the radio what had already taken place to fulfill the conditions of the ceasefire and pointed out that we have to do everything to eliminate the distrust that exists between the Soviet Union and Finland. He also touched on the placement of those who had been disbanded back into the workforce, the plan for a new law for compensation, the colonization issue, etc.

The lack of housing in Helsinki was severe. People with larger apartments were forced to rent out rooms to others. This is how the mandatory boarding and lodging started. Many were glad to help others and crowded together, and many situations were resolved with sympathy. But it also happened that dishonest individuals were forced upon good folks who regarded their homes as sacred. Old couples and single people suffered the most in the crowded conditions, staying in one or two rooms, with the rest of the house filled with strangers, either families or single people. There also was a shortage of coals which resulted in difficulties producing electricity.

Persons who, due to their leftist affiliations, had been imprisoned were freed and political gatherings were allowed again. The Finland-Soviet Union Association was formed, and local departments soon emerged in all larger communities.

In the entire country, gigantic collections of clothes have been organized for the evacuated. In our community, the Lottas participated in the work. I took part in sorting massive amounts of clothing in an ice-cold apartment.

Rovaniemi was conquered on October the 18th. The Germans were retreating but destroyed everything in their path. Even Sodankylä was soon free, and in Rovaniemi bombs with timers were exploding long after the Germans had left. The blackouts were stopped in the whole country. Communities in the heart of the country had earlier been relieved of this regulation, now it was expanded to the South Coast and the Kymmene valley.

The fishermen in the Nyland County in the South were discussing how to help the Porkkala inhabitants. An urgent request for voluntary surrendering of fishing waters and housing was presented.

Fifty thousand Finnish children are still in Sweden. The value of just the Swedish care is estimated at forty million crowns. Whole families have fled from the Baltic States, mainly from Estonia, both via Finland or directly across the Baltic Sea to Sweden in motorboats and other small vessels. The newspaper reported that a family had crossed the sea in a rowing boat. There are also rumors that some of our countrymen have made the trip to Sweden without passports or permits to leave the country in similar fashion as the Baltic people.

Among them are single people, families, and deserters of the colors. Not everyone's nerves have held up under the pressure. One should maybe not blame those who are in panic, as one did not know anything about the future.

There are also those who have been put in prison and the mood is fearful in many places.

A newspaper article announced that the country's universities and higher learning institutions have started their operations. For those who had been disbanded, the most important question was the continuation of their studies:

"The Helsinki University so-called inauguration festivities had been moved to the large auditorium's 'new side', and it was probably the first time in the university's history that the old tradition, to gather in the now destroyed main hall to listen to the president's inscription address, had to be broken. Rarely had it been as crowded as this year. The large auditorium had about five hundred seats. One had to now crowd together so that there were two to each seat. The rest were standing in the walkways and along the walls. Still, the doors had to be shut in front of long lines of people who could not come in.

During the recent years one had gotten used to seeing almost only female students on the benches during these inauguration ceremonies. But this time, one really was alarmed over the masses of women that filled the auditorium. One had the impression that, at the most, five percent of those present were male students. And completely unsought the thought came to mind: how would the disbanded warriors returning home react to this overwhelming majority of women? How were they going to make room for those coming back?"

Present at the semester opening was also the little seventeen-year-old student Pi, that is, the mathematics student Britta Knutsdotter von Troil. She must have felt lost, but it would not be long before she would make some friends and feel right at home. Pi would always do well in all transitions in life.

WITH HEAVY STEPS INTO THE FUTURE

According to the ceasefire agreement the Russians demanded that several organizations and associations be dissolved. The 3rd of November, the Defense Corps was given the death blow. The 6th of November, the commander of the guard, Lauri Malmberg, published an Order of the Day, where, among other statements, the following was said:

1: According to the law set forth on November 3rd, 1944, the law about the Defense Corps Organization from 12.22.1927, and all later amendments, has been abolished.

2: I hereby want to express my warmest gratitude to the corps' commanders, lieutenant commanders, and volunteer forces for the long and self-sacrificing operations to the benefit of our nation's defense, as well as for the trusting work together. I also want to thank the volunteer and, in essence, people-minded Lotta-Svärd organization for its strong support, without which the Defense Corps could not have operated on such a large scale and reach such a high degree of efficiency, which the result of a quarter of a century of work proves. Lastly, I want to thank the benefactors and all the people in the Defense Corps, old and young, and all those who in one way or another have contributed to the work of the Defense Corps.

The Lottas all over the country were waiting with anticipation to see if their organization would fall victim to the same fate. So far, there was no news. We held our meetings as usual.

One day, in the beginning of November, the Kymmene factory Lottas invited the colleagues from the War Hospital #13 for a get together. The atmosphere was good and intimate. Coffee surrogate with wheat buns were served and we sang a few songs.

The 23rd of November the blow came. The Lotta organization also had to be dissolved. We had, up until the last moment, hoped that this was not going to happen. After this day no more meetings were held. We did not even have a farewell moment where everyone could have been together one last time. Not even a church service was held. One simply could not. Only the board had their last meetings to make sure the break up was carried out.

It was as if one was at a funeral - to bury a dear friend.

I took out my Lotta dress and removed the ten-year badge, the course star, and the section band and put them together with the pin in a box, which I hope to be able to keep for future generations.

Everything was carried out so quietly, there was no fuss about it. And then it was over.

Even the Boy Soldier Corps, which should have had about sixty thousand members in the whole country, was dissolved.

I thought about Mi up in Joensuu. She did not have any civilian clothes with her, but if she removed the pin from the dress and picked off the cockade from the cap, even she would be a civilian again. She had a home to come to, but she had a friend who had lost her home up in the far north. Her friend wore everything she owned. Where would she go, how would she start her life anew?

The War Hospital #13 was dissolved and the disbandment of the troops had started. The general population was asked to, as far as possible, limit their travel so that the disbandment could be carried out as planned. The trains had, for some time, been overcrowded. I had planned to travel to Kristinestad to pick up our belongings but subsequently cancelled my plans. The boxes were returned with the Kymmene Company officials' and worker's things that had been evacuated to Närpes.

We again had extremist communists in congress. Finland was like a tower that was leaning to the left. How long would the leaning hold up?

I am here finishing my book about the Kymmene-Troils War Experiences. The war is over. We have had to endure a lot, but there are others who have seen more and have been exposed to worse things than we have. We still have our home, and, above all, we have each other.

Our poor country and its people– what will become of us? The times have a new face, much of what we thought was right and sacred is now of no importance.

But even if everything was going to fall apart, we hope that the people of Finland never will forget their fallen heroes, their invalids, their widows, those without fathers, and the grieving parents.

We are like a cork drifting at sea, there is nothing we can do. We have to mindlessly follow the stream. We don't know anything about the future and only have to hope and try to become happy at some point.

But in this month of November in 1944, we are walking out into a fog that is sweeping over the land with a breeze out of the east.

EPILOGUE

Stella von Troil

BRITA AND PULLE

Pulle continued to work for Kymmene and after he retired my grandparents moved to Helsinki, where they lived across the street from the Finlandia Concert Hall giving them access to live classical music. Pulle died in 1964, he was 72.

Brita continued to spend her summers in Mustaniemi. Even though she did have a heart problem at a young age, she continued to live a relatively healthy long life and died in 1990 at the age of 87.

MÄRTHA (Mi)

Mi, or Misse, as she was called in her later years, married Adolf (Atte) Tigerstedt in a double wedding with her sister Pi. Her husband became a Supreme Court Justice in Finland. They did not have any children, but her love for her nieces and nephews was easily noticeable. She worked as a secretary for the Bensow Company in Helsinki. She died in 2004 at the age of 82.

BRITTA (Pi)

Pi went on to study economics and became the CEO of the Elfving Company in Helsinki. She also held the position of Chairman of the Board at Sparbanken, now Aktia Bank in Finland. She was married to Björn Sjöblom, they had a son, Bo, and a daughter, Marianne. I remember Pi as an avid dancer and she was very good at the various card games played in Mustaniemi. She died in 1997, she was 70.

Sten (Trolle)

Trolle, my father, became a paper engineer, working for Kymmene early in his career. Later he became a consultant and Chairman of the Board at Pöyry, a paper engineering consulting firm. He married Ulla Meyer and they have three children: my sister Birgitta, my brother Holger, and myself Stella. Like his father Trolle loves hunting. But his favorite pastime, at the age of 86, is taking care of the forest and maintaining the wood supply for the fireplaces and the sauna.

When Mustaniemi was outgrown by the steadily increasing number of family members, my father decided to leave Mustaniemi as a summer residence. Instead, we moved to an island west of Helsinki, where we are looking out toward the west over the Porkkala Peninsula, which was returned to Finland after 12 years, even though the original lease agreement was for 50 years. We still have a small Russian boat flag that we found on the property. When we have the traditional yearly summer crawfish party, you can hear us sing our favorite schnapps song all the way to Porkkala, the song is called: "And Now We Will Take a Russian to His Grave".

Mustaniemi

Lake Urajärvi is still today the idyllic summer vacationing spot with its clear water and peacefulness. After my father left Mustaniemi, the sisters Pi and Mi cared for it and spent their summers there with their families. After they had passed, the main house was sold. The new owners have restored the villa beautifully, maintaining its old country charm. Bo Sjöblom, Pi's son, kept part of the property on which he built his own summer cottage.

Kuusankoski

Kuusankoski today has been joined with Kouvola under the name Kouvola. It has become a medium sized town by Finnish standards with about 85,000 residents. It remains an important railroad crossing and the Kuusankoski Paper Mill remains one of the main employers, and, yes, even McDonalds has arrived.

Helsinki

Helsinki has become a culturally and architecturally respectable European capital city famous for its buzzing market place next to the Presidential Palace overlooking the harbor. Hundreds of tourists arrive daily at the nearby port on cruise ships from Sweden, Germany, and the Baltic States. You can actually walk from the port to the market place and all the shops in the heart of the city, including the Stockman Department Store. And if you want to visit Russia, St. Petersburg can be reached by high speed train in 3 ½ hours.

Finland

The political system in Finland is based on democratic principles, and various rights of the individual are undeniable. This includes healthcare, which is considered an inalienable right.

Finland is well known for its excellent educational system, its students regularly top various rankings, especially in mathematics. Literacy is high and infant mortality is among the lowest in the world. The highly educated population is the basis for an industrialized society, which in the past was dominated by the paper industry. Nowadays, ship-building and Nokia produce the most recognized products worldwide.

In the business world Finland is known for its high ethical and quality standards.

Some may still remember the long-distance runner Paavo Nurmi, the Flying Finn. Now, ice hockey and motor sports produce most of the sports stars.

But maybe most importantly the Scandinavian countries, including Finland, are known to be among the happiest nations in the world.

Finland celebrates its 100th year as a free democratic nation on December the 6th, 2017. The Centennial Independence Day will undoubtedly bring back memories from the war in those who survived it and are still alive today, among them my father. I would also like to acknowledge my father's cousin, Margaretha, whose married name is Berghell. She had a very distinguished Lotta career and is mentioned in the book many times. She celebrated her 96th birthday this summer and has been invited to the Presidential Palace for the Independence Ball.

Margaretha Berghell
Sitting in the Lower Right Corner

It is with pride that we will sing the Finnish National Anthem, "Our Country", on December the 6th. We will remember the heroes that with their sacrifice gave us our freedom. We have been lucky, but we have also carved the path for our future with our hard work and our "Sisu", our grit.

Stella von Troil

Dec 2, 2017, Pensacola, FL, USA

83035746R00226

Made in the USA
Columbia, SC
10 December 2017